IMPERIAL GERMANY

The Birth of

THE GERMAN REPUBLIC

1871-1918

IMPERIAL GERMANY

The Birth of
THE GERMAN REPUBLIC
1871-1918

by ARTHUR ROSENBERG

Translated from the German by IAN F. D. MORROW

BEACON PRESS

BOSTON

TRANSLATOR'S PREFACE

AS reporter of the Reichstag Commission for the investigation of the causes of the German collapse in the World War, Dr. Rosenberg enjoyed exceptional opportunities both for hearing from the leading soldiers and politicians their own explanations of the downfall of the Empire and for examining a great collection of documents bearing upon the subject. From these two sources Dr. Rosenberg has written the following impersonal and scholarly narrative of the events leading up to the establishment of the German Republic in November 1918. A narrative that cannot fail to be of interest and value to all who wish to know something of the historical background to the present political and economic situation in Germany.

No change whatever has been made in the original German text of Dr. Rosenberg's book. Dr. Rosenberg has been kind enough to supplement the bibliography in the German edition with the titles of some recently published works containing information not available to him at the time when he wrote his book.

TYROL.   IAN F. D. MORROW.
January 1931.

PREFACE

I WAS prompted to write this book by the fact that I was a member of the Reichstag Committee of Inquiry into the causes of Germany's collapse in the World War. I was a member of this Committee from 1925 to 1928 in addition to being reporter for the so-called 'stab in the back' theory (*Dolchstossfrage*). It was an opportunity such as is not often granted to an historian for getting material at first hand. The members of the Committee belonged to the most various political Parties; but in spite of differences of opinion they were at one in their desire to discover the real historical truth. I wish particularly to thank two of my former colleagues on the Committee: Professor Bredt by his special report on 'The Reichstag during the World War' opened up a number of new problems; and Professor Bergsträsser was of great assistance in his communications to the Committee on the subject of racial psychology.

I chose November 10, 1918, as the closing date for my study, although it would have been scientifically better to have brought it down to the acceptance of the Weimar Constitution by the National Assembly. For research purposes the line of division still comes on November 10—the documents for scientific investigation being largely available before but not after that date. To write a critical history of Germany after November 10, 1918 is impossible at present. The work of the Committee was limited to the years after the outbreak of the World War. Nevertheless, in order to make the whole development comprehensible, I was obliged to go back in my study as far as the year 1871.

Up to November 10, 1918 I belonged to no political party or organization. My personal experiences during that time were so unimportant that they could not have given me any permanent bias. I have written this book without consideration for any Party opinion or Party prestige. I do not think that my political activity has predisposed me to deliver unjust judgements. In writing this book I have only had a single aim in view: to expose historical untruths, whether they emanated from the Right or from the Left. Obviously my book can in no way be considered as a publication of the Committee of Inquiry—the responsibility for it is mine alone.

The peculiar nature of the political development in Germany

has caused empty political claptrap, illusions, and improvisations to play a much greater part here than with other nations. If I am able to help my readers in their battle with these fantasies I shall have achieved all that I set out to accomplish in this book.

The quotations and references, printed in the Notes attached to each chapter, make no claim to completeness. They are intended, especially in controversial matters, to indicate to the reader where he may find reliable sources of information. Chief among such sources are the publications of the Reichstag Committee of Inquiry. The fourth of these publications bears the title: *Die Ursachen des deutschen Zusammenbruches im Jahre* 1918, and has been prepared by Dr. Philipp with the assistance of the Secretaries to the Committee, Drs. Fischer and Bloch. Vols. i–iii (1925) treat of the military collapse; vols. iv–vi (1928) deal with the general causes and nature of the internal collapse in Germany; vols. vii–viii (1926–8) are concerned with the Reichstag during the World War; vols. ix–x discuss the part played by the navy in the collapse; vol. xi will treat of social grievances within the army; and vol. xii has for its subject the problem of annexations.

The fact that I have not considered the 'stab in the back' (*Dolchstoss*) trial at Munich nor the proceedings at Magdeburg in connexion with an alleged insult to Ebert as scientific material will hardly need further explanation.

BERLIN-ZEHLENDORF.   A. ROSENBERG.
August 1928.

ADDITIONAL BIBLIOGRAPHY

Since the appearance of the first German edition of this book in 1928 the following works have been published which present supplementary material on the subject.

The Report of the Committee of Inquiry: Bd. IX–X: 'Marine Unruhen', 1917–18. Berlin, 1928.

Bredt: *Die belgische Neutralität und der Schlieffensche Feldzugsplan.* Berlin, 1929.

Bergsträsser: *Die preussische Wahlrechtsfrage im Kriege.* Tübingen, 1929.

Scheidemann: *Memoiren eines Sozialdemokraten.* Dresden, 1928.

Haase, Ernst: *Hugo Haase: Sein Leben und Wirken.* Berlin, 1929.

Bülow, Fürst: *Denkwürdigkeiten.* Bd. I–III. Berlin, 1930–1.

Volkmann: *Revolution über Deutschland.* Oldenburg, 1930.

TRANSLATOR'S NOTE

To economize space the following abbreviations have been introduced throughout to indicate works frequently referred to in the notes.

REPORT = the publications of the Committee of Inquiry.

GP = *Die Grosse Politik des europäischen Kabinetts, 1871–1914.*

BGE = Bismarck's *Gedanken und Erinnerungen* (1898).

CONTENTS

I

SOCIAL FORCES UNDER BISMARCK

THE Bismarckian Empire, proclaimed in the Hall of Mirrors at Versailles in 1871, was in 1919 destroyed in that same Hall. Yet the German Republic by which it was succeeded, and of which the Constitution was drafted in Weimar, resembled the Empire in many important aspects. Fundamentally, however, the Republic was the embodiment of much that was new. The chief innovation was not, indeed, the disappearance of the House of Hohenzollern and of the other reigning Houses: Bismarck's Empire could have continued to exist with an elected President at its head. Nor did the innovation consist in the fact that, under the Republic, Social Democrats could become Ministers: they had already held office in the last days of the Empire. Neither were the new frontiers given to Germany in the Peace Treaty of Versailles of importance from this special standpoint: Bismarck founded his Empire without Alsace-Lorraine; and the relation of Germany to Poland and to Austria could have been regulated differently. The chief innovation is to be found in the destruction of the old Prussian army by the military defeats on the Western Front, by the Revolution, and by the Treaty of Versailles.

The Bismarckian Empire and the Prussian army formed an indissoluble entity. Bismarck himself thought his greatest achievement was his winning over of the King of Prussia and of the Prussian army for the ideal of a national unified Germany. He thought the failure of the Revolution of 1848 in Germany lay in the fact that the middle classes sought with their own strength to bring about the establishment of the Empire, regardless of the German dynasties and, above all, without regard to the historic evolution of Prussia. Bismarck chose another path. He united the military aristocracy of Prussia with the German middle class, placed the Hohenzollerns at the head of the whole edifice, and so gave the Empire its peculiar stamp.[1] The history of the revived German Empire is made up of the reciprocal attraction and repulsion of the two elements which Bismarck thus brought together. The end came when the Prussian military caste collapsed in 1918 and the middle class took over the government.

Was Bismarck's conception of making Prussia serve the cause

of German unity a false one? Was the situation in 1871 such that
the German Empire could only be realized as a middle-class State
based on liberal and parliamentary foundations—and in no other
way? Did the Junkers and the middle class stand to one another
as fire to water between whom no compromise is possible? Did
Bismarck sacrifice his real convictions to a romantic dynastic ideal?
It would be easy to answer these questions in the affirmative—and
it would be exceedingly mistaken. The Revolution of 1848–9
showed that the German middle class was not capable of conquer-
ing by its own strength alone. The agrarian and military, the
dynastic and bureaucratic, and even the clerical, elements in the
old order in Germany were far stronger than at first appeared in
the excitement of the March days of 1848. And, behind the middle
class, the proletariate of the cities emerged as a new political entity
ready to fight with the middle class against the governing aristocracy. But nevertheless it was possessed of ideals which were not
those of the liberal middle class. The explosive force latent in the
Labour movement was at that time far more apparent to impartial
observers than to the workmen themselves.

It was in these circumstances that a realist politician of con-
servative-socialist tendencies as was Bismarck believed it possible
to reconcile the middle class with the old ruling forces by means
of a clever compromise, to achieve national unity through the
co-operation of the two, and at the same time to raise a strong
bulwark against the 'Red' revolution. Any one who occupied
Bismarck's position in 1871, and who made such a calculation,
was not overrating the existing forces in Germany. Even in the
unprecedentedly favourable conditions of November 1918 the
German working class itself was unable to seize the reins of power in
the State. Far less could it have done so in the past. Moreover,
until the outbreak of the Revolution in 1918, there was little sign
in the German middle class of a Jacobin spirit seeking to sweep
away the privileges of the Crown and the nobility. For the failure
of Bismarck's ideal neither the opposition of the working class
nor of the middle class was necessary. The Bismarckian Empire
was mortally ill from the day of its birth. The glamour of military
victories and commercial prosperity scarcely availed to conceal the
political crisis existing from the *Kulturkampf* to the Chancellorship
of Max of Baden: a crisis for which no solution was ever found,
continually taking to itself new forms and dimensions, and which
in the end destroyed the whole of Bismarck's work.

What caused this long-continuing political crisis? Bismarck was unable to weld together into an organic whole the various elements present in the German people: indeed he never once made a serious attempt to do so. The conflicting classes and forces in Germany were to be held together by the superimposed strength of the Empire. Up to 1890 Bismarck's power and the Imperial authority were synonymous. The personal dictatorship lived and died with the dictator himself. When in 1890 the old dictator was compelled to resign, when he saw in the weak and vacillating William II the thunderbolt that was to strike him down, the doom was sealed. Its coming became only a question of time and circumstance. Powerless to avert it, Bismarck from his retirement at Friedrichsruh beheld the storm that threatened to destroy his life-work. It is often said that Bismarck's successors ruined his creation. That is true in so far as the Bismarckian Empire could not exist without a Bismarck. But in that very fact lies the severest criticism of Bismarck himself.

The German Empire was not doomed to failure because it arose from a compromise between the German middle class and the Prussian military aristocracy, but because it embodied that compromise in the form of the Napoleonic autocracy. In order to avoid having to hand over his authority to the Imperial Chancellor, the King of Prussia had to be both by inclination and birth a Bonaparte. That Bismarck bound up the political life of the German nation with his own person, indeed with his own personal relation to William I, was an historical mistake of incalculable consequence. It must, nevertheless, be admitted that in the peculiar situation in Germany in 1871 Bismarck's mistake was a very natural one. At the time of the establishment of the Empire the liberal middle class was possessed of the intelligence, the commercial and industrial ability, of the Germany of that day. The vast masses of manual labourers and of the lower middle classes, the great majority of the factory workers, even a considerable part of the peasantry and a few of the nobility, adopted the nationalist and liberal ideals of the middle class and did service to its political mottoes.[2] In opposition to this undoubtedly powerful force stood the Prussian army, the King, the corps of officers, the hierarchy of the Prussian bureaucracy, the great territorial magnates from east of the Elbe, a group of liberal nobles and the agrarian population dependent upon their landlords. How could a compromise be achieved between these two forces?

In Prussia the King and the military aristocracy wielded supreme power. Military discipline in the generation prior to 1871 had successfully emerged from the severest test; neither the Revolution of 1848 nor the wars of the sixties had seriously undermined the discipline of the Prussian army. The King chose his Ministers in accordance with his personal inclination. The Civil Service and the Police were firmly controlled by the Government. If a recalcitrant Parliament refused supplies, the King carried on the government without a parliamentary budget; and the wars of the sixties had clearly demonstrated his ability to do so. Confronted by the disciplined Prussian army, a popular rising was foredoomed to failure. Even the recruit inspired with subversive ideas submitted himself to the discipline of the army; and the iron institution of the Prussian corps of officers and non-commissioned officers displayed no cracks anywhere. Although here and there throughout the land a liberally-minded judge was to be found, nevertheless the machinery of the Law from the President of the Supreme Court to the last recruited policeman was entirely subservient to the Government.

Thus feudal and conservative Prussia held all the political trumps in its hand. A compromise was only conceivable if the military caste voluntarily surrendered an important part of its rights and privileges to the middle class, and this might be accomplished in two ways; either the middle class was given a share in the actual government in Prussia, or the middle class shared in the government of the Empire to such an extent that a counterpoise was thereby created to Prussia. At the establishment of the Empire, Bismarck avoided both these paths. He left Prussia untouched— that is to say, the King and the military aristocracy retained all authority—and he raised an Imperial constitutional edifice from which Prussia ruled the Empire, and not the Empire Prussia.

It would be erroneous to ascribe Bismarck's conduct to narrow pride of caste. Bismarck never entertained any special regard for the Prussian Junkers, and he never underrated the importance of the middle class. But he believed that in consequence of the perilous international situation in which it found itself the German Empire could not live without a powerful army. And an efficient German army, which would be able in case of need to defend the Empire on its eastern and western frontiers, could only be created with the help of Prussia. The destruction of the Prussian military system implied a defenceless Germany. But in a defenceless

Germany it would be impossible to control the domestic political conflict. Bismarck therefore became a convinced supporter of the old Prussian military system. He championed the military dictatorship of the King of Prussia in Germany and the undisputed authority, free from all parliamentary control and interference, of the King over the army.

With Prussia as the military dictator of Germany, however, it was excessively difficult to induce the Prussian military caste to make concessions to other and unarmed sections of the nation. Even if Bismarck had ever desired to do so, it is improbable that he could have induced William I to renounce an important part of his prerogative. It was a misfortune for the subsequent evolution of Germany that the constitutional conflict in Prussia ended in so complete a victory for the Royal authority. Feudal Prussia hurled back the attack of middle-class liberalism along the entire front. The King of Prussia and his army were victorious in 1864, in 1866, and in 1870–1, and by their victories alone the German Empire was rendered possible. Was it conceivable that after such victories the King would renounce his prerogative in·favour of a parliament? Hence Bismarck left Prussia untouched and entrusted it with the leadership of Germany.

The secret of the Imperial Constitution lay in the fact that in reality no Imperial Government was ever called into being. The place of an Imperial Government was taken by the Federal Council (*Bundesrat*), the organ of the individual State governments, with the Imperial Chancellor as its advisor and representative. From the very outset Bismarck must have known that the Federal Council, which was no more than a 'Council of Ambassadors', was utterly incapable of governing. Thus the Federal Council became the constitutional camouflage for Prussia's governance of the Empire, while the Imperial Chancellor, who was also President of the Prussian Council of Ministers, formulated German policy. If a State, for example Bavaria, put forward definite demands, the matter had to be settled by diplomatic channels; and not once in the whole course of its history was the policy of the Empire determined by a collaboration between any of the component States. The corner-stone of Bismarck's edifice—the government of the Empire by the Federal Council—was from the outset an avowed fiction.

The Reichstag, indeed, could debate publicly all political questions. The army and foreign policy, however, were excluded from its sphere of influence. The Emperor—actually the Imperial Chancellor—formulated foreign policy without any regard for the speeches delivered in the Reichstag. Moreover, the right of voting army credits possessed by the Reichstag was in no circumstances permitted to infringe upon the Emperor's absolute authority over the armed forces of the Empire. In domestic affairs the Reichstag found its influence circumscribed by the special rights assured to the individual States as well as by its own complete lack of control over the actions of the Government. When the Reichstag, for example, found itself in disagreement with the Government's policy, the most that it could do was to refuse to pass the budget. But the struggle in Prussia between the King and the Parliament had shown plainly that the Government could continue to discharge its functions without the aid of supplies obtained in a constitutional manner. Hence the sole weapon in the possession of the Reichstag was from the very beginning useless.

Neither in the Prussian Parliament nor in the Reichstag were the middle classes able to exercise any real influence upon the course of German policy. Nevertheless, Bismarck knew very well that the German Empire could neither be established nor maintained against the will of the middle classes to whom, however, no constitutional rights were to be accorded at the expense of the Crown. Hence it was to be the duty of the executive power— theoretically the Emperor, actually the Imperial Chancellor—to ensure that the just demands of the liberal middle classes were fulfilled. The ideals of the middle-class patriots no less than the economic requirements of Industry and Commerce were to be realized in the nationalist character given to the German Empire. The demands of the Liberals for a modern, intelligent, and straight-forward form of government were to be satisfied as far as possible. Bismarck himself was prepared to go even further by entrusting certain portfolios in the Prussian Cabinet and important administrative posts in the Empire to prominent Liberals; and by working in a sincere collaboration with the Liberal groups in Parliament. In reality, however, all this was made to depend upon the arbitrary will of the Emperor, i.e. of his most influential advisers. Bismarck wished to retain for himself and his successors in office the possibility, if necessary, of being able to crush the Liberals as they had been crushed in the days of the struggle in Prussia.

From the middle class Bismarck demanded that it should be content with such concessions, and that it should realize the peculiar and exceptional nature of the situation in which Germany found herself in regard to politico-military and international affairs. The military power placed in the hands of the Emperor afforded the capitalist middle class the best defence against the danger of a proletarian socialist revolution. The Commune in Paris had made a profound impression upon Bismarck's mind. He was convinced that a middle-class parliamentary system—much less a republic—did not possess within itself sufficient powers of resistance to cope with the attack of the proletarian masses. For this reason alone the middle classes ought to rally round the existing conservative State, notwithstanding the fact that they might be dissatisfied with this or that detail in the Constitution of the German Empire.

At the same time Bismarck considered it to be no less essential that the old Prussian aristocracy should adapt itself to the new order. The Junker must learn that the German Empire could not be governed by the same methods that were employed in the working of an estate to the east of the Elbe. He must learn to reconcile himself to the existence of Liberal Ministers and to the growing wealth and power of the municipalities. He must be brought to recognize the power that lay in his hands through the undiminished prerogatives of the Prussian Crown. Finally, the Junker must be ready to support the Emperor and the Imperial Chancellor in all emergencies, even though at the moment he might not understand the meaning and purpose of this or that governmental action. In Bismarck's opinion the healthiest political situation would be that in which a large 'Old Prussian' Conservative Party worked in collaboration with a large Liberal Party. It must, however, be left to the Government in each individual instance to decide how the balance of forces could best be maintained. If necessary, the Government must be prepared at one time to seek support from the Left and at another from the Right; but it should always bear in mind that its principal aim was the reconciliation and collaboration of the two fundamental forces in the Empire.

It is easy to see that the working of this system depended entirely upon the personality of the two Heads of the Executive. In order that the balance of forces should be maintained it would always be necessary to have a chancellor like Bismarck or a king like Frederick the Great. If the leadership were wanting, the whole system would dissolve in pieces. The balance of forces that had been achieved in England by the Revolution of 1689 depended

upon the existence of a compromise between the landed aristocracy
and the townsfolk. An organic collaboration and evolution of these
two classes in the nation was attained in England. The two classes
divided the task of governance between them; the squire exercised
magisterial authority in the country districts as a Justice of
the Peace, &c., while the mayors and aldermen ruled over the
cities. In the House of Commons the two classes met as representatives of town and country boroughs. Each respected the
privileges of the other because each recognized that the privileges
of the one presupposed the privileges of the other. They watched
in common over the integrity of the Constitution and they united
to form the Government. The foundation-stone of the English
system—autonomy—was wanting in Germany, where its place was
taken by the all-powerful bureaucracy. The supreme power of the
House of Commons resulted from the collaboration of all classes
in the nation in the governance of the country. The impotence of
the Reichstag forbade the conclusion of an effective compromise
that would have resulted in a united governance of the Empire.
In the Reichstag, as constituted by Bismarck, a parliamentary
coalition could only achieve positive results for so long as it worked
in collaboration with the Government. The most that could be
achieved by a coalition of parties and classes inimical to the
Government's policy was the annoyance of the Imperial Chancellor
by the adoption of obstructionist and pin-pricking tactics.

Under the influence of the victory won in the Franco-Prussian
War of 1870-1, the liberal middle class became reconciled to the
Imperial Constitution and was prepared to give the Chancellor
parliamentary and moral support. It was not long, however, before
a crisis arose which was intensified by the fact that the two forces
on whose collaboration Bismarck wished to make the governance
of the Empire depend were not the only forces in the State.
Alongside the 'Old Prussian' Conservatives were ranked the 'Old
German' Conservatives from the district left of the Elbe, while
beside the liberal middle class arose in ever-increasing numbers
and rapidly growing class-consciousness the industrial proletariate.
The statesman who sought to maintain a balance of forces within
the Empire found himself called upon to juggle with not only two
but four elements each of which was incompatible with the others.

Until 1866 Vienna was the centre of the Old German Conservatism. The ruling bishops of the former German Empire had seen
in the House of Habsburg their natural overlord as had also the

Imperial knights who owed allegiance directly to the Emperor and not to a territorial prince. Although these two estates of the old Empire had lost their power with the destruction of the Empire by Napoleon I, the Catholic Church in Germany, as well as the great nobles in southern Germany and the Rhineland, continued to look upon Austria as their leader and the natural champion of their interests. The old Empire was very imperfectly restored in 1815 in the shape of the German *Bund*. The territorial sovereigns within the *Bund*, and especially the smaller principalities, continued nevertheless to look upon Prussia as their obvious enemy and Austria as their predestined friend. For in their eyes an increase in the power of Prussia was synonymous with a reorganization of Germany on centralized lines, whereas the maintenance of the Austrian hegemony guaranteed the continuance of German federalism.

German federalism found its support not only amongst the ruling Houses, aristocrats, and priests, but also in the masses of the agrarian and lower middle-class population who were averse to paying taxes to Berlin, and disliked the notion that their administrative and social traditions should be destroyed by the hegemony of Prussia. The conservative elements in the old Germany from Hanover to Munich made common cause in the war of 1866 against Prussia. Victory crowned the Prussian arms. Austria was excluded from Germany. Hanover, Hesse, and Nassau were annexed by Bismarck. The liberal-minded middle classes everywhere proclaimed itself in favour of Prussia and German unity, and Liberal and Nationalist feeling was strong enough in 1870 to compel the south German States to participate in the war with France.

At the foundation of the Empire Bismarck sought to render the Conservatives in the old Germany harmless by making the German dynasties an essential factor in the new order. Thus in order to gain over the House of Wittelsbach Bismarck gave his consent to the special privileges accorded to the Bavarian army. The federal character of the *Bundesrat* left the smaller dynasties in possession of as many privileges as it was possible to accord them under the changed circumstances. Success crowned Bismarck's work. From 1871 onwards he never met with any serious difficulties on the part of the non-Prussian ruling Houses. Bismarck, for example, could never have fought the *Kulturkampf* unless he had had the King of Bavaria and the Bavarian Government as steadfast allies.[3]

If the west and south German dynasties were thus easily won

over to the new 'Protestant Empire', it was very different in the case of the deeply conservative elements in the nation. The Catholic priesthood, the great nobles, and vast numbers of peasants and labourers in southern and western Germany united to form an imposing defensive front, and the Centre Party arose as the party of the German Catholics. Nevertheless, the *Kulturkampf* in its essentials was not a sectarian conflict. The Protestant farmers in Hanover, who also wished the independent existence of the old Guelph kingdom to be restored, ranged themselves in the ranks of the Centre Party, while the Catholic burghers of the towns in the Rhineland and in southern Germany were supporters of Bismarck. At the same time the National Liberal elector in Munich or Cologne did not desert his own Church. The peculiar character of the Centre Party received its embodiment at the time of the *Kulturkampf* in Windthorst, a Catholic and former Minister of the King of Hanover.

Besides its Guelph supporters the Centre possessed two allies whose friendship with it was specially unwelcome to the Bismarckian Government. The defence of Catholicism against an Executive Power with strong Protestant leanings had brought about an alliance between the Centre and Poland. Moreover, the Catholic Church in Germany had for more than a generation past begun to organize the Catholic workmen. An independent Labour movement in Germany was brought into existence by two parallel forces. Beside Marx stood the Catholic Church. It is even questionable whether the ruling classes in Germany in the seventies were more alarmed by the Social Democrat Labour movements in Berlin and Saxony than by the Catholic Labour movements in Upper Silesia[4] and in the Rhineland. In Upper Silesia, where the Polish-Catholic workman was opposed to the German-Protestant factory manager, class distinctions manifested themselves with peculiar sharpness.

In its social composition the Centre was—even in the days of the *Kulturkampf*—a multi-coloured organization. Nevertheless all its members, from whatever class they sprang, were united in opposition to the middle class. The priest and the nobleman no less than the peasant and the workman had in common nothing to gain by furthering the middle-class capitalist evolution in the cities; and they were as one man in their opposition to the militarist, autocratic, Prussian centralism. Hence it came about that the Centre was the predestined anti-Bismarck Party. Every single

principle embodied in the Bismarckian Empire was denied by the
Centre. It was of fateful import for the Bismarckian Empire that
the Old German Conservatism after 1866 was not merely spread
like a fairy haze over a number of Rhenish castles, convents, and
small courts, but that broad masses in the nation, as represented in the
Christian Peasants Society and the Christian Trade Unions, should
have associated themselves with the Catholic Federalist movement.
The Bismarckian Empire thereby added another heavy burden
to that already imposed upon it by the irreconcilable conflict
between the middle class and Prussianism.

Bismarck's *Kulturkampf* was no more than the continuance of
the war of 1866 under a new guise and with other weapons. Of the
truth of that statement Bismarck himself was well aware. For some
years, indeed, he feared lest Germany might be faced with a war
of revenge on the part of clerical France and the Habsburgs. In
such an event the intellectual leadership of the attack would come
from the Papacy in Rome, while the Centre, the Poles and the
Guelph Party would come forward in Germany as the allies of
Viennese and Parisian desires for revenge.[5] Bismarck's suspicion
that the then leaders of the Centre were hatching treasonable
projects was wholly unfounded, although it is obvious that a defeat
in a war with Austria and France would have resulted in a reorganization of Germany on federalist lines and the destruction
of all that had been achieved through the wars of 1866 and 1870-1.

The *Kulturkampf* resulted in a more complete understanding
between Bismarck and the Liberals than any hitherto or subsequently achieved. The liberal middle class threw itself with fervour
into the battle, partly because anti-clericalism fully accorded with
its own notions, and partly—indeed above all—because the
Kulturkampf seemed to afford an opportunity in which to realize
parliamentary government and to take the reins of power into its
own hands.[6] It seemed as if the moment had come for the middle
class to retrieve their losses in 1871 at the time of the establishment
of the Empire and the drafting of the Constitution.

Many of the Prussian nobility who had failed to comprehend
Bismarck's policy since 1866 were alarmed at this development. It
seemed to them that Bismarck was doing all that lay in his power
to augment the authority of the municipalities at the expense of the
countryside. The millions received from France as war-indemnity
had disappeared into the hands of Jews and speculators on the
Stock Exchange. Profiteers and company promoters grew rich

while the earnings of the peasantry and labourers decreased. What was to become of the Empire that had been born on the battlefields of Metz and Sedan? Nor did the evil end there. Bismarck was seeking to destroy the moral and intellectual authority of the Church. Although it could not be gainsaid that he had declared the *Kulturkampf* to be waged solely against Catholicism, nevertheless the new laws for the secularization of the schools and the introduction of civil marriage were equally offensive to the Protestant Church. On Falk's assuming the ministry of religion and education in 1872 Prussia came under the domination of Liberal free-thought. The mistaken policy which Bismarck was pursuing seemed likely to result in his having to adopt the very parliamentary system which he had rejected at the time of the constitutional conflict in Prussia. In such circumstances it seemed natural to the Prussian nobles that all right-thinking men of the old Prussian stamp should unite in opposing Bismarck. An end must be made to the *Kulturkampf*. The Protestant and Roman Catholic Churches in Germany must combine to present a united front against the attacks of Liberalism, Free-thought, and Profiteering. The most intelligent champion of the Conservative opposition to Bismarck, Stocker, who was Court Chaplain, went even further in declaring it to be the duty of Prussia and of the Protestant Church to come to the aid of the city proletariate, crushed down as it was by Jews and capitalists, by seeing that their just demands were fulfilled. An end would thus be made to the Social-Democrat agitation which was menacing the existence of the Empire.

Hence it came about that at the very moment in which in alliance with the Liberals he was engaged in a hot struggle with the Centre, Bismarck found himself attacked from behind by the majority of the Prussian nobility and the Protestant clergy. This conservative opposition to Bismarck was but the outward expression of an inner narrow-mindedness and blindness of heart. The Prussian aristocracy refused to recognize what it owed to Bismarck and to acknowledge that its exceptional position within the Empire could only be maintained—if indeed it could be maintained at all—by Bismarck's methods. The conservative attack was the most dangerous of all those to which Bismarck[7] was exposed inasmuch as an enduring enmity on the part of the Conservatives in the Empire might result in the destruction of the foundations on which Bismarck had built up his power. Notwithstanding all the polemics against Bismarck in the *Kreuzzeitung*, William I firmly supported his Chancellor. But would the King of Prussia be able to rule permanently in opposition to all the monarchist and militarist forces in Prussia? If the battle waged between the King and Bismarck on the one hand and the Centre and the Conservatives on the other became a standing dispute, the result would be parliamentarism, the assumption of the reins of government by the liberal middle class, and the opening up of an opportunity for the defeated forces in the constitutional struggle to obtain their revenge. Although a formal truce was subsequently achieved between Bismarck and the Conservatives, the former never regained the confidence of the powerful Prussian Conservatives; and the minority by which he was overthrown in 1890 was composed of Conservatives of the Christian-Socialist and Stöcker stamp. Herein is revealed the inner weakness of the Bismarckian Empire. If the Prussian military aristocracy had so little confidence in Bismarck that he could scarcely make the smallest concessions to the middle-class Liberals, what was to become of the German Empire? That being so the Prussian aristocracy must continue to be a foreign element in the political life of Germany, and their exceptional position be doomed to destruction by the first serious attack made upon it.

The Liberals naturally recognized the difficulty in which Bismarck found himself by reason of the *Kulturkampf*, and they sought to turn it to their own advantage by demanding concessions amounting in effect to the establishment of a Liberal parliamentary régime in Prussia and the Empire.[8] A choice was thus forced upon Bismarck. As was only to be expected, he rejected a parliamentary middle-class form of government. Not that Bismarck himself ever shared in the narrow self-righteousness of his own caste who believed that all was well with the world so long as the Prussian Guards were on duty in Berlin and Potsdam and the crowd on the streets continued to be obedient to a policeman's orders. Bismarck knew that the Empire could not continue to exist unless it were assured of the willing and voluntary support and co-operation of powerful elements in the population. Hitherto Bismarck had waged war on the various political parties in their character as representatives of the different classes in the State. He had fought with them all—Liberals and Conservatives no less than the Centre—and in no quarter could he find really influential and trustworthy supporters. If he had ignored the politicians and addressed himself directly to the peasants instead of to the editor of the *Kreuzzeitung*, or to the manufacturers and workmen instead of to the Liberal lawyers and professors, he might possibly have achieved better results.[1] Moreover, would not a systematically pursued governmental policy along the lines desired by the agrarians have confronted the Catholic peasants of the Centre with a new situation?

His customs policy was the means chosen by Bismarck to reconcile himself with the industrial and economic interests. Bismarck offered a protectionist tariff to the newly born and thriving German industry with which it could overcome the all-powerful British competition. He offered increased duties to the agrarians by which they might defend themselves against the swamping of the German market with agricultural produce from eastern Europe. The tariff question in a recently industrialized country like the Germany of 1879 was of quite a different nature from the same question in the Germany of 1928. Moreover, Bismarck could then bring forward weighty arguments in favour of his customs, policy. The Liberal politicians were opposed to customs duties out of regard for the example of England and owing to the fact that commercial were stronger than industrial influences within their ranks. The agrarian influence, however, among the Conservatives and the Centre was so powerful that it overcame all other oppositional currents, and enabled Bismarck to carry his tariff law through the Reichstag with the support of these two parties against the opposition of the Liberals.

The policy pursued by Bismarck after 1879 brought about a great increase in the strength of the Prussian Conservatives. From being an aristocratic Court clique they developed into a broad party devoted to agrarian interests. The Liberal Party daily lost ground with the peasants, while for the first time the country districts to the east of the Elbe became the strongholds of the Conservatives.[9] This development in the grouping of the parties was reflected in the composition of the Prussian Parliament. The overwhelming Liberal majority at the time of the constitutional struggle had only been rendered possible by the fact that large numbers of the peasants placed themselves under the leadership of men of intellect and capacity from the cities.[2] All that was now changed. The peasants began to elect representatives pledged to support agrarian interests; and in the Protestant electorates of Prussia that meant a Conservative. The electoral divisions in Prussia had been designed to favour the country districts as compared with the towns: a matter of indifference, politically speaking, so long as the country-

folk and the towns pursued in general the same political programme. When, however, the agrarian population and the townsfolk were divided in their political principles, then the distribution
of electoral divisions became a matter of the greatest importance.
Henceforth the agrarian Conservative Party dominated the Prussian
Parliament,[10] and into the hands of the ruling class in Prussia fell
the control over the three law-making powers in the kingdom—the
King, the Upper House, and the Lower House. The Prussian
State in all its aspects thus became the bulwark of the Conservatives
against the attacks of the middle class and the workmen.

Moreover, Conservatism in its agrarian dress achieved an immense success outside the limits of Prussia itself. The Protestant
peasants in Hanover and Hesse-Nassau as well as throughout the
whole of southern Germany cut themselves free in ever-increasing
numbers from their former political allegiance. Until 1918 there
sat in the German Reichstag, which was elected in accordance with
universal and equal suffrage and by a secret ballot, among the
ranks of the Prussian feudal aristocrats, peasant representatives
from Bavaria, Würtemberg, Baden, and even Alsace-Lorraine.[11]

Bismarck's tariff policy also resulted in a far-reaching change in
the character of the Centre; a change to which the concordat
between the Papacy and the Empire contributed its share. The
danger of the formation of a Catholic League inspired with desires
for revenge against the German Empire was dispersed as a result
of the suppression of the clerical monarchist party by the Republicans in France and the conclusion by Bismarck of the alliance
with Austria which henceforth formed the foundation-stone of his
foreign policy. Thus the quarrel between Bismarck and the Centre
ceased to be of international importance. A secondary object of the
Austro-German alliance in Bismarck's eyes was the conciliation of
the reactionary conservative—so-called Pan-German—movement
with the German Empire. The alliance between Austria and
Germany was intended to restore to life the German *Bund* in those
aspects in which it had proved itself to be of value.

Bismarck thus brought it about that the Centre was reconciled to
the German Empire in its existing form and was ready to confine
itself to defending by constitutional means the federal institutions
and the Catholic Church. The former offensive power of the Centre
had been transformed into a loyal defensive force. The *Kulturkampf* ended with a victory for Bismarck, who began forthwith
to repeal the laws against the Catholics. Moreover, the agrarian

majority in the Centre were converted into supporters of the Government's economic policy. In these altered circumstances the Centre became a political factor in many respects by no means unwelcome to Bismarck. The Centre and the Catholic Church were able to control in a political sense large numbers of the city populations, especially the proletariate, which would otherwise have been found in the ranks of the Social Democrats or the Left Wing Liberals.[12] The Catholic nobility, which had become reconciled to the Empire, played an important part in the Centre and was naturally disposed to collaborate with the Prussian Conservatives. Any one who at that time regarded political questions solely from the standpoint of a political tactician might very well have come to the conclusion that the foundations of the German Empire could be strengthened by a close coalition in Parliament between the Conservatives and the Centre. Since the day when the Conservatives had been absorbed in the great Protestant Agrarian Party, which was also supported by the loyalist, anti-capitalist, anti-Semitic town populations, a fairly reliable majority composed of Conservatives and the Centre was available in the Reichstag. Moreover, the demands made by the Centre were extremely moderate. The Centre demanded neither parliamentary government nor any alteration in the old Prussian State organization; it was content if now and then a professing Catholic could become a *Landrat* or a judge in Prussia. The chief demands of the Centre were that the Constitution should not be altered in order to effect greater centralization; that no inimical policy should be pursued towards the Catholic Church; and that reasonable concessions should be made to the Christian workmen. There was nothing in these demands that could offend the Government and the Prussian Conservatives. Hence the Conservatives were always ready to prefer a coalition with the Centre to one with the Liberals.

Bismarck with unreasonable obstinacy refused to build up the German Empire upon the basis of a coalition with the Centre.[13] He believed that the west and south German Catholics were as good Germans as the Protestants. Nevertheless, while the peasants in Pomerania and east Prussia were attached to the Hohenzollern Empire both by inclination and interest, the same could not with truth be said of the Upper Bavarian peasants and the Christian miners of the Ruhr district. Since peace had been concluded between Church and State the supporters of the Centre had become loyal citizens of the Empire, yet in a great political crisis it was always possible that they would be ready to support another form for the Empire than that given to it in 1871. While Bismarck was prepared for this reason to maintain friendly relations with the Catholic Church and to co-operate with the Centre in Parliament, he was at the same time determined that the existence of the Empire no less than the proper functioning of its governmental system should never be made dependent upon the collaboration of the Centre. The Emperor in the gravest crises must always be free to carry on the government without the co-operation of, and even in opposition to, the Centre.

To carry on the government by means of a coalition between the Centre and the Conservatives involved the exclusion of the middle-class. But, in Bismarck's opinion, the German Empire could not be maintained without the active co-operation of the educated and propertied middle class. If the middle class were driven to take up an oppositional attitude, the King of Prussia would find himself isolated with the military aristocracy the moment a crisis arose. For Bismarck believed that the alliance with the Centre would not survive the first severe test. While the Government must be in a position to refuse in case of necessity exorbitant demands on the part of the Liberals, and to carry on the government without them, Bismarck looked upon a permanent snubbing of middle-class Liberalism as impracticable,[13] and he sought to bring into existence a new Bismarckian Liberal Party in place of the old Liberal Parties which were animated by the idea of parliamentary government. This new Liberal Party was to represent industrial interests, support his customs and Colonial policy, and to adopt a conservative attitude in all constitutional questions. He was successful in so far as there came into being in the eighties a National Liberal Party which had little more in common with the National Liberal Party of 1871 than the name.

Certain inimical elements were to be found in the middle class: the commercial classes, for example, which were not interested in his customs policy, and such men as were opposed to the military-aristocratic character of the German Empire and upheld the traditions of the constitutional movement. This 'Progressive Party', which was led by Eugen Richter, occupied the same place within middle-class Liberalism as did the Stöcker group within Conservative circles. These two groups were the chief opponents of the Bismarckian coalition. The Stöcker group wished to detach the Conservatives from all alliance with the Liberals, while Eugen

Richter sought to free the middle class from 'Junker' domination. Because in these two men Bismarck glimpsed the two forces that threatened to destroy his work from within the hatred with which he pursued the *Kreuzzeitung* Conservatives was no less bitter than the enmity he brought to bear upon Eugen Richter and the Progressives.

It is conceivable that both these groups speculated upon a third factor in German politics—the Centre. The Conservatives put forward the idea of a Conservative-Clerical coalition as a substitute for Bismarck's system, while the Liberal opposition became accustomed to voting with the Centre in the Reichstag. In the eighties the opposition to Bismarck in the Reichstag concentrated itself under the leadership of Richter and Windthorst. Was it inconceivable that an active alliance between the Liberal middle class and the Catholic Party could be brought into existence? During the *Kulturkampf* the Centre had felt the pressure of the existing system only too heavily—was it therefore not possible that the Centre might be induced to support parliamentarism? Could not a Cabinet be formed in Germany after the model of Gladstone's[14] Cabinet which had relied for its support upon an alliance between the English Liberals and the Catholic Irish? Such a Cabinet would have found supporters amongst those in Court circles who were inimical to Bismarck: for Bismarck's enemies at Court were divided into those with liberal and those with clerical sympathies. From an historical standpoint the idea of a German Cabinet on the Gladstonian model is extremely interesting, inasmuch as in this idea are to be found the beginnings of the coalition that subsequently resulted in the majority for the Peace Resolution of 1917 and the Weimar Coalition of 1919. But in the eighties the prospect of achieving a new governmental system out of an opposition composed of the Windthorst-Richter-Social-Democrat Parties was an extremely limited one. Throughout the years 1881–6 the Opposition in the Reichstag did in fact possess a majority, and, in the event of a change of rulers, it was conceivable that a Cabinet might have been formed which could have relied for support upon this majority with the exclusion of the Social Democrats. Nevertheless, in order to create a new and efficient governmental system, it would first have been necessary to destroy the power of the military aristocracy in Prussia; and no one was to be found who was ready to attempt that task.

Moreover, the Centre was not at that time prepared to enter into such a combination and preferred a peaceful co-operation with the Conservatives to any such revolutionary course of action. Then, too, the desire for power had steadily sunk in the middle class throughout the preceding decades. The objects for which the middle class had unsuccessfully striven from 1848 to 1866 with all their energies, and at the cost of great sacrifices, had been achieved by the King of Prussia and Bismarck by a few forcible actions. Since 1871 the nation had seen Bismarck build up the German Empire without permitting himself to be greatly distracted by the party politicians; Germany from year to year becoming more and more of a World-Power without waging war; industry and commerce steadily increasing; and the domestic situation seemingly stabilized. Thus the great majority of the middle class, especially the educated and academic elements, came to distrust their own political judgement. Instead they became increasingly disposed to believe that the Government in Berlin would always do the right thing.

Although it is unquestionable that Bismarck and William I achieved more and were of greater importance as statesmen than either Lasker or Eugen Richter, yet it was this very fact that gave rise to the doctrine of Prussia's historic mission and Prussian infallibility. The truth is that the backbone of the German middle class was broken in a political sense about 1880 without the employment of either physical or moral coercion. Despite the political oppression under which the German middle class suffered from 1815 to 1848, it remained in unbroken opposition to the Government and in continued possession of its self-confidence. After 1871 the pressure exercised by the Government upon the middle class was of the slightest. What comparison was there between a few prosecutions for *lèse-majesté* and for libels uttered against Bismarck, and the systematic persecution of the popular leaders in the March Revolution? Apart from some errors in taste, the Government could confront the middle class with an unprecedented political record that had resulted in the fulfilment of their own national ideals. When faced with this stupendous achievement, the opposition of the middle-class broke in pieces: while thanks to the feeling produced by the Government's record support for the Bismarckian National Liberals was forthcoming in other circles besides that of the industrialists. Moreover, this feeling both rendered the opposition of the Progressives innocuous and made of the notion of a 'Gladstonian Cabinet' under Bismarck a dream without any substance.

At the same time the attitude of the German middle class towards the Imperial Government was unhealthy for the Empire as a whole. The intellectual capitulation of the middle class before William I and Bismarck could perhaps be justified; but before William II and Bülow it was an absurdity. The obvious result of such a feeling of inferiority in comparison with the Government was that, on the occurrence of a serious crisis, the middle class simply looked dumbly to the Government and waited for it to act. If the Government failed it, the middle class was incapable of acting on its own initiative. After 1890 Bismarck was made furious by the submissiveness displayed by the populace towards William II, with the exception of the Social Democrats who were opposed in principle to the Bismarckian Empire, and by the lack of any serious opposition to the Government, yet Bismarck himself must have admitted that this deplorable condition was the result of his own political education of the German middle class.

Meanwhile, in the daily business of government, everything proceeded in accordance with Bismarck's wishes. At the Reichstag elections in 1887 the Bismarckian Coalition of Conservatives and National Liberals won a great victory. Bismarck found himself in possession of a majority both in the Prussian Landtag and the German Reichstag. Throughout the country he could rely on the agrarian Conservative movement as well as on his faithful supporters, the middle-class National Liberals. The quarrel with the Centre had lost its former bitterness; and Richter's party was in consequence no longer a danger to Bismarck. Two other dangers, however, threatened Bismarck's governmental system. First, the die-hard Conservatives under Stöcker, although they had failed both to raise themselves to the status of a party and to prevent the official Conservative Party from joining with the National Liberals, had nevertheless continued unreconciled to the Bismarckian system, and on the accession of William II in 1888 they became a great power at Court. Then, secondly, despite all the measures taken for its suppression, the Social Democrat Labour movement had become so powerful that it endangered the entire Bismarckian system. It was the simultaneous conflict with the Stöcker Conservatives and the Social Democrats that led to Bismarck's downfall.

The independent class movement of the German proletariate grew during the seventies and eighties of the last century in proportion with the growth of German industrialism. In those days the Social Democrats fought above all else to improve the miserable economic condition of the working class, and the drawing-up of their plans for a seizure of political power, and for the transformation of Germany into a Socialist Workers' Republic, were only of secondary interest to them. Moreover, owing to the small percentage of Social Democrats in Germany, their goal still lay in the dim distance. Until 1887 the Social Democrats were scarcely more strongly represented in the Reichstag than was the Polish Nationalist Party. All thoughts of attaining their goal by a *Putsch* were far removed from them; they carried on their propaganda within the limits set by the law; and they were not in any way implicated in the two attempts made in 1878 to assassinate William I. Although both these attempts originated with the Anarchists and Russian Social Revolutionaries, Bismarck made use of the feeling aroused to pass a special law to control the Socialist movement.

Bismarck in truth could neither tolerate nor make use of a proletarian class movement in his governance of the Empire.[15] He failed to understand the working-class demand for the betterment of social conditions, and he had no sympathy with endeavours to secure a Sunday holiday and a limitation on the employment of child labour in factories. Although German social legislation had its beginnings within the period of his government, Bismarck himself remained sceptical as to the value and importance of such measures. He was even less disposed to accord the working class a voice in the government of the Empire. The structure of the Empire did not, indeed, permit of anything but the repression of the working class. Even the right of the middle class to a voice in the government was never expressly admitted. If the propertied middle class could not be granted a share in the government, what could the working class expect to obtain in answer to its political demands?

Moreover, the demands of Labour implied a fight with the industrialists that was exceedingly abhorrent to Bismarck, who intended that the industrialists should be the picked troops within the ranks of the middle class. The industrialists were behind the National Liberals; to affront the industrialists was synonymous in Bismarck's mind with affronting the middle class—a course of action likely to result, in his opinion, in the substitution of governmental experiments by the Christian Socialist-Stöcker groups for his well-tried system of a balance of political forces. Hence the enmity of the workmen was in Bismarck's eyes a lesser evil than the

hostility of the capitalist middle class: for without the middle class
the German Empire could not continue to exist. Bismarck further
believed it to be well within the bounds of possibility that the
political labour movement could be crushed by means of force.

The only form of State organization which met with Bismarck's
approval, and which he held to be sane and prudent, was one in
which the propertied classes, grouped around a monarchy, held all
power in their own hands. He was convinced, on the other hand,
that rule by the poor and non-propertied masses must inevitably
result in chaos and lead to the military dictatorship that was the
invariable result of 'pure democracy'; and that therefore the task
of wise statesmanship must be to guard European society from
the calamity of such a revolution.[16] Bismarck's political theories
bore a startling resemblance to those of Prince Metternich—only
Metternich was far more of a doctrinaire than Bismarck, and in
consequence more rigid in his use of methods. Bismarck feared
that the Paris Commune of 1871 might be repeated in Germany.
He had made common cause in 1871 with the middle-class French
Republican Government against the Commune, and had urged
on, and assisted by every means in his power, the French Government in their efforts to suppress the Paris workmen by force.
Bismarck, like Metternich, believed in the necessity for the European Governments presenting a united front to the menace of
the 'Red Peril', although he never suffered his conviction to lead
him into political adventures.

The attempts made to assassinate William I were sufficient proof
for Bismarck that a 'Commune' in Germany was within the range
of possibility. Accordingly he struck at the Social Democrats as
being the party which had proclaimed its solidarity with the Paris
Commune. Bismarck's law against the Socialists brought misery
to hundreds of workmen and their families; the Socialist Press
was suppressed and Socialist Associations disbanded; yet since it
could not annul the mandates of the Social Democrat members of
the Reichstag, nor prevent Social Democrats from carrying on
propaganda in the electorates, the law failed to effect its purpose.
Despite the loss of newspapers and official organizations, the
Social Democrat Party continued to flourish by means of personal
contact between the workmen in the factories; and with each
triennial Reichstag election the Social Democrat Party once again
came before the public eye. Although it brought great hardship
to individuals, the law against the Socialists was in reality a piece

of bluff rather than a genuinely repressive measure. Even during the period 1878–90, throughout which they were the object of persecution, the Social Democrats determinedly refrained from acts of violence. As long as the strength of the Social Democrat Party did not grow rapidly, Bismarck believed that no useful purpose would be served by intensifying the repressive measures against it. But the Reichstag elections of 1890 brought an entirely new situation into existence; the votes cast in favour of the Social Democrats increased by a single leap from three-quarters of a million to one and a half millions. The Bismarckian system was in consequence shaken to its very foundations. To the millions of votes cast for the Centre—a party regarded by Bismarck as being inimical to his system—were added those cast for the Social Democrats. If to these were added the votes cast for the opposition groups of Poles, Alsatians, Danes, and Guelphs, then it at once became clear that notwithstanding the extraordinarily prosperous economic condition, and the brilliant international position, of Germany, forty per cent. of the population had cast their votes in a sense hostile to the Bismarckian Empire. If that occurred in a time of peace and plenty, what would happen on the occurrence of the first grave crisis? The work of 1871 had been jeopardized, and there ensued a battle of life and death.[17]

It was wholly logical and inevitable that Bismarck should thus judge the situation which arose in 1890: either the Empire of 1871 must crush the labour movement or else go under itself. There was no other alternative. Any attempt at a compromise would place the rudder of the ship of State in the hands of the middle class, and therewith the fabric of the constitution of 1871 would be torn from its supports. Moreover, Bismarck was convinced that the labour question in Germany was incapable of being solved along the lines proposed by Stöcker and the Christian Socialists. In holding such a belief Bismarck was completely in the right inasmuch as the class-conscious socialist proletariate were not to be converted into loyal supporters of the Prussian State organization by means of quotations from the Bible and a few laws framed in a socialist sense. Besides, the working-class supporters of the Centre were in principle as deeply opposed to the governmental system of Prussian-Germany as were the Social Democrats. Any one who studies the situation in 1890 from the standpoint of the consequences it was inevitably bound to bring in its train attains to a realization of the historic inevitability of the Revolution in 1918.

It is no longer possible to form any notion of the measures which Bismarck, if he had remained in office after 1890, would have employed against the Social Democrats. Probably he would have increased the severity of the law against the Socialists for the purpose of rendering the Social Democrat mandates and votes null and void.[18] If he had done so, it would scarcely have been possible for the workmen to rise in rebellion, and for some years at least Bismarck would have been able to enforce his will. He would doubtless have rendered it impossible for the Social Democrats to engage publicly in politics, and by thus banishing the Social Democrats from political life he would have robbed the Centre of its powerful position in the Reichstag. Such a policy, however, could only in the long run have had the effect of creating in Germany the atmosphere of a Russian Tsarism and of hastening the Revolution.

Since 1871 the pursuance of a policy of peace in foreign affairs had come to have the authority of a dogma in Bismarck's eyes owing to the grave dangers threatening the Empire from within and the lack of political education in Germany. After 1871 Bismarck no longer entertained thoughts of further conquests on the Continent, while he regarded the acquisition of further territories inhabited by a non-German population as an evil to be avoided. Moreover, a union of German Austria with Germany would have resulted in such a strengthening of the Catholic minority in the Empire that the balance of forces desired by Bismarck would have been disturbed. But he was not averse from the acquisition of colonies overseas, and he was successful in acquiring these on a considerable scale without involving Germany in a war with any European Great Power.

It was England who chiefly stood in the way of Germany's colonial expansion. Bismarck was of the opinion that England could be forced to give way and to make territorial concessions overseas by confronting her with a united Europe. For his disputes with England Bismarck needed the help of France—of a powerful France[19]—and he looked upon any further crippling of France beyond the restrictions placed upon her in 1871 as hurtful to German interests. It was obvious that the policy of playing off France against England needed to be pursued with caution. Bismarck did not believe that France would be reconciled to the loss of Alsace-Lorraine within a lifetime. If Germany were to be involved in a war with another Great Power, it was only to be expected that France would seize the opportunity to attack Germany. Hence Bismarck never allowed his disputes with England over colonial questions to go to such lengths that a breach of the peace was rendered possible. It had always to be borne in mind that, although France gave Germany diplomatic support against England, she might, in the event of a crisis arising, be suddenly found on the other side. Even when he made common cause with France and Russia against England in colonial and overseas questions Bismarck was invariably cautious! He would have looked upon an attempt to carry out a colonial policy in opposition to France and England as insane. Without permitting himself any illusions as to the feeling prevalent in the French middle class, Bismarck did all that lay in his power to improve Franco-German relations. He refused to give any support whatever to plans for a monarchist *coup d'état* in France, since he looked upon the middle-class Republic in Paris as more likely to pursue a peaceful foreign policy than either a clericalist monarchy or a Bonapartist dictatorship. Bismarck furthered all the wishes of the French Government in foreign affairs, and especially in colonial questions, in as far as it was possible for him to do so. For the more deeply France engaged herself in Morocco[20] and China the farther she was diverted from thoughts of Alsace-Lorraine and *revanche*.

Apart from France, the two possible enemies of Germany on the Continent were Russia and Austria-Hungary. According to Bismarck the chief aim of German policy must be to avoid Germany's being involved single-handed in a war with several Great Powers at the same time. From a military standpoint the German Empire was thoroughly capable of engaging in war with a single enemy; but a war with two or more Great Powers simultaneously must create an exceedingly precarious situation for Germany. In Bismarck's opinion the natural foreign alliance for Germany was the alliance with Russia, which accorded with Prussian tradition prior to 1871, since it was solely owing to the friendly attitude of Russia that Prussia had been able to wage her wars with Austria and France. Moreover, there existed no serious political differences between Russia and Germany, who were indeed bound together by common monarchical-conservative interests and a common enmity towards the Catholic-Polish movement. In alliance with Russia Germany could face an Austro-French alliance, inspired with a desire for revenge, with equanimity. If, however, Austria refused under the influence of the events of 1866 to enter such an alliance, and instead joined herself to the conservative Russo-German alliance, then an alliance of the Three Emperors afforded Bismarck the best guarantee of peace that he could wish for.

The events of the years 1875–9, however, forced Bismarck to place less reliance upon the support of Russia. Under Prince Gortschakoff's leadership Russia clearly perceived the dilemma confronting Germany. Gortschakoff demanded Bismarck's unconditional support, even at the risk of a war with Austria and England, for Russia's policy of expansion in the East. If Germany hesitated to participate in such an adventure, then Russia almost openly threatened that in alliance with France, and perhaps even with Austria and England, she would attack Germany. For Russia in those days could realize her traditional policy in the East in two ways: either by directly making war upon her rivals in the East with Germany protecting her in the rear or by leading a victorious coalition of the European States against Germany.

In the latter instance, as the arbitrator of Europe, Russia would be able to arrange the frontiers of the Balkan States according to her own wishes. The beginnings of the subsequent Entente lay in the seventies when, on the one hand, Gortschakoff sought an alliance with France and, on the other hand, Gladstone was prepared to solve the Eastern Question in a common understanding with Russia.

In order to release Germany from her dangerous dependence upon Russia Bismarck from 1879 onwards made the Austrian alliance the basic principle of his foreign policy. Nevertheless, he avoided breaking the connecting link that bound Germany to Russia, and, after a brief period of ill-feeling between Berlin and St. Petersburg, he extended the alliance with Austria by means of the Reinsurance Treaty with Russia. Bismarck was successful in maintaining the treaty with Russia in force for as long as he remained in office. The twofold alliance thus created was based upon a very simple premiss. Germany would not tolerate a Russian attack upon Austria, although in the event of an attack by Austria upon Russia Germany would remain neutral. As compensation Russia bound herself not to attack Germany.[21]

The secret of Bismarck's retention of Russia's friendship, despite many disagreements and periods of ill-feeling, lay in the fact that he never encroached upon or injured a vital Russian interest. He steadily supported Russia's claims to a protectorate over Bulgaria and to the Dardanelles. Russian statesmen had only themselves to

blame for the fact that during the reign of Prince Alexander of
Battenburg Russian influence declined in Bulgaria, and that they
failed to solve the Straits Question in the Russian sense. For these
failures they could in no wise blame Bismarck. Bismarck never
once interpreted the Austro-German Alliance in such a way as to
accord Austria a free hand in the Balkans. Austria could only
indulge in Serbian and Bulgarian adventures at her own risk, and
without any hope that she would receive the military support of
Germany.[22] Finally, Bismarck never even contemplated Germany's pursuing an active policy in Turkey.

The desire of Italy to join herself to Germany and Austria encountered Bismarck's opposition. Italy was inspired by the desire
to reinsure herself for her anti-French Mediterranean policy.
Bismarck took care to see that the Triple Alliance did not involve
Germany in any avoidable quarrels with France in regard to
French interests in the Mediterranean. The ease and skill with
which Bismarck manipulated his international system cannot blind
one to the fact of its complexity. The steering of a middle course
first between Austria and Russia, and subsequently between
France and England, required an experience and suppleness of
which none of Bismarck's successors were possessed. Despite the
conflicts that arose from time to time, Bismarck was successful
after 1871 in arousing an unusual degree of confidence in the
unselfishness and pacific aims of German foreign policy, and this
trust was reposed in him not only in Vienna and Rome, but also
to a very high degree in St. Petersburg, London, and even in
Paris. It was solely owing to his pursuit of a peaceful and sensible
foreign policy that Bismarck was able to resolve the domestic
problems in Germany from 1871–90 in accordance with his own
wishes and to give an appearance of stability to the internal situation in Germany.

NOTES TO CHAPTER I

1. Bismarck's basic sociological conception is most clearly expressed
in BGE, ii (1898), p. 59: 'The greater caution of the more intelligent classes
may quite likely arise from the materialist basis of preservation of property:
. . . but for the security and advancement of the state, it is more useful
to have a majority of those who represent property. . . . Every great
community in which the careful and restraining influence of the propertied
classes is lost on material or intellectual grounds will always develop
a pace that will cause the ship of state to founder, as happened in the case
of the first French Revolution.' Bismarck said in Munich on June 25,
1892: 'If I possess the respect of the young people and of the educated

middle class among my countrymen, then I am assured of the only thing
which I still strive after in my private life.' Compare with this Bismarck's
speech in Friedrichsruh on April 8, 1895: 'The results of national development in every country are chiefly dependent on the minority of educated
people which the country contains. . . . Unrest among the lower classes
may cause an acute illness for which we have remedies; but unrest among
the educated minority will develop into a chronic disease whose diagnosis
is difficult and whose convalescence is wearisome. It is for this reason that
I feel that the most important consideration in any country is the up-
bringing and the outlook of the educated classes.' For Bismarck's views
on the necessary co-operation between agriculture, industry, and trade,
see his speech of July 9, 1893, in Friedrichsruh; also his speech of June 9
1895, at the same place. The political manifestation of the welding
together of these powers upon which the State depends was in Bismarck's
opinion the Conservative-Liberal Coalition. See his speech in Kissingen
on July 24, 1892; also his speech on April 14, 1891, in Friedrichsruh.

2. The political currents in Prussia during the constitutional struggle
can be understood by a study of the extremely interesting statistics of
the elections for the Landtag of October 20, 1863, reprinted in the
Zeitschrift des königlichen preussischen statistischen Bureaus for 1867,
p. 240. Votes were recorded in the whole country as follows (in thousands):
for the Liberals 536, Conservatives 336, Poles 132, Catholic Party 23,
indeterminate 72, total 1,099. The Party statistics were extraordinarily
difficult to compute, owing to the complicated 'three-estates' suffrage
system. This is the explanation of the great number of votes which
appear in the statistics as 'indeterminate'. It is clear that in those days
the Liberals had an absolute majority in Prussia. The results of the
election statistics are arranged according to urban and agricultural
districts. The Liberals obtained large majorities in all the towns; except
in the province of Posen where the Poles were in the majority. Particularly
interesting are the election results in the country districts: in east and
west Prussia the votes were recorded as follows, in percentages of the
total number of votes: Conservatives 30%, Liberals 37%, Poles 23%,
indeterminate 10%. In Brandenburg: Conservatives 54%, Liberals 43%,
indeterminate 3%. In Pomerania: Conservatives 61%, Liberals 33%,
indeterminate 6%. Liberal majorities in country districts were also found
in the provinces of Saxony and Westphalia; a Conservative majority in
Silesia, a Polish majority in Posen. The three divisions at that time
showed roughly the same political picture. The considerable success of
the Liberals in the country districts of east Prussia, for example, prove
that a great number of the peasants were actually of the Opposition.
The election results of the rural districts of the Rhine province were
astonishing: Liberals 60%, Catholic Party 8%(!), Conservatives 20%
indeterminate 12%. Thus the Catholic peasantry of the Rhineland was
unreservedly in opposition to the Prussian Government. There was then
no Church and State controversy. Hence the Catholic peasant voted
for the candidate who would be likely to oppose most strenuously the
Prussian system. At that time that would have been the Liberal and not
the Clerical candidate. After 1871 the picture changes. The Liberals

had meanwhile become pro-Prussian and anti-Clerical. Henceforward the Catholic peasant voted only for the Centre.

3. BGE, iii, p. 16: 'The parliamentary Opposition would gain fresh power if the exclusiveness which has hitherto prevailed in the Federal Council were to come to an end, and Bavaria and Saxony would make common cause with Richter and Windthorst.'

4. For a description of the class-warfare in Upper Silesia see Bismarck's speech in the Prussian Landtag on February 9, 1872.

5. BGE, ii, p. 169: 'If, after the Treaty of Frankfurt, a Party favouring Catholicism, whether of royalist or republican tendencies, had come to the fore in France, we should hardly have succeeded in postponing the renewal of war as long as has actually happened. In that case we should have had to fear that our two vanquished neighbours, Austria and France, would have approached one another on the ground of their common Catholicism, and would have made a joint attack upon us; and the fact that in Germany there were nearly as many people as in Italy whose religious feeling was stronger than their national feeling would have served to encourage and strengthen such a Catholic alliance.'

6. Bismarck, speaking in the Prussian House of Commons on January 31, 1872, said: 'As long as we are expected to rule constitutionally, we must have a majority in order to pursue any given policy. As I mentioned yesterday, we shall not get this majority if we follow the course suggested by the honourable members opposite.' (He meant the members of the Centre.) See also his speech in the Prussian Landtag on February 9, 1872.

7. Bismarck on the Conservatives, on Stöcker, and the *Kreuzzeitung*: BGE, ii, pp. 153, 156; iii (1919), pp. 19 and 22.

8. Bismarck's break with the Liberals: a thorough analysis in BGE, ii, pp. 180 et seq.

9. As examples of the decay of Liberalism in the rural districts, we may cite some east Prussian electorates. During the constitutional struggle the Liberals were in a majority in the country districts of east Prussia. At the Reichstag elections of 1871–8 the district of Ragnit-Pillkallen, for example, was represented by a Liberal. At the Reichstag elections of 1903 in the same place the Conservatives polled 11,000 votes, the Liberals 1,200. Stallupönen was represented by a Liberal from 1874 to 1877; in 1903 the Conservative obtained 12,000 votes and the Liberals 1,300. Lötzen-Angerburg had a Liberal representative from 1874 to 1877; in 1903 the Conservatives polled 9,000 votes, the Liberals 700. Sensburg-Ortelsburg returned a Liberal in 1871–5, 1877–8, 1881–4; in 1903 the Conservatives polled 11,600 votes and the Liberals 1,100.

10. In the Prussian Landtag in 1913 there were 202 Conservatives, 73 National Liberals, 40 Independents. The Centre had 103 members, the Social Democrats 10, the Poles, Danes, and Lithuanians 15 between them.

11. At the Reichstag elections of 1903 Conservatives, or members of allied parties, were returned from the following south German electorates: in Homburg-Kusel in the Palatinate a representative of the Landowners' Association; in Ansbach a Conservative; in Dinkelsbühl (Franconia) a

Conservative; in Rottenburg a.d. Tauber, a Protestant member of the Peasants' Association; in Heilbronn a Conservative; in each of the two Würtemberg electorates of Backnang and Gerabronn a member of the Landowners' Association; in the Alsatian electorate of Zabern the German Imperialists' candidate was successful. Of the provinces of New Prussia, Hesse-Nassau in 1903 elected five representatives of the Right. The Conservatives only got one representative in Hanover and Schleswig-Holstein respectively in 1903. Nevertheless, in most of the other electorates of these two provinces, they had considerable minorities. At the Prussian Landtag elections, which gave the peasant proprietors the advantage, the Conservatives achieved a much greater success: at the Landtag elections of 1913 Hanover elected 36 representatives among which were 18 Conservatives; and in Schleswig-Holstein of 19 representatives 11 were Conservatives.

12. See Bismarck's speech in the Reichstag on December 3, 1884.

13. In his speech at Jena on July 31, 1892, Bismarck said: 'I consider the Centre as an enemy to the country in its tendency even if not in all its members. There are plenty of good Germans amongst them, but the general tendency is such that I consider them as a danger to the country. If the Government were to choose its authoritative advisors from the Centre Party and formulate its policy so as to please the Centre, a procedure which can have no lasting stability, it would be a misfortune for the Fatherland.'—Bismarck on a coalition of the Conservatives and the Centre: see his speech in the Reichstag on December 3, 1884.

14. The 'German Gladstonian Cabinet': BGE, ii, pp. 134, 188, 197.

15. BGE, iii, p. 51: 'It went against my principles and experience to interfere to such an extent with the independence of the worker, his means of earning a livelihood and his rights as head of a family, as to forbid him by legalization to make use of his working-powers and those of his family at his own discretion. I do not believe that the worker at the bottom of his heart is grateful to those who forbid him to earn money on such days and at such times as he chooses. . . . I have by personal inquiry discovered that workers will only agree to the prohibition of Sunday work in the cases when they are assured that the week's wages will be just the same for six days as they were for seven. As regards prohibition or curtailing of work for non-adults, the parents of those who were forbidden to work did not agree, and among the non-adults themselves only individuals whose tendencies were unsatisfactory.'(!)

16. On the subject of the Constitution see Bismarck, BGE, ii, p. 60.

17. At the Reichstag elections of 1887 a total of 7,541,000 valid votes were recorded. The Centre received 1,516,000, and the Social Democrats 763,000. In 1890, 7,229,000 votes were registered, of which the Centre received 1,342,000 and the Social Democrats 1,427,000.

18. In vol. iii of BGE Bismarck does not give details of the methods by which he intended to fight the Social Democrats. On p. 57 he speaks of the need for making the laws against Socialists more severe. He was probably referring to decisions which he had already taken in 1878, but had not then been able to carry through. See Bismarck's letter to Tiedemann on August 15, 1878, printed in BGE ii, p. 190: 'I consider further

that, if the law is to be effective, it is impossible permanently to allow such individuals as are legally defined as Socialists the right to vote and to be elected and the enjoyment of the privileges of members of the Reichstag.' At the same time Bismarck was planning a change in the Imperial suffrage system which was to substitute open balloting for secret. See BGE, ii, p. 59, and Bergsträsser, *Geschichte der politischen Parteien in Deutschland*, 4th edition, 1926, p. 85. If Bismarck had carried through all these projects, every elector who openly voted Socialist would thereby have forfeited his right to vote; apart from the fact that none of these votes would have counted!

19. See GP, vi, p. 177. Bismarck to the Ambassador von Schweinitz, on February 25, 1887: 'France's continuance as a Great Power is just as necessary for us as that of each of the other Great Powers. If only on the ground that for certain contingencies we need a counterpoise to England's sea-power. . . . Thus in the next war, if we win it, it will be wise to treat (France) leniently, just as we did Austria in 1866. If I have said anything to the contrary in the Reichstag, it is to discourage the idea of war. If this does not succeed, we should offer France peace on favourable terms after the first battle we win.'

20. GP, iii, p. 397. Prince Hohenlohe, then acting Secretary of State for Foreign Affairs, on May 6, 1880, sent to Count Solms, the German Ambassador in Madrid, the following instructions regarding the International Morocco Conference which was then meeting in Madrid: 'The Imperial Chancellor is of opinion that it will be better for us not to come into the foreground at the discussions over this question, but rather on general political grounds to go hand in hand with France, who has justifiable interests to uphold in Morocco on account of her neighbouring Algerian possessions.'

21. GP, vi, p. 62. Memorandum by Count Rantzau dictated by Bismarck on December 20, 1887: 'Our system of secret treaties sets a premium on friendly demeanour, because we stand by Austria if Russia breaks the peace, and stay neutral according to the Russian treaty if Austria commits a breach of the peace. Thus we neither can nor may promise the Austrians anything, no movement of troops, no mobilization, if Austria is the aggressor.'

22. GP, vi, p. 57. Bismarck to von Albedyll, the Chief of the Military Cabinet, on December 19, 1887: 'The efforts of Austria, or at least of those Austrian statesmen and militarists who wish to seize the opportunity to earmark the German army for specific Austrian purposes, or any purposes as have no interest for Germany, are directed towards the extension and prolongation of our treaty. It is impossible for us to agree to this.' On December 27, 1887, Bismarck wrote to the Ambassador Prince Reuss (GP, vi, p. 66): 'Our entry into a possible future war will depend chiefly on a Russian attack on Austria. A simultaneous declaration of war or mobilization, such as have been the subject of military discussion, could therefore not occur, because Austria will already have been attacked by Russia and be at war with her, if a *casus foederis* exists for us.' In view of what happened in 1914 it is particularly interesting to consider the situation in 1885, when Austria was preparing to invade Serbia during

the Serbo-Bulgarian War. If the Austrian troops had then invaded Serbia, Austria would have come into serious conflict with Russia. In a memorandum to Prince Reuss, the German Ambassador in Vienna, on December 6, 1885, Bismarck draws attention to the fact that, according to the Treaty of June 18, 1881, Austria can only invade Serbia with the consent of Russia. Bismarck continues (GP, v, p. 26): 'If the breach with Russia should be caused by an Austrian invasion of Serbia without previous agreement according to the treaty, we could not very well make the matter the excuse for a Russo-German War.' The actual facts of the cases must be taken into account in considering the difference in the situation in 1885 and 1914; also the circumstance that the treaty of 1881 was no longer in force in 1914. Nevertheless this letter of Bismarck's indicates how he would have behaved in a situation like that in July 1914.

II

INTENSIFICATION OF THE INTERNAL POLITICAL CONFLICTS IN GERMANY UNDER WILLIAM II

THE Emperor William I died on March 9, 1888. His was unquestionably an outstanding personality. He completely understood the Bismarckian system and he possessed sufficient foresight, notwithstanding his strong dynastic feeling, to permit the Chancellor to govern. Up to his ninetieth year he watched closely over the course of political events and invariably formed an independent judgement upon them. His greatest trial of strength with Bismarck occurred in 1879 when the Chancellor turned from Russia to Austria in his desire to make the Austro-German alliance the basic principle of his foreign policy. The fact that William I would not tolerate any break in the friendly relations between Germany and Russia does honour to his political judgement. Although the old Prussian military traditions exercised a powerful influence over his mind, he was ready to assent to every concession to middle-class demands and changed circumstances that Bismarck held to be desirable. If he now and then betrayed his amazement in individual instances, the aged Emperor never permitted himself to be influenced in important questions by the views of his courtiers or his family.

The Imperial Constitution of 1871 made the German Emperor the most powerful man in the world. His power both at home and abroad was so immense that it inevitably aroused alarm and suspicion. Hence the German Emperor acted most wisely when he did not allow his enormous powers to be clearly perceived; the simple and unpretentious habits of thought and life of William I achieved this result. He was looked upon not as an autocratic military sovereign but as the first civil servant of the Empire, and foreign States had confidence in his peaceful intentions. Nevertheless, in the furtherance of Bismarck's policy, William I had waged three wars and frequently intervened in a ruthless manner in domestic affairs. Since he was no puppet, but a man of independent judgement, William I bears before History the full responsibility for the harshness that marked the constitutional struggle in Prussia, the *Kulturkampf*, and the anti-Socialist Law. But he ruled in silence. Never once did he wound or threaten his opponents by braggart speeches. Under William II the exact opposite took place. He laid bare before the world the vast Imperial power in his pompous and boastful speeches which were not followed up by deeds. Thus he made himself a laughing-stock and destroyed the prestige that was bound up with the most powerful position in the world.

The Emperor Frederick's brief reign brought about no real change in the situation in Germany. Although as Crown Prince Frederick had been more in sympathy with the Liberals than was his father, he was still a convinced believer in the Bismarckian system and, even had he reigned longer, he would hardly have altered it in any way.

On June 15, 1888, William II ascended the throne. From the standpoint of constitutional law his reign lasted from 1888 to 1918, but in reality two years must be deducted from both the beginning and the end of the period. From 1888 to 1890 Prince Bismarck, and from 1916 to 1918 General Ludendorff, governed in the name of William II, whose real reign only lasted from 1890 to 1916. At the very outset of and throughout his whole reign William II felt himself called upon to formulate Imperial policy. Since William II refused to allow himself to be guided by Bismarck, the Chancellor was faced with the alternative of either becoming a mere tool in the Emperor's hands or else of quarrelling with him. Bismarck chose the latter alternative and was speedily overthrown.

Why was Bismarck unable to defend his position, which he had occupied for thirty years with unprecedented success, against a young man who had nothing in his favour other than his royal title? Why did Bismarck not dispose of the refractory monarch in exactly the same manner as a thousand years before the Imperial Chancellor Pippin had disposed of the Merovingian king? The answer is to be found in the state of the Prussian army. The Prussian Corps of Officers was under an enormous debt to Bismarck; yet it felt itself bound to render obedience to the King and not to the Chancellor. Bismarck had never taken the trouble to gain a direct control over the military system. The Prussian army was a State within a State, commanded by the King through the intermediary of his Military Cabinet and the General Staff without any regard for the Government, and the professional jealousy of the generals was so great that they took care that no civilian, not even Bismarck, obtained any control over the army.[1] As long as William I lived Bismarck was in no danger, since the army was always at the service of his policy at the King's command. When, however, a monarch ascended the throne who was opposed to Bismarck that monarch could count upon the support of the army if he quarrelled with the Chancellor. If the generals had been on Bismarck's side, the relative strengths of the two opponents would have been other than they actually were; and he could have deposed the Emperor. As it was William II had all the real power in his own hands. Although this situation was in the highest degree unpleasant for Bismarck, it must be admitted that there was in it nothing contrary to the spirit of the Imperial Constitution: whether Emperor dominated Imperial Chancellor or vice versa was a matter of indifference; what was indispensable was that one or other should be the embodiment of the vast executive power. William II's determination to be his own Chancellor must of itself sooner or later have brought about the conflict with Bismarck. Moreover, there existed a real divergence of opinion between them as to the conduct of domestic and foreign policy.[2]

Even before he had ascended the throne William II had been brought in contact with and had assimilated the ideas of the Stöcker Conservatives. Although the irresistible advance of the Social Democrat Party had aroused in him feelings of alarm, William II refused his assent to Bismarck's plans for the forcible suppression of the Social Democrats. He wished to pursue a policy of social reform and to rule with an Imperial Government inspired by Stöcker's ideas. Among the chief exponents of these ideas was the Chief of the General Staff, Count Waldersee, who looked upon a war with France and Russia as inevitable, and under whose influence William II refused to countenance Bismarck's endeavours to maintain treaty relations with Russia. At the outset of his reign William II wished instead to prepare for a defensive war against Russia and France by a close alliance with Austria and possibly even with England. Bismarck dissented entirely from both the domestic and foreign policy laid down by William II. He was in consequence dismissed.

After 1890 William II not only interested himself in all the details of German foreign policy but actually determined its course, and he laid down at least in broad outline the course to be followed by domestic policy in Germany. While the Emperor displayed no lack of energy in dispatching the business of State, his technical knowledge was small, and the nervous hesitation and irritability to which he was subject rendered the steady pursuit of any line of policy impossible. Although he permitted his Ministers to oppose him in matters of detail, William II never suffered any one to pursue a definite course in domestic and foreign affairs. Moreover, his changeability was only heightened by the numerous influences at Court which were brought to bear upon him. Thus it came about that Germany from 1890 to 1916 had in reality no Government, and that the business of the day was discharged in a chance fashion and without regard to any principle. Nevertheless, a work of a real and lasting value was accomplished in many directions through certain laws that were placed upon the statute book. There was, however, no guiding personality capable of grasping the general situation in Germany and of working towards a definite goal. Political chaos resulted from William II's methods of government, and it was solely the chance that until 1914 Germany was not involved in war on a large scale that prevented the catastrophe from coming sooner than it did.

The fact that this catastrophe ultimately overwhelmed Germany was less the fault of the Emperor himself than the outcome of the Constitution of 1871. In constitutional monarchies the personality of the monarch plays no decisive role, and even autocracies have contrived to survive the government of utterly inefficient and incapable rulers. It is only necessary to call to mind the Austria and the Russia of the Napoleonic era to realize that the Emperor Francis I of Austria and the Emperor Alexander I of Russia were not the men to inspire their peoples with a feeling of confidence and security. The situation of Austria after the Battle of Wagram in 1809 was almost as hopeless as that of Prussian-Germany in the autumn of 1918; while the situation of Russia in 1812, when Napoleon was in Moscow, was equally grave, yet neither in Austria nor in Russia was there any sign of a revolutionary movement. Absolute monarchies can only be stable and secure so long as they are the traditional expression of the will of the politically and economically powerful class in the population.

In the old Austria and the old Russia absolutism meant the rule of the aristocracy. The emperor was only outwardly an autocrat: he was forced in reality to carry out the traditional policy of his Empire in domestic and foreign affairs, within the carefully defined limits that had been handed down to him. If he himself was incapable of doing this, then his Ministers were at his side ready to advise him in accordance with the political traditions of the Empire. In event of his sabotaging and paralysing the business of

State through his caprices he was deposed by the aristocracy as in the case of Peter III and Paul of Russia. Nobody, however, ever dreamt of altering the Constitution of the State. Instead a new 'absolute' monarch, who had learnt the limits of his power from the fate that had overtaken his predecessor, took the place of the deposed emperor and pursued the traditional lines of policy. Hence it came about that for hundreds of years autocratic monarchs could pursue a continuous line of policy without its suffering any real interruption through the accession to the throne of an incapable ruler.

The German Empire was neither a constitutional monarchy nor an autocracy with strong traditions; and the forces out of which the Empire arose lacked cohesion. Moreover, Bismarck's ideas had not in the slightest degree become part of the political 'make-up' of the governing classes. The Emperor was the pointer in the balance between the Prussian military aristocracy and the other forces in the Empire. The Bismarckian Empire was a Napoleonic creation whose prosperity depended to a very large extent upon the personality of the ruler—the Emperor or the Imperial Chancellor. After his dismissal Bismarck became a ruthless critic of William II's mistakes, yet he himself bore a share in the responsibility for them inasmuch as he was the architect of the Constitution which placed the destinies of Germany in the hands of William II.

Under William II the great territorial magnates in Prussia strengthened the ties that bound them to the Protestant peasantry throughout the Empire: the 'Landlords League' became a great power in the political life of Germany. The various attempts made to organize an association of the smallholders to oppose the Landlords League met with no success. Until the outbreak of the World War the Protestant villages continued to be Conservative, although a number of the farm labourers voted 'Red' at the Reichstag elections. When Bismarck's heavy hand had been removed, the Prussian Conservatives could not be brought to make concessions to the townsfolk and the working class; they resolutely defended their privileged position in the Army and the Civil Service; and the customs duties and taxes had to be framed in accordance with their wishes. The most valuable weapon in the Conservative armoury was the three-class-suffrage system in force in Prussia, and this they defied any one to destroy. William II lacked both the will and the power to diminish the aristocratic Prussian influence in the government of the Empire. Not that the Prussian Conservatives were invariably in agreement with the Emperor's actions; indeed many Conservatives capable of an independent judgement entertained grave misgivings as to many aspects of the Emperor's personal government, and especially as to his foreign policy. But the Conservatives as a whole never contemplated any reform of the Constitution which would have resulted in a curtailment of the Emperor's power, since they believed that any constitutional reform must weaken their own position. Instead they allowed everything to go on as before.

During William II's reign the liberal middle class steadily gained in economic strength, although its influence in Parliament diminished. The agriculturists dominated the Prussian Landtag, while at the Reichstag elections the municipal and industrial electorates returned Social Democrats in ever-increasing numbers. It was only with great difficulty that the Liberal Party managed to retain chiefly in the lesser towns a certain number of seats. To have introduced parliamentarism into Germany would have necessitated in the first place the transference of power from the agrarian Conservatives to the middle-class Liberals, but the weakness of the Liberals in the Reichstag, where they occupied at most a fourth of the seats, caused the prospects of a parliamentary régime to appear even more forlorn than they actually were. The influence of the middle class upon Imperial policy was achieved not through the Reichstag, but by means of pressure brought to bear upon the Emperor.

William II was personally very friendly with the leaders in commerce and industry, inviting them to Court and ennobling them, and when a great firm contrived to bring its foreign interests before the Emperor's notice in an interesting way, it could always reckon upon obtaining its desires. For William II was invariably prepared to protect a great industrial undertaking with the whole authority of the Empire as, for example, in the case of the Deutsche Bank's Baghdad railway project. As in other political spheres, so here William II was utterly devoid of foresight and never paused to consider the consequences that might arise out of such actions. Notwithstanding the influence wielded over the Emperor by such men as Ballin, the middle class as such was politically powerless, and stood aside while Germany was ruled by the Agrarians and Conservatives. Nevertheless the National Liberal industrialists retained the sense of loyalty to the Crown which had come to them as an inheritance from the Bismarckian era. In 1890 it seemed for a time as if the Emperor intended to pursue a policy of social reform even against the wishes of the industrialists. When, however, William II saw that neither his speeches nor his small concessions had the effect of winning over the Social Democrats he speedily changed his course, and in future social reform during his reign was confined within the limits set to it by the industrialists. Hence the National Liberals continued to be constant supporters of the Government in the Reichstag, approving the naval and colonial policies, and joining with the Conservatives and the Centre to form a majority to pass the protective customs duties. The manufacturers, on the one hand, saw in a strong government their best defence against the workers, while the 'free-thinking' merchants, on the other hand, who were not so sharply opposed to the working class, disapproved of the protective system. But in the Reichstag they were unable to offer any effective opposition to the Government which, especially after Eugen Richter's death, was always able by taking pains to assure itself of their votes.

It would nevertheless be wrong to judge the state of opinion among the middle class in Germany during William II's reign from the actions and speeches of the Liberal members of the Reichstag. As a whole the middle class was loyal to the Constitution and opposed to any attempt to reform it by force. Everything went on very much as it had done in the days when under Bismarck the political power of the middle class had been broken, although disapproval of the existing governmental system made itself manifest in the most varied ways.

Throughout the years 1890–5 a Bismarck 'cult' steadily arose in Germany, especially in middle-class and academic circles, from which the Prussian nobility as a whole remained aloof. Although this idolization of Bismarck was for the most part only the expression of Imperialist and Nationalist emotions, yet it afforded an outlet to an undertone of middle-class opposition to William II which Bismarck was quick to seize upon and stimulate by all the means in his power; and, especially, through the medium of the newspapers and journalists under his influence. If the Reichstag had in those days been the faithful reflection of middle-class opinion, a strong Bismarck Party would have been found in the ranks of the Opposition. Of this, however, there was no trace. In one of the Hanoverian electorates the National Liberals returned the old Prince to the Reichstag, but, although he accepted the mandate, Bismarck never made any use of it. His son, Prince Herbert Bismarck, was also elected to the Reichstag.[3] Yet an organized Bismarck Party never came into existence.

The most brilliant exponent of Bismarck's ideas was the editor and publisher of the journal *Zukunft*, Maximilian Harden, who combined the most unsparing criticism of William II, his Court, and his advisers with the expression of the upper middle-class desire for power in world politics. Thus—entirely in accord with Bismarck's own ideas—Harden was simultaneously the deadly enemy of the Emperor and of the Social Democrats. Although for obvious reasons Harden never formally declared himself in favour of a German Republic, nevertheless his constant and amazingly successful discrediting of the Emperor and his friends must have daily aroused republican feelings. If the question be asked who did most during the reign of William II to pave the way for the present German Republic, the answer must be returned that it was Maximilian Harden. A long way behind him came Erzberger, while Karl Liebknecht had no share in the task of preparation whatsoever.

The merchants in the great cities, especially in Berlin, were prominent among the opposition to William II. Their hatred of the 'Junker' power in the civil administration and army alike was united to their derision of and annoyance with the want of culture displayed by the governing classes. William II's ridiculous campaign against modern art, naturalistic drama, and the Secession, only had the effect of rendering Hauptmann and Liebermann the idols of the populace. The 'Siegesallee' was as unwelcome a sight in the eyes of the Berlin citizens as was the Chief of Police. The Protestant orthodoxy, which was all-powerful at Court, sought in alliance with the Centre to strengthen clerical influence in the schools and to exterminate the so-called 'obscene' literature and art. The modernist wing of the middle class met these attacks with angry resistance, and in doing so made common cause—as in the case of the 'lex Heinze'—with the Social Democrats.

The spirit of opposition among the citizens of the great towns found its expression in newspapers like the *Berliner Tagblatt* and *Simplicissimus*, and was directed towards a reform of the German Constitution along the lines of the English Constitution. The alliance between the Left Wing of the middle class and the Social Democrats was not confined to matters of art and education alone —a sphere in which the younger writers dealt with the social question in the spirit of 'Weber', but was interpreted to mean a far-reaching co-operation with the Social Democrats in the fight against the half-absolutistic, aristocratic government clique. This opposition movement was scarcely represented in the Reichstag, since the liberally-minded Reichstag deputies were for the most part returned by electorates composed of the lesser cities and country towns.[4] During William II's reign these deputies came as a rule from Lower Silesia, Würtemberg, Oldenburg, Danzig, Nordhausen, &c., while Berlin, Hamburg, Frankfurt am Main, and Munich almost invariably returned Social Democrats to the Reichstag. Nevertheless, the powerful radical Press, by the influence which it wielded over these deputies, rendered easier co-operation at the hustings between the Social Democrats and the Left Wing Liberals. The supporters of a coalition of the parties of the Left had before their eyes the example of Baden, where in the Landtag elections the co-operation between all the Liberal groups and the Social Democrats had placed the Centre and the Conservatives in the minority.

At the same time the power of the Left Wing Liberal opposition was limited inasmuch as the industrialists supported the Government, and their sole importance from a political standpoint consisted in the possibility of a coalition with the Social Democrats. It is true that in a crisis the Government was not defeated by the mere fact that middle-class opinion was behind the Social Democrat millions. It was, however, in order to maintain itself in power forced to rely upon the Centre. Hence the greater the increase in the strength of the Social Democrats the greater became the importance of the Centre as an indicator in the balance. And this was true not only of the relative voting strengths of the parties in the Reichstag, where since 1907 a reliable majority for the Government had been unattainable without the Centre, but also and to a far greater degree in regard to the relative strengths of the rival parties in the nation at large. If the Centre and the Social Democrats, supported by the sympathies of the middle-class opponents of the Government, had once united against the Government, a state of revolution would have been brought into being. But William II did not share in Bismarck's fear of making the Centre the pivot on which depended the existence of the German Empire. Hence it came about that from 1895 to 1906 the Centre was the chief support of the Imperial Government,[5] and its leaders were invariably in close touch with the Imperial Chancellor. Hohenlohe and Bülow always discussed the draft of any new measure of importance with the leaders of the Centre before submitting it to the Reichstag; and even admitted them to some extent into the secrets of the Foreign Office.

It would nevertheless be a great mistake to see in this relationship between the leading party in the Reichstag and the Government a step on the road towards the establishment of parliamentary government in Germany. In the first place the Reichstag dared not infringe upon the authority of the Emperor, and in the second place, notwithstanding the fact that information was occasionally given to its members, the foreign policy of Germany lay completely in the hands of the Emperor and the Imperial Chancellor. It is significant in this connexion that in 1914 the Reichstag had no knowledge whatever of the course of the diplomatic negotiations between the European Great Powers from the day of the Archduke Francis Ferdinand's murder in Sarajevo to the outbreak of the World War.[6] The Party leaders themselves knew nothing more of these matters than what they read in their newspapers. Hence it is impossible to speak of the existence of a parliamentary system in Germany before the War.

The influence wielded by the Centre in the Reichstag was disproportionate to its numerical strength in the electorates. The Centre was supported by the Catholic minority among the agriculturists and by the minority organized by the churches amongst the factory workers. The middle class was hardly represented in the Centre. The demand for a parliamentary system in Germany meant in reality the transference of power from the Prussian aristocracy to the German middle class rather than from the Emperor to the Reichstag. Thus the anti-middle-class coalition between the Centre and the Conservatives during the years 1895–1906 and 1909–14 for the purpose of forming a majority for the Government in the Reichstag had in reality only the effect of hindering the introduction of parliamentary government in Germany.

The leaders of the Centre throughout the reign of William II were in truth opposed to the introduction of a parliamentary system in Germany. The peace concluded under Bismarck between the German Empire and the Catholic Church now began to bear fruit. During William II's reign the Centre was led by a clique of Catholic civil servants who adopted a thoroughly die-hard attitude towards the existing political situation in Germany. Their attitude was shared by a number of the Catholic hierarchy. In men like

Spahn, von Hertling, and Cardinal Kopp the basic principles of national conservatism were united with the belief that the German Empire in its existing form afforded the best possible conditions of livelihood for German Catholicism. An entirely different standpoint from that held by the leaders of the Centre in the days of the *Kulturkampf*!

The Conservative group in the Centre was able to rely in ordinary times upon the agrarian interests of the voters for the Centre. Nevertheless the Roman Catholic peasantry of southern Germany, despite their patriotism, was not wholly bound up with the existence of the Hohenzollern Empire; and this was even truer of the Catholic workmen. Social democracy had made rapid strides even in the Catholic districts during the reign of William II, and before the War the great majority of the workmen in cities like Munich, Cologne, Düsseldorf, and Mainz were already Social Democrats. Among the Catholic miners in the Ruhr, however, the Social Democrats met with a stiffer resistance, as also among the Catholic workmen's organizations in the district of Munich-Gladbach, but ever since the Centre shared in the responsibility for the agrarian-conservative course taken by Imperial policy its hold upon the workmen became more and more precarious. Thus the majority of the miners in Upper Silesia went over in these years to the Radical Polish Party.

The fierce competition with the Social Democrats and the Independent Trade Unions forced the Catholic organizations to lay special emphasis upon their differences with the Social Democrats. Nevertheless their common enmity for Prussianism and capitalism brought together the Social Democrat and the Catholic workman. It is significant that the campaign waged by the Social Democrats against the Prussian three-class suffrage met with the fullest sympathy and support of the Catholic workmen.[7] As a party the Centre was not affected by the Prussian suffrage system, since with the help of its voters amongst the middle class in the towns and in the country the Centre was able to secure proportionately as strong a representation in the Prussian Landtag as in the Reichstag. But the removal of civil rights from the workmen who came within the third category was equally wounding to the Social Democrat and the Catholic workman.

The opposition of the Catholic workmen found expression in a Left Wing of the Centre whose more youthful leaders did not approve of the tactics of the die-hard Party chiefs. The most active and influential man among the leaders of this Left Wing of the Centre was Matthias Erzberger. Although it must be admitted that in many decisive issues his judgement erred, and that his political career was characterized by many changes of opinion, yet Erzberger had a remarkable gift for appreciating the realities in a situation and for extracting from that situation whatever it was possible to extract. But Erzberger was not the man to fight a long battle against Prussianism; on the contrary, he frequently worked in harmony with not only the old system itself but also with the soldiers who administered it. But the emergence of a crisis was sufficient to rouse him to such an extent that he became capable of making the most tremendous attacks upon the existing order. His quite exceptional energy assured to him the leadership of the German middle-class revolution. Alike in the Left Wing of the Centre, and in the radical middle-class opposition, he was recognized as a man who—while of no importance himself—became the deadliest enemy of the old order whenever he entered into alliance with the Social Democrats.

During the reign of William II the voting strength of the Social Democrats increased from one and a half to four and a quarter millions.[8] On the outbreak of the War a third of the population of Germany was enrolled within the ranks of the Social Democrats. After the repeal of the Socialist Law, William II never again attempted to suppress the Social Democrats by force, although Social Democrat leaders and workmen were constantly condemned by the magistrates on charges of *lèse majesté*, breach of the peace, &c. But in general the formation of Social Democratic organizations was carried out without interference by the State authorities. The Social Democrat associations and newspapers as well as the powerful and independent Trade Unions covered Germany as with a network. The Social Democratic Party Council became a sort of secret shadow Government and August Bebel at the height of his power a 'shadow-Emperor'. At the same time the Social Democrats were careful to keep the letter of the law. Since the repeal of the Socialist Law had given them back their freedom, the Social Democrats were all the more desirous of adding to their numbers by means of legitimate propaganda, although this was not to be interpreted to mean the abandonment of revolutionary methods nor of the seizure of power. If the German Empire and the Prussian Government did not feel themselves strong enough to destroy their deadly enemy, it would certainly have been sheer foolishness on the part of the Social Democrats to have precipitated a life and death struggle and therewith to have run the risk of a defeat like that experienced by the Paris Commune. The only real statesman possessed by the Social Democrat Party in the nineties, Friedrich Engels, laboured under no illusions as to the exact nature of the situation.[9] It would have been hopeless for the workmen to have engaged in street warfare with the entire Prussian army armed with all the latest lethal devices. With the growth in the strength of the Social Democrats at the elections of 1887, 1890, and 1893, however, there came a proportionate increase in the numbers of Social Democrats in the army. A time was therefore bound to come when there would be so many Social Democrats in the ranks of the army that it would be incapable of being used against the workmen. But if war should break out Germany would find herself in the same situation as France in 1793: the workmen would take over the reins of government amidst the ruins of an *ancien régime*, and a working-class Germany would victoriously repulse Russian Tsarism and its allies, even as France had defeated the united forces of monarchical Europe in the wars of the French Revolution.

As a realist politician and the possessor of a ruthless ambition, Friedrich Engels was the equal of Bismarck. The workmen became Social Democrats primarily in order to improve their miserable conditions of livelihood, and—thanks to the resolute fight put up by the Trade Unions—their wages were raised during the reign of William II. The concessions made by the Government to the working class were only wrung out of it by the pressure exercised by the Social Democratic Party. Moreover, the workmen understood little of the connexion between the capitalists and the military and police régime; they fought against Prussian 'militarism' and the three-class suffrage system in Prussia; nor were they inspired by a real wish to assume the upper-hand themselves. The proletariate is indeed often far more dependent in an intellectual sense upon the middle class than is conceded—thus revolutionary Socialism in Russia in the twentieth century could never have developed as it did were it not for the century-old revolutionary tradition of the Russian middle-class intelligentsia. And the fact that the English working class of to-day is able to form so clear and definite a judgement in all political questions is due to the example afforded it for centuries past by the English middle class. Among the German middle class no such tradition existed; and the foundations laid in the years 1848–71 of what might have developed into some such tradition were destroyed under Bismarck. It was no mere chance that without the revolutionary movement of 1848 the careers of the pioneers of Social Democracy in Germany —Marx, Engels, Lassalle, Wilhelm Liebknecht—would have been impossible. At school, in the army, and in the factory, the German workman only learnt to write and to read, the technique of his employment, discipline, and organization. He never achieved a political cosmogony. He had no conception of how the political, economic, and social revolution for which he longed could be accomplished, and no knowledge of which road would lead him out of his present distresses to a better future. Nor, although in some respects it accomplished much, was the educational activity of the Social Democrat Party able to fill in these gaps.

The rank and file of the Social Democrat Party were thus inspired by a strong class feeling and a willingness to sacrifice themselves for the Party on which they had become dependent: they were further inspired by a determination to better their economic condition and by a profound dislike for the Prussian governmental system. These feelings spread upwards from the rank and file to the officials and the General Council. At the same time the Party as such adhered to a policy of criticizing existing conditions and of 'wait-and-see'. Apart from its arrangements for the electoral campaign before each Reichstag election, the Party had no plans whatever for the immediate future. This passive official policy of the General Council was attacked from two quarters—by the Left Wing Radicals and by the Revisionists. The Radicals, under the leadership of Rosa Luxemburg[10] and Franz Mehring, recognized the fact that Europe was approaching an unprecedented crisis; they foresaw the World War and the Revolution which it was to bring in its train; and in their eyes the Russian Revolution of 1905 had opened a new and eventful period in history—a period in which German workmen must not be content with mere electoral campaigns but must prepare themselves for a revolutionary struggle. The German workman must be made skilful in the use of that weapon—a general strike—which had been used by the Russian proletariate in its fight against Tsarism. The Revisionists, under Eduard Bernstein, were no less convinced that pacifist methods must be abandoned, and that the policy of waiting for an immediate collapse of the capitalist system was both speculative and unreasonable. The Revisionists held that the working class had very definite tasks to accomplish within the limits imposed by the capitalist State. It was the duty of the workers to fight more strongly and more methodically than hitherto for the realization of economic and political reforms. According to the Revisionists, the Social Democrats would achieve a great deal more were they to win for themselves allies among the middle class, since in alliance with the radical elements in the middle class they would obtain a majority in the Reichstag and strike terror into the ranks of the Prussian militarists. The conclusion of such an alliance would of itself be a great achievement for the working class.

When the division within the ranks of the Social Democratic Party before the War is considered in retrospect, it must be confessed that both the Radicals and the Revisionists rightly judged in many important respects the course subsequently taken by events; and that the General Council on the whole comes out badly from any such survey. The General Council, indeed, lacked both understanding and foresight. It allowed itself to be surprised by the outbreak of the War and to become the slave rather than the master of circumstances during the War. Theoretically speaking, a coalition directed against the General Council could have been formed between the Radicals and the Revisionists; but not even Rosa Luxemburg recognized the importance of reform from the standpoint of the working class. Moreover, the conclusion of an alliance with even a section of the middle class for the purpose of overthrowing the dominant military feudality was in direct contradiction to the orthodox principles of Marxism. The Radicals might indeed with advantage have learnt much from the far more practical solution put forward by the Revisionists. But an unbridgeable gulf separated the two groups on a matter of principle. The Revisionists refused to listen to Radical warnings of an approaching catastrophe; and they refused utterly to believe in the immediate outbreak of a life and death struggle between Capital and Labour. The Radicals for their part were so convinced of the approach of decisive events that they regarded with derision the tactics and ephemeral triumphs of the Revisionists. Hence the battle between Revisionists and Radicals was fought out at the Party Congresses while the comfortable role of arbitrator between the contestants fell to the General Council, which was supported by the less class-conscious members of the Party as well as by the Trade Unions. The two active groups counted among their members the intellectual independents and academic thinkers of the Party, and, in both groups, the number of 'intellectuals' was considerable. Among the broad masses of the workmen, however, the Radicals enjoyed little support, while the Revisionists—thanks to special circumstances—were influential in the south German States. In Bavaria, Würtemberg, Baden, and Hesse no military aristocracy of a Prussian type existed to dominate the administration; and, apart from the working class, there existed a Conservative peasantry and a middle class inspired by Liberal principles. Moreover, the Civil Service was far more identified with the middle-class than with the clericalist peasants: a statement also true of the ruling dynasties. The Grand Ducal dynasty in Baden was famous for its old liberal traditions, and in Munich, Stuttgart, and Darmstadt there was no feeling of opposition as between the Court and the middle class.

Experience has taught that a middle-class government finds it much easier to come to terms with the working class than does an aristocratic and military government. Deep as is the gulf between employer and employed it is never so deep as that between a governing aristocracy and the masses. Not that the character of the individual contributes to the creation of this dissonance. The landowner and officer often outdoes the manufacturer in generosity towards the poor. Nevertheless, while the relationship between Capital and Labour is looked upon by the European of the twentieth century as being in the nature of things, a feudality is in his eyes something incomprehensible and intolerable.

Thus it was that the Social Democrats in southern Germany were less fanatical than their northern brothers, giving their assent to the budgets in the various States, and so contributing to bring about the much discussed movement of the Social-Democrat farm labourers towards the south German estate-owners. The most important development took place in Baden,[11] where the long-standing Liberal majority in the Landtag was threatened by the Centre. The Liberals in Baden allied themselves with the Social Democrats in order to keep the Centre in the minority, and, in the Grand Ducal Government, Liberals and Social Democrats worked together without any very grave differences of opinion. Various reforms advocated by the Social Democrats were put into effect, and they in return voted for the budget they had helped to draft. Further they were no longer in a position to boycott the Grand Duke. Thus Baden was transformed into a Revisionist stronghold, and the 'Grand Coalition of the Left', composed of National

Liberals, Independents, and Social Democrats, became a model opposition to William II in the eyes of all Germany.

This experiment in Baden constituted a deliberate departure from the Bismarckian tradition on the part of an important State in the Empire. Bismarck himself possessed an unrivalled and unerring instinct for ferreting out all those who were inimical to his creation. Although in his lifetime nobody dreamt of the 'Grand Coalition' in Baden, Bismarck recognized the danger to his system implied in the strength of the Liberal movement in that State.[12] The development in Baden was not in truth a step on the road to the socialization of Germany; it was a blow delivered against the governing Prussian aristocracy. At the Congress of the Social Democratic Party the General Council, with the help of the Radicals who were the protagonists of disciplinary measures against the 'insubordinates', passed a motion disavowing the proceedings in Baden.

It was a matter of indifference for the Empire and its rulers alike whether the Social Democrats pursued an active or a passive policy: the mere existence of a Social Democratic Party with a membership that ran into millions was itself the danger. In times of peace, indeed, the authority of the Prussian State was sufficiently strong to be able to deal effectively with any menace from the Social Democrats, as was shown in the case of the demonstrations organized by the Party, under the influence of the Russian Revolution of 1905, for the purpose of forcing a reform of the electoral system in Prussia. The Prussian police everywhere held the demonstrators in check, the military were not called upon to intervene, and the Prussian electoral system remained unaltered. What, however, would happen were the day to dawn when the proud battalions of the Prussian Guards were shot to pieces between Metz and Verdun, and when the working-class masses had to be called to the colours to serve in the *Landwehr* or in garrison battalions? The failure of the Imperial Government in the first grave crisis that arose would of a certainty have as its consequence the transference of power to the 'shadow' government, the General Council of the Social Democratic Party, and, were that to happen, the Left Wing of the Centre and the opposition Liberals would as a matter of course unite with the Social Democrats. After 1890 Bismarck had again and again prophesied this development.[13] Two courses were open to the Government by which they might master the situation: either to suppress the Social Democrats brutally after the manner of Bismarck—a course which after 1890 nobody had the courage to follow—or to pursue a policy of compromise that would, in the first place, accord a share in the government to the middle class and then, after that had been achieved, lead to an attempt being made to come to terms with the working class. But William II and his Chancellors—Caprivi, Hohenlohe, Bülow—adopted neither of these alternatives and simply let matters take their course. Then, in 1906–8, Chance once more gave an opportunity to the old order in Germany to save itself.

A conflict arose in the Reichstag in 1906 between Prince Bülow and the Centre over certain questions of personnel in the Colonial Service at whose head stood the former Berlin bank director, Dernburg. Since his appointment to a high office of State was looked upon at the time as a concession to the middle class, Dernburg could rely, in his fight with the Centre, upon the sympathies of the National Liberals and the Progressives in the Reichstag and upon those of all middle-class Liberals throughout Germany. The Centre, indeed, had not the slightest intention of engaging with the Government in a struggle over matters of principle. Although Erzberger took part in the attack upon the Government, its leader was a member of the ultra-Conservative group in the Centre, Roeren. On failing to obtain their demands, the Centre vetoed a part of the financial estimate for the defence force in South-West Africa and, as the Social Democrats voted with the Centre, the Government found itself in a minority in the Reichstag. At this very time the troops in South-West Africa were engaged in suppressing a native rebellion. The Government therefore declared that the number of troops for which the Centre was prepared to vote the money would not suffice to put down the rebellion. How was it that this issue was allowed to develop into a sharp contest between Bülow and the customary supporter of his policy, the Centre? A few minor concessions on the part of Bülow would have sufficed to placate the Centre. But, in truth, the higher officials in the Imperial Civil Service were unwilling to acknowledge the slightest control by the Reichstag—even so slight a control as that implied by the action of the Centre. Bülow seized the opportunity to raise his dispute with the Centre and the Social Democrats to the dignity of a question of 'national' interest. The Reichstag was dissolved. The Conservatives, the National Liberals, and the Progressives united to form a 'Block' in order to assure a majority at the elections without the Centre. At the election of 1907 the

Centre held its own. Although the number of votes cast in their favour remained the same as in the election of 1903, the Social Democrats lost about forty seats owing to the fact that many electors abstained from voting. A certain majority was thus assured in the new Reichstag to the coalition of Conservatives and Liberals.

Through a number of fortunate coincidences William II and Bülow were thus able to return to the policy followed by Bismarck in 1887; and Bülow's forces were even stronger than those of Bismarck had been. In the Liberal camp Bismarck could only reckon on the support of the National Liberals whereas Bülow could also count upon that of the Progressives. The middle-class Liberals had supported the Government solely in the belief that Dernburg's appointment, and the breach with the Centre, meant the beginning of a new period in German politics. Everything now depended upon this hope not being disappointed. Bülow, however, who was no statesman but only a clever tactician, never envisaged a reform of the German Constitution. Nevertheless Fate gave Prince Bülow and his supporters still another unprecedented opportunity in which to reform Germany.

In 1908 occurred the episode of the *Daily Telegraph* interview.[14] William II permitted an interview with him to be published in the *Daily Telegraph* in which he protested his friendship for England. Apart from other observations, the article contained the following remarks by the Emperor: the German fleet was not being built against England but against Japan; at the time of the Boer War, when Russia and France had secretly inquired of Germany whether she would make common cause with them against England, he had not only refused but had revealed the whole plot in a letter to Queen Victoria; still more—at a moment when the English army found itself in a critical situation in South Africa he had, in collaboration with the German General Staff, drawn up a plan of campaign indicating the way in which the Boers could best be defeated which was dispatched to London, and which advised the employment of almost the same tactics as those by which Lord Roberts subsequently defeated the Boers; yet, despite all this, he continued to be looked upon as the enemy of England. Before the Emperor gave his consent to the publication of the article in the *Daily Telegraph*, he sent the text to Prince Bülow with orders to read it through and to make such alterations or omissions as he thought desirable. As Bülow subsequently admitted, he did not himself peruse the article, owing to pressure of work, but he sent it instead to the Foreign Office with instructions to go through it carefully. The Foreign Office proposed a few slight alterations, and announced its consent to its publication when these had been made. Bülow reported in this sense to the Emperor, and the article, with the desired alterations, was published on October 28 in London.

In raising no objections to the publication of a thoroughly blameworthy article the Foreign Office assumed a heavy responsibility. Although it was in a position to do so from the documents in its own possession, the Foreign Office had not even corrected the fantastical tale of the Emperor's alleged plan of campaign. The Foreign Office was actually in possession of a copy of the document which William II had sent on February 4, 1900, to the Prince of Wales (later King Edward VII). This document contained 'Twenty-two Aphorisms on the Conduct of the War in South Africa' from the pen of William II—completely harmless observations of a general nature from which the English generals could not have derived the slightest benefit—and there is nothing to show that the German General Staff had had any hand in their compilation. William II, in order to display his friendship towards England, was guilty in 1908 of a gross lapse of memory. Yet so great was the veneration in which an Imperial memorandum was held in the Foreign Office that not a single official dared to make any real alterations in its text. Or was it that they were so devoid of political sense that they did not appreciate the results likely to ensue from its publication? That Prince Bülow passed on the document unread revealed unheard of carelessness on the part of a great State official inasmuch as he at least must have known the Emperor's foibles. The *Daily Telegraph* affair furnishes a classic example of the way in which Germany was governed throughout the reign of William II.

The publication of the interview aroused a storm of fury against the Emperor in the entire German nation from the Conservatives to the Social Democrats. The man who autocratically laid down the foreign policy of Germany unwarrantably provoked Japan, deprived all the Powers of any feeling they may have possessed that they could with safety make a confidential communication to Germany, and, finally, boasted that he had betrayed a small and friendly nation in time of war by going behind its back to its enemy with his famous 'Plan of Campaign'. The Emperor found himself confronted with the gravest crisis that occurred in Germany until

1918, and, in the debates in the Reichstag on November 10–11, with a united front of all the political Parties. Prince Bülow did not attempt to defend the Emperor, and even joined in the Reichstag's expression of its desire that the Emperor should maintain a greater reserve in the future. On November 17 the Emperor received Prince Bülow in audience. William II was infuriated with his Chancellor and—humanly speaking—rightly so. For he had sent the unfortunate article to the Imperial Chancellor for his approval and had only allowed its publication on receiving Bülow's consent. Thus the constitutional responsibility for the *Daily Telegraph* interview rested upon Bülow's shoulders—no matter whether he had read the text or not. Nevertheless William II did not dare to dismiss Bülow in view of the state of public opinion. The outcome of the audience on November 17 was an official announcement in the *Reichsanzeiger* in which William II gave an assurance that in future he would 'ensure the stability of Imperial policy by respecting his constitutional obligations'—an announcement that read like an abandonment by the Emperor of autocratic government.

Now or never was the moment in which to carry through a reform of the Bismarckian Constitution. Foreign policy must be placed under the control of a foreign minister answerable to the Reichstag, and an Imperial Cabinet constructed which would also be responsible to the Reichstag for its actions. Since the Emperor's hands were tied as those of none of his predecessors had been since 1848, Bülow and his supporters had only to proceed as a united body in order to achieve all. But the introduction of parliamentary government and the limitation of the Imperial power was impossible without the consent of the Conservatives who would have had to surrender voluntarily a part of their authority to the middle class. Moreover, it would have been necessary to form both a Liberal-Conservative Imperial Cabinet and a Liberal-Conservative Cabinet in Prussia. If the Bülow 'Block' had been capable of raising itself from a purely political combination formed for tactical reasons into an organism in which all the chief forces in the Empire were united, the basic defect in the Bismarckian Constitution might have been remedied in the eleventh hour. In similar situations the English Conservative Party behaved in such a manner. The Prussian Conservatives showed themselves to be still possessed by the same narrow-mindedness which had characterized their fight against Bismarck. They absolutely refused to forgo one jot or tittle of their historic privileges. They were filled with anxiety at the prospect of the continued existence of the Bülow 'Block' and at the spectre of a reform of the Prussian franchise that had once more made its appearance. The very slightest alteration in the Prussian franchise system must of necessity involve a loss on the part of the agrarian Conservatives. Who, moreover, was ready to guarantee that the Liberals would not become more greedy in their demands if they were looked upon as an indispensable element in the building of a Government majority? Finally, the natural support of the Conservatives in their fight against 'Democracy', and for the maintenance unchanged of the old Prussia, was above all else the undiminished Royal power. The Conservatives only joined in censuring the Emperor for his part in the *Daily Telegraph* affair on the understanding that now as formerly they refused to assent to any parliamentarization of Germany.[15]

Hence the great national movement against the Emperor vanished like a puff of smoke. For a reform of the Bismarckian Constitution by legal means and along the path of evolution was only possible with the co-operation of the Conservatives. If the Conservatives refused their assent to any alteration in the Constitution, then revolution became the sole means open to those desirous of reform. Although its inevitability was determined in that eventful year, even though those then living did not clearly apprehend the significance of what had taken place, neither the psychological nor the material conditions for a revolution were present in 1908.

The Conservatives, indeed, desired to leave the dangerous 'Block' and to return to their well-tried alliance with the Centre which had been guided through the crisis by its conservative-minded leaders. At the election of 1907 the Centre was forced for tactical reasons to side with the Social Democrats, especially in the case of second ballots at which the Opposition Parties continued to help one another against the 'Block'. This co-operation at the polls between the Centre and the Social Democrats did not lead to any political alliance between them. The leaders of the Centre did not wish to close behind them the door that opened upon a possible return to their alliance with the Government, and it was with feelings of relief that they beheld Bülow at loggerheads both with the Emperor and the Conservatives.

A quite unimportant event in 1909 led to the dissolution of the Bülow 'Block'. The Conservatives refused their support for a death duty proposed by the Government; and were supported in their refusal by the Centre. Bülow found himself in the minority and his 'Block' dissolved. The decisive factor in inducing the Conservatives and the Centre to oppose the death duty was not so much the unwillingness of the landowners to shoulder an additional financial burden as their common desire to overthrow the 'Block'. Bülow resigned on finding himself without a majority in the Reichstag.

William II saw in this event a personal triumph.[16] The fact that Bülow had been overthrown by a vote in the Reichstag was taken by the Emperor to mean that the Reichstag acquiesced in his part in the *Daily Telegraph* affair. The nation had been for a time deceived by Bülow and rendered inimical to the Emperor. Now, however, it had returned to its loyalty to the Emperor. The effect produced upon William II by the national indignation in 1908 at once disappeared, and he resumed his old system of autocratic government unchecked by any limitations. Bülow was succeeded in the Chancellorship by a typical bureaucrat, Bethmann-Hollweg, who was not in the least likely to have ideas of his own nor to seek to endanger the Emperor's authority. The severest charge that could be brought against the *ancien régime* in Germany is that such a man as Bethmann-Hollweg was Imperial Chancellor in July 1914.

On his resignation Bülow was the recipient of an ovation to which he was not in the least entitled, and he came to be looked upon by a great part of the nation as the champion of a modern and reformed Constitution which would put an end to William II's autocratic government and the power of the reactionary landowners. But Bülow had in truth only engaged in the battle with the Centre for purely tactical and opportunist reasons and not from any far-reaching political motives. Moreover, Bülow himself shared in the responsibility for the *Daily Telegraph* affair and had only brought pressure to bear upon the Emperor because he (Bülow) was too weak-willed to stand up against the people's fury. So great was the reputation with which he left office in 1909 that an influential current of opinion sought in 1917 to restore him to the Chancellorship in the belief that he would prove the saviour of Germany.

The middle-class Liberals were deeply embittered by the dissolution of the Bülow 'Block' inasmuch as they beheld the last possibility removed by which the intolerable political situation in Germany might have been reformed. Yet the Liberals did not take to the barricades any more than did the Social Democrats. But the desire grew stronger in them to ally themselves with the Social Democrats in the fight against the Prussian Junkers and the half-absolutistic governmental system in Germany. The Reichstag elections of 1912 saw a formal co-operation at the polls between the Progressives and the Social Democrats and between the National Liberals and the Progressives. The Social Democrats received four and a half million votes and won one hundred and ten seats, while the Liberals almost entirely made up at the cost of the Conservatives and the Centre for what they lost to the Social Democrats. This changed relationship in the strengths of the various Parties was at once made apparent on the assembly of the Reichstag in the voting for the election of a President. This election was by no means a mere formality in as much as the President was brought into personal touch with the Emperor between whom and the Reichstag he acted as intermediary. In view of the existing relations between the Social Democrats and the Emperor the election of a Social Democrat to the presidency could only be interpreted as an insult to the Emperor. On this occasion the Reichstag elected Spahn, the leader of the Centre, as its President by a narrow majority. His opponent, Bebel, received the support not only of the whole Progressive Party but also of twenty members of the National Liberal Party. As Vice-President the Reichstag elected the Social Democrat, Scheidemann, who was also supported by some of the National Liberals,[17] although he was compelled to resign his office a few weeks later on his refusing to go to Court. If he had been supported by the whole National Liberal Party, his election would have been tantamount to a public demonstration in favour of a republic. As yet, however, matters had not gone to such a length—but what a change had come over the political scene since 1890! What must have been the feeling among the German middle class when loyal, patriotic National Liberal members of Parliament, who had been returned as the representatives of industry, saw no other course open to them except to vote for Scheidemann and Bebel! But the Emperor, Bethmann-Hollweg, and the ruling Prussian nobility shut their eyes to what was going on around them in Germany. Then in the winter of 1913–14 a new crisis arose. Once again an event of no very great importance in itself gave rise to a bitter conflict between the governing caste and the rest of the German nation.

In the little Alsatian garrison town of Zabern a dispute arose between the inhabitants and some young officers from the garrison. Street demonstrations were held in order to protest against the officers' conduct. The Colonel of the Regiment then in garrison in Zabern, von Reuter, who considered that the civil authorities had neglected to take proper measures to protect his officers, gave orders to his men to seize a score or more of the demonstrators and confine them in the barracks for the night. By thus acting the Colonel gravely exceeded his authority, since under no circumstances was an army officer authorized to place civilians under arrest, although he could plead in extenuation of his offence that he had acted in good faith and of necessity. At other times, and under different political conditions, the incident at Zabern would merely have been looked upon as a regrettable local disturbance. But in the existing political tension in Germany the Zabern affair stirred the German nation to its very depths. The majority of the population felt itself to be physically and legally defenceless against high-handed actions on the part of the military aristocracy. As chance would have it Zabern was the sole district in Alsace-Lorraine in which the Protestants were in the majority over the Catholics. It was in Zabern that an emotion of loyalty towards the German Empire first began to display itself, and for many a long year it was the only electorate in Alsace to be represented by a Conservative member. Despite all this—such was the treatment which the inhabitants of Zabern had to suffer at the hands of the German army! In the debate that ensued in the Reichstag the action of the military authorities was sharply and brutally defended by the Minister for War, von Falkenhayn, as also by the Imperial Chancellor, von Bethmann-Hollweg, in his customary weak and ineffectual manner, and there arose a storm of indignation in the Reichstag against the Corps of Officers the like of which had never before been known in the whole history of the German Empire. The Centre joined with the Social Democrats and the Liberals in censuring the action of the military in Zabern, and it was actually a member of the Centre, Fehrenbach, who delivered the most effective attack upon the military régime. The Conservatives found themselves completely isolated. On December 4, 1913, by a majority of 293 over 54 with 4 abstainers, the Reichstag condemned the action of the Government in the Zabern affair.

The most important political lesson to be learnt from the Zabern incident was that even the cautious leaders of the Centre were forced to go with the crowd on the occurrence of any great mass movement in opposition to the Government, and that the Prussian Conservatives and the Prussian governmental system could not rely upon the support of the Centre in a serious crisis. William II, Bethmann-Hollweg, and the Corps of Officers regarded the Zabern incident as bound up with the prestige of the existing governmental system, and held that the military authorities had from beginning to end acted in a perfectly correct and justifiable manner. On January 10, 1914, Colonel von Reuter was acquitted by a court martial in Strasbourg. The majority of the nation and the Reichstag were forced to reconcile themselves as best they could with the verdict. Six months later came the World War.

On the outbreak of war the German nation found itself in an intolerable state of political tension. The enmity between the ruling aristocracy and the masses had steadily increased from year to year throughout the past six years. Although incidents like the *Daily Telegraph* interview, the 1912 election, and the Zabern affair did not of necessity point to a revolution, yet nevertheless they were typical of a pre-revolutionary period. If the war had not broken out in 1914, the conflict between the Imperial Government and the majority of the German nation would have continued to intensify to a point at which a revolutionary situation would have been created. The immediate consequence of the war was to bridge over, although not to close, the breach between them. But it was obvious that the longer the war lasted, and the greater the burdens and miseries it brought in its train, the more powerful would become the forces that threatened the truce that had been concluded between the rivals until the day should be reached when War and Revolution would be synonymous terms.

It had been Bismarck's opinion that the Hohenzollern Empire could hold its enemies in check, notwithstanding all difficulties, only for so long as peace was maintained. William II was equally desirous of maintaining peace. Although in 1890 he had believed that a war between France and Russia was inevitable, he had later become more and more convinced that peace could be maintained. In his opinion, however, a will to peace was not sufficient of itself to preserve peace—a clever policy directed towards that end must also be pursued. Neither William II nor his Imperial Chancellors from Caprivi to Bethmann-Hollweg nor his immediate entourage ever desired war. But by the unprecedented mistakes of which they were guilty they were responsible for leading Germany along the path that led to July 1914.

The domestic policy and the foreign policy of a State cannot be distinguished from one another since both alike are the expression of the social forces in power in the State. The balance of political forces in Germany as arranged in the Constitution resulted in placing the final decision in all matters of policy in the hands of the Emperor, even though he might be as undiplomatic by temperament as was William II whose impulsiveness and infirmity of purpose aroused mistrust everywhere. Foreign Powers began to doubt whether it would ever be possible to pursue a steady course in common with the Germany of William II. Thus the confidence in German policy which had been awakened in foreign Powers by William I and Bismarck was destroyed. Although his fiery speeches were never followed up by deeds, yet William II's love for rousing and menacing words only served to increase the general mistrust in which he was held.

In his speeches William II did his best to improve Anglo-German and Russo-German relations, and he was devoid of the least enmity towards France. Nor should certain occasional strongly-worded *marginalia* from his pen on diplomatic dispatches be taken too seriously. But the fact remains that he failed to bring Germany into a state of political stability either at home or abroad. Yet, without recourse to a revolution, there was no means of depriving the Emperor of the control of foreign policy that had been placed in his hands by the Constitution. The Prussian aristocracy for their part had no reason for desiring to pursue an imperialistic and warlike policy. The east Prussian landowner had neither commercial interests at stake in China nor coal-mines in Morocco. The real cause of the difficulties in which Germany found herself abroad lay far more in the power of commercial expansion displayed by the German middle class and the jealousy which that aroused in Germany's competitors, and nowhere more notably than in England. If Germany had had a middle-class government like England or America, then the middle class would have organized and regulated its policy of expansion in accordance with a definite plan. Being itself responsible for guarding its own political interests, it would have reflected carefully over what was and was not attainable: it would not have dissipated its own strength; and it would certainly not have simultaneously aroused enemies against itself in all quarters of the globe.

Although the middle class failed to exercise a continuing influence on German foreign policy under William II, individual firms having overseas interests competed with each other for the protection of the Emperor and the Imperial officials who believed it to be their duty to fulfil the demands of industry and commerce. The lack of direction which characterized German foreign policy was due to two causes: the fitful and muddle-headed way in which William II conducted the business of State and the senseless conflicts between rival firms.

William II began his period of autocratic government by refusing to renew the Reinsurance Treaty with Russia. As a result the Dual Alliance between Russia and France, which Bismarck had worked successfully for two decades to prevent, came into being. Even were Russia and France to refrain from military action against Germany the political situation in which Germany found herself from that time forwards was an extremely precarious one; for she was forced to depend upon the friendship of Austria and England. Until the Russo-Japanese War and the outbreak of revolution in Russia in 1905, the Franco-Russian alliance was directed at least as much against England as against Germany. The old-standing rivalry between Russia and England in Central Asia seemed likely to provoke a crisis at the very time that England was engaged in disputes with France over territorial claims in Africa that reached a climax in the Fashoda incident.

At the close of the nineteenth century English statesmen were prepared to conclude an alliance with Germany notwithstanding the fact that England was being made uncomfortably aware of the growing competition of German trade. The danger, however, that the Tsar would one day seize China and India and so deal the British Empire her death blow was still greater. Hence came Chamberlain's plan for an Anglo-German-Japanese alliance directed against the Franco-Russian alliance. Germany's role in such an alliance with England would not have been a pleasant one, since she might have found herself compelled to fight in a world war at England's side for English interests without at the same time being protected against those sudden changes that take place in English policy with every change of Government. Nevertheless, Bismarck himself had in the last days of his Chancellorship reckoned upon joint action on the part of the Triple Alliance and England as against the danger threatening from France and Russia. Although Germany would have found herself in no ideal situation in an alliance with England, yet she would have been incomparably better off than in the situation in which she found herself in 1914.

William II and his advisors rejected the English alliance. It must be admitted that they could advance good reasons for their action. Nevertheless, if they were determined to take up the challenge of an economic and naval rivalry with England, there was only one course open to them: an agreement with Russia and France for the purpose of creating a continental alliance directed against English naval supremacy. For the construction of a German navy could only be of value in that the German navy in alliance with the French navy would be too powerful for the English fleet. It was utterly impossible to create a German navy capable of fighting at one and the same time against England, France, and Russia. A Franco-German understanding, despite Alsace-Lorraine, could have been achieved if William II had been prepared to act in the Bismarckian tradition and support all France's colonial projects. As it was, in her most important colonial ambition, in Morocco, France encountered the fiercest opposition on the part of Germany. German foreign policy was sacrificed to serve the interests of a few private individuals. William II's policy with regard to Russia was equally senseless. Although William II was filled with the friendliest feelings for the Tsar personally, Russia invariably found Germany standing in her path wherever she attempted to achieve a success abroad. At the time when Russia had concentrated her entire strength in northern China, Germany occupied Kiao-Chow and dispatched an army under Waldersee to Pekin. When Russia turned her attention to the Near East, she found Germany had been before her in Persia and the signal posts of the German-Baghdad Railway covering the Asiatic provinces of the Ottoman Empire. Finally, when Russia again embarked upon an active policy in the Balkans, Germany not only supported Austria by all the means in her power, but went farther and took up her stand as an independent factor in Turkish affairs by the dispatch of military missions. Bismarck had always contrived to avoid conflicts with Russia by never injuring a vital Russian interest. William II, on the contrary, everywhere either undermined Russian policy or openly came forward in opposition to it. Yet nothing was further from the intention of William II, Bülow, and Holstein, who held all the strings of foreign policy in his hands, than to provoke a war with Russia or France. These three men, who exercised the decisive influence upon German foreign policy, were solely concerned with defending Germany's so-called 'place in the sun', and, from a moral standpoint, Germany had unquestionably the same right as the other powers to interest herself in China, Morocco, &c. At the same time Germany could only challenge France and Russia in event of her being able to count upon the support of England. In any other circumstances it was no more than a risky speculation and was bound to end with an Anglo-Franco-Russian alliance against Germany. Moreover, the actual results achieved by German foreign policy were small, since the Emperor always gave way when he found that he could only achieve his aim by means of war. Kiao-Chow was the sole acquisition made by Germany in China, while she was compelled to abandon her interests in Morocco in return for a territorial compensation of more than dubious value in Central Africa. In Persia Germany retreated before England and Russia. Notwithstanding the German military missions in Turkey, William II did not afford any support to the Sultan in either the Tripolitanian or the Balkan wars. Foreign capital was admitted to share in the Baghdad Railway project. But these German concessions and withdrawals were ineffectual in making good the injury inflicted upon France and Russia by the behaviour of William II.

The defeat of Russia by Japan did away with the danger that threatened England from Russia in Asia. While in the Moroccan affair a Franco-German arose in place of the former Anglo-French colonial dispute, and thus the opportunity was given for English statesmen to render German competition harmless. King Edward VII brought the Entente Cordiale into being, and from then onwards English tactics became perfectly clear. England had indeed no intention of attacking Germany, but was resolutely determined that, in event of Russia and France being involved in war with Germany, she would be found among Germany's opponents. One real cause of the World War is to be found in this decision on the part of England. For had Russia and France not been absolutely certain of English support Russia would never have dared to attack Germany and Austria. It is true that England was not formally a partner in the Dual Alliance, but declarations on the part of the English Government existed that covered all eventualities. This situation must have been completely clear to the eyes of German statesmen in the year immediately preceding the outbreak of the World War. The German Ambassador in London, Prince Lichnowsky, left no doubt as to this in his dispatches. The seriousness of the situation was nevertheless not recognized in Berlin, and it was believed to be possible to divert the English Government from their warlike intentions by concessions in individual questions. No one was more under the influence of such illusions with regard to England than the Imperial Chancellor, von Bethmann-Hollweg. The English Government was always willing to conclude advantageous agreements with Germany over special questions, African colonies, Baghdad Railway, &c., and was further prepared to conclude a naval agreement by which both States would have bound themselves to slow down the rate of their naval construction. All this did not, however, influence the standpoint of England in the decisive question.

In no circumstance were English statesmen prepared to allow Germany to emerge victorious from a war with France and Russia, since, in that event, Germany would have become not only the paramount power on the Continent, but also so powerful that England would have found herself in the utmost danger. English statesmen of both Parties were determined to prevent such an eventuality, and were therefore unalterably resolved to make common cause with France and Russia in a continental war.[18] It is easy to see that England was thus not primarily influenced in her policy by the strength of the German Fleet. The danger for England lay in the possibility that Germany might one day dominate the western coast of Europe from St. Petersburg to Brest and not in whether Germany had a few cruisers more or less. From the standpoint of England's interests, this was a perfectly logical train of thought and there is no justification for accusing her of 'hypocrisy' and 'disloyalty'. It was not the fault of England if William II and Bethmann-Hollweg did not understand her policy. At the same time the notion that the World War would never have come if Germany had slowed down her rate of naval construction is no less false. It is true that the refusal of the German Government to conclude a naval agreement with England had a powerful effect on English public opinion and contributed not a little to render it easier for the English Foreign Office to pursue an anti-German policy.

How would an intelligent German policy have dealt with England? If Germany desired to keep the peace, she must of necessity avoid injuring France or Russia in any way. Since the unfortunate Morocco crisis had been terminated, there no longer remained any very acute issue between France and Germany. Yet at that moment Germany permitted herself to become involved in the Balkans in a serious conflict with Russia. The Anglo-Franco-

Russian Entente forced Germany into a hopeless dependence upon Austria-Hungary. Bülow and Holstein believed that Germany was doomed should her one trustworthy ally, Austria-Hungary, be defeated in a war; and, with some reservations, William II shared in this opinion to which Bethmann-Hollweg also subscribed. Although they completely misunderstood him and his policy, they called upon the name of Bismarck to support their theory. This was to do an injustice to Bismarck's memory in more than one respect. In the first place Bismarck would never have allowed Germany to be involved in such a way that her existence was at the mercy of Austrian statesmen. In the second place Bismarck never interpreted the Austrian alliance to mean that the German army was at Austria's disposal for any of her Balkan adventures. Finally, although Bismarck deemed the existence of Austria-Hungary a necessity for the German Empire, yet that was not to be taken to mean that Germany must inevitably take part in an Austro-Russian war. Indeed, Bismarck had in the most emphatic manner repeatedly declared that Germany would remain neutral should Austria be the aggressor; for in that case Germany would be quite powerful enough to defend the existence of Austria at a subsequent Peace Conference. William II and his advisors, on the contrary, placed such an interpretation upon the Triple Alliance that the Austrian Cabinet was able to include the German army in calculating Austria's war strength. This was ominously shown in 1908 at the time of the Annexation Crisis. The very clever and energetic Austrian Minister for Foreign Affairs, Baron von Aehrenthal, took the opportunity afforded him by the Young Turk Revolution to annex the two Turkish provinces of Bosnia and Herzegovina of which Austria had been in occupation since the Congress of Berlin. Legally Aehrenthal was in the right as against Russia, who at the Congress of Berlin had handed over the two provinces to Austria by a secret agreement and had further renounced any right of protest against their subsequent annexation. In the meanwhile, however, Serbia had exchanged the protection of Austria for that of Russia. The Serbian nation demanded that it should be united with its co-racials in Bosnia, and Russia supported the Serbian demand in the interests of its own Balkan policy. Thus the annexation of Bosnia gave rise to a grave conflict between Austria and Russia.

Cleverly and coolly Aehrenthal played his hand. He knew that he could rely upon Germany and that Russia was at that time not prepared for war. He refused to make any concessions, and induced the German Government to hand in a Note at St. Petersburg in which it declared that it shared the Austrian standpoint to the full and placed the responsibility for any failure of the negotiations on Russia.[19] At the time the question as to whether Germany's politely-worded note amounted to an ultimatum or not gave rise to much discussion; but that was after all a question of purely academic interest. What was of real importance was that Russia was no longer left in any doubt that, in the event of an outbreak of war over the Bosnian issue, Germany would be found on the side of Austria. Although Russia could already reckon upon the certain support of France and England, the Russian Government felt that its military preparations were not yet in a sufficiently advanced state, and accordingly yielded. The Entente had retreated before the Central Powers. Germany and Austria had won a diplomatic victory—but at what a price! The policy pursued by William II and his Ministers in the Annexation Crisis was an unpardonable mistake. From this time forth the Russian Government was convinced that in Balkan questions they would always find Germany taking the side of Austria. Russia was determined not to suffer a second humiliation; but to strengthen her army and to take the opportunity of the next Balkan dispute to go to war. Bethmann-Hollweg, on the contrary, added yet another to his many illusions by his belief that Russia would always yield before a forceful policy on the part of Germany, and that in this manner peace could be maintained. The doom was thereby sealed.

Then came the assassination by Serbian conspirators of the Archduke Francis Ferdinand. William II and Bethmann-Hollweg were convinced that the existence of Austria was once more at stake. Unless Austria received satisfaction at the hands of Serbia, her Slav provinces would fall away from her, and German interests required the maintenance of Austria-Hungary as a Great Power and an ally. Hence the German Government gave their support to the Austrian Government in its action against Serbia. At the worst William II and Bethmann-Hollweg only reckoned upon a local war between Austria and Serbia, and no one anticipated that Russia would offer any opposition to Austria's justifiable course of action. Still less did anybody think that England would be found fighting on the side of Russia in such a cause. Thus it came about that the German Government stumbled helplessly, blindly, and through sheer incapacity, into the World War.

It is untrue that William II and Bethmann-Hollweg deliberately worked to bring about the World War. If William II had wished to go to war in order to achieve German hegemony in Europe, he would have attacked France either at the time of the Russo-Japanese War or in 1905 on the outbreak of the first Russian Revolution. Russia was then powerless in a military sense; and Germany would probably have defeated France in her then isolated position in Europe. The pacific attitude maintained by the German Government in 1905 is a sufficient answer to the accusation of German war guilt. Apart from any other reasons, William II was far too nervous and lacking in self-confidence to wish to take upon himself the terrible responsibility of conducting a world war; nor was Bethmann-Hollweg—haunted as he was by anxieties and fearful of responsibility—the man to provoke a war. The Secretary of State for Foreign Affairs, von Jägow, sought from the very first day of the war to bring it as speedily as possible to a conclusion.[20] No military clique clamouring for war was to be found in 1914 at the Court of William II. The Chief of the General Staff, von Moltke, was not only ill but felt himself unequal to assuming the conduct of operations. How could he have forced a war? The Minister for War, von Falkenhayn, was a soldier who confined himself to the affairs of his department, and who was lacking in the ambition necessary to have induced him to mix himself up in political questions. The Secretary of State for the Navy, von Tirpitz, was away from Berlin during the decisive weeks in July 1914, and subsequently strongly disapproved of the manner in which the war was begun. Finally, the Chiefs of the Emperor's Military, Civil, and Naval Secretariats—von Lyncker, von Valentini, and von Müller—who exercised a considerable influence over the Emperor, were all branded as 'procrastinators',[21] and as such fiercely attacked during the war by the supporters of unrestricted submarine warfare, the Supreme Command, and the Crown Prince. While the men who ruled Germany in 1914 are thus to be absolved from any moral responsibility for the war, the political incapacity of William II and Bethmann-Hollweg must be condemned all the more strongly. That Germany should have supported Austria's action against Serbia was an unprecedented mistake, and one that was contrary to all the traditions handed down to them by Bismarck. Austria declared war on Serbia on learning of her rejection of the Austrian ultimatum. Russia thereupon mobilized her armies notwithstanding the warning she had received from Germany. Although from a political standpoint it was of vital importance for Germany to let Russia assume the responsibility for breaking the peace, the problem was handled in Berlin as if it were purely a question of tactics.

It was with the gravest anxiety that the German General Staff found itself confronted with a war upon two fronts. Alike in numbers and equipment the French army was approximately the equal of the German army, while the Russian army far outnumbered it and—thanks to the efforts of the Minister for War, Suchomlinow —was properly equipped. The Austro-Hungarian army, on the contrary, was so weak in properly trained men and modern artillery that it could only hold in check a fraction of the Russian army. Since no help was to be expected from Italy, Germany found herself called upon to wage war on two fronts against vastly superior forces. The German General Staff believed that the war could only be won by carrying out the plan which had been drawn up by Count Schlieffen, the former Chief of the General Staff. According to the Schlieffen Plan the whole military strength of Germany, with the exception of some divisions, was to be concentrated upon the Western Front in order to overrun France in a few weeks; and only after that had been achieved was the main army to be transferred to the Russian Front. That the General Staff looked upon the situation of Germany as exceptionally grave is shown very clearly by the Schlieffen Plan, which demanded for its successful execution that within a few weeks Germany should defeat her equal in strength and valour—France. No one can say with certainty if and how that could have been accomplished. What is certain, however, is that a General Staff called upon in event of hostilities to solve such an apparently insoluble problem is not likely to be desirous of war. In order to make use of the Schlieffen Plan, which the General Staff thought to be Germany's only chance of salvation, it was imperative that hostilities should be commenced on the Western and Eastern Fronts immediately after the Russian order for mobilization had demonstrated the inevitability of a conflict. From a purely military standpoint such an argument was unquestionably right; but, on the other hand, reasons of policy demanded that the odium of having taken the offensive should fall upon the enemy. William II and Bethmann-Hollweg lacked the courage to take upon themselves the responsibility for such a decision, and therefore they declared war upon France and Russia. At the same time there can be no question that the war was begun before the formal German declaration of war by Russia's attack upon Austria. Nevertheless, Germany's political situation was prejudiced from the very outset by the fact of her declaration of war. When, in addition, she proceeded to violate the neutrality of Belgium in pursuit of the Schlieffen Plan, the English Government was provided with an excellent excuse for England's participation in the war on the side of Russia and France. Thus the German Empire became involved in the very war out of which Bismarck had prophesied the emergence of a Socialist Republic.[22]

NOTES TO CHAPTER II

1. On the subject of the antagonism between Bismarck and the Generals see BGE, ii, p. 94, where the laughable boycott of Bismarck by the General Staff in 1870 is mentioned; see also BGE, iii, p. 111.

2. The circumstances which led to Bismarck's fall are fully explained in the third volume of the BGE. Not only Bismarck's motives are given, but also William II's views, in the original letters of the then Prince William of December 21, 1887 (on the subject of Stöcker see pp. 7 et seq.) and of January 14, 1888 (p. 23 also about Stöcker), again on May 10, 1888 (p. 136 on the relationship with Russia). This is not the place to enter upon a discussion of the much-debated individual questions.

3. Bismarck was elected to the Reichstag by Hanover on April 30, 1891. See his interesting speech to a delegation from the electorate on May 2. Prince Herbert Bismarck was elected by Jerichow, in the province of Magdeburg, in 1893.

4. At the elections for the Reichstag in 1903, Greater Berlin, for example, elected seven Social Democrats and one Independent; Hamburg three Social Democrats; Munich two Social Democrats; Frankfurt-am-Main one Social Democrat; Greater Leipzig two Social Democrats; Breslau two Social Democrats. At that time the Social Democrats had a total of eighty-one seats. The Progressives, who were split into four groups, received thirty-seven seats. Of these, eight members were from Lower Silesia, five from Würtemberg, two from Oldenburg. The remaining 'independent' electorates were scattered over the whole kingdom. The National Liberals at that time won 51 seats, the Centre 100, the various Conservative groups 94, the small Parties—Poles, Guelphs, Alsatians, &c.—34 between them. (The Imperial Reichstag had 397 members.)

5. For information on the subject of the Centre during William II's reign see REPORT, vii, pp. 227 et seq., statements by the German Nationalist Reichstag member, Dr. Martin Spahn, the son of the former leader of the Centre, Peter Spahn. Highly characteristic is a remark of Peter Spahn to his son, p. 229: 'You younger men must also consider the situation of

the German Empire as it is now. Everything is as brittle as if it were made of glass. Things can only be arranged with the greatest care according to each individual case.'

6. Bell, a member of ·the Reichstag, REPORT, vii, part i, p. 218: 'I do not know if it is everywhere realized that the historical events and the diplomatic negotiations, which took place between the murder at Sarajevo and the outbreak of war on August 1, 1914, were never brought to the knowledge of the Reichstag before August 4, 1914. The Reichstag never sat at all during this time. The Government did not consider that it was necessary to convene it or even at least to inform a committee or the Party leaders confidentially. Thus, on August 4, 1914, we were confronted with accomplished facts.'

7. At the Reichstag elections of 1903, 9,496,000 valid votes were recorded. Of these the Social Democrats received 3,010,000 and the Centre 1,875,000. At the elections of 1907 the number of recorded votes rose to 11,263,000. The Social Democrats received 3,259,000 and the Centre 2,180,000. At the elections of 1912, 12,208,000 votes were registered. The Social Democrats rose to 4,250,000, the Centre had only 1,997,000. If to the votes of the Social Democrats and the Centre, are added a few hundred thousand votes for the Poles, Guelphs, Alsatians, and Danes, it is seen that during the last decade before the War there was a clear majority of the people against Bismarck's governmental system.

8. On the subject of the Prussian suffrage question see the observations of Joos, a member of the Centre (leader of the Christian Trade Union) in REPORT, vii, part i, pp. 100 and 323.

9. See especially the political letters of Engels, published in 1920 under the title *Friedrich Engels Politisches Vermächtnis*, by the *Verlag der Jugendinternationale*. In a letter of October 24, 1891, Engels writes (pp. 24 et seq.): 'If in spite of everything the French bourgeoisie should begin such (a war) and should put themselves at the disposal of the Tsar of Russia for this purpose, who is really the enemy even of the bourgeoisie of all Western Europe, it would be a betrayal of the revolutionary mission of France. It is our duty, on the other hand, as German Socialists, who will come into power within a decade if peace is preserved, to maintain the position we have won in the van of the Labour movement not only against enemies at home but also against those abroad. If Russia wins, we shall be crushed. Rise, therefore, if Russia begins a war—rise against Russia and her allies, whoever they may be! ... We have not forgotten the glorious example of France in 1793, and if we are compelled, it may happen that we celebrate the centenary jubilee of 1793 by proving that the German Workers of 1893 are not unworthy of the Sansculottes of those days.' The same idea occurs in the letter of September 29, 1892 (pp. 38 et seq.). In a letter written as early as December 11, 1884 (p. 18), Engels discusses the question whether the Socialist Labour Government will follow direct on the Empire in Germany, or whether a middle-class democracy is a necessary intermediate stage: 'The matter may very well follow a different course (than in France in 1848) and on military grounds: external attack, as things are at present, is not likely to come from any-

where except Russia. If there is no attack from without and Germany is the aggressor, the revolution can only start in the Army. An unarmed people against a present-day army is from a military standpoint a purely vanishing quantity. In such a case, when our reserve from the ages of 20-5, who do not vote but who do drill, came into action, a "pure democracy" might be eliminated.'—See further Friedrich Engels's famous preface to Marx's book *Der Bürgerkrieg in Frankreich*. In this Engels was, of course, obliged, on account of the Public Prosecutor, to confine himself to references and comparisons.

10. The best account of the dissensions within German Social Democracy itself before the War is given in vol. iii of the collected works of Rosa Luxemburg, published by Clara Zetkin and Adolf Warski in 1925. Rosa Luxemburg and Bernstein, ibid., p. 92 f., and the South German tactics, pp. 408 ff.

11. For the great coalition in Baden see Bergsträsser, *Geschichte der politischen Parteien*, p. 106.

12. Bismarck and Baden: see BGE, iii, pp. 28 et seq.

13. See Bismarck's significant remark in BGE, iii, p. 131: 'At any rate to satisfy completely those allies which the Prussian monarchy and the Protestant Empire might find in the Centre and among the Jesuits, will be found to be as impossible as to satisfy the Socialists; and in case of danger and necessity we shall find ourselves in a situation analogous to that at the time of the decay of the Teutonic knights in Prussia when they could not pay their mercenaries.' The comparison of the Centre to 'unpaid mercenaries' is true Bismarckian venom. Nevertheless the political meaning of the remark is clear. If the German Empire were ever to suffer such a military catastrophe as befell the Teutonic knights at Tannenberg, then the Centre and the Social Democrats would strive for a new political system in Germany just as did the mercenaries and the vassals of the Order in Prussia.

14. All documents relating to the *Daily Telegraph* Affair are now published: GP, xxiv, pp. 165 et seq.—See also xv, pp. 551 et seq.

15. On November 6, 1908, a declaration against the Emperor's policy was published by the Conservative Party leaders. However, the *Kreuzzeitung* wrote on the subject: 'It is seen by the attitude of the Party towards parliamentarization that the Party leaders have not waited for the parliamentary action. This affair must not turn into a trial of power between Crown and parliament. It is not parliamentarians who are here expressing the wishes of the people with regard to the throne; it is the elected leaders of a monarchically-minded Party.' (See Schulthess, *Europäischer Geschichtskalender* for November 6, 1908.)

16. Stresemann in REPORT, vii, part ii, p. 301: 'The overthrow of Prince Bülow, to which the Conservatives contributed by rousing a fanatical opposition on the part of agriculturalists to a relatively small tax on direct inheritance, must have appeared to the Emperor as an atonement for the attitude of Prince Bülow. The people themselves in demonstrations at visits and addresses by the Emperor took absolutely no notice of the criticism of the Reichstag, but cheered him wherever he appeared, so that the Emperor's entourage could justifiably encourage the impression

that the Reichstag's mood was artificial and found no response among the people themselves.'

17. At the election of a chairman of the Reichstag on February 9, 1912, Spahn received 196 votes, Bebel 175. At the election for the first Vice-Chairman, Scheidemann received 188 votes and Dietrich, a Conservative, 174. On February 10 Spahn resigned his office. On March 8 the final election took place. The Progressive Kaempf was elected chairman, or President, with 192 votes. Spahn received 187. The National Liberal Paasche became First Vice-Chairman with 197 votes. Scheidemann this time only got 155.—See the notes by von Richthofen in REPORT, vii, part ii, p. 248. Richthofen at that time belonged to the National Liberal Party in the Reichstag and himself voted for Bebel.

18. Prince Lichnowsky's reports from London are best seen in GP, xxxix, pp. 119 et seq.

19. The decisive instruction of Prince Bülow to Count Pourtalès, the German Ambassador to St. Petersburg, on March 21, 1909, can now be found in GP, xxvi, part ii, p. 693. Prince Bülow demands that the Russian Government should declare its unreserved consent to the suppression of Article 25 of the Berlin Treaty, which upheld the Turkish suzerainty over Bosnia. Amongst other things Bülow writes: 'Your Excellency will please tell M. Iswolsky (the well-known Russian diplomat, at that time Minister for Foreign Affairs, later Ambassador in Paris) very firmly that we expect a definite answer—yes or no. We shall be obliged to regard any evasive, provisional or vague answer as a refusal. In that case we should withdraw and let things take their course.'

20. Von Richthofen in REPORT, vii, part ii, p. 215: 'It is noteworthy that von Jägow, the Secretary of State, has always been a great pessimist. I remember that he said to me during an interview at the Foreign Office, I believe only a day or two after England's entry into the World War, that it must be the aim of German foreign policy to get out of this most unfortunate war as soon as possible.'

21. See the Crown Prince's letter of July 18, 1917, to Dr. Michaelis, the Imperial Chancellor, published in REPORT, vii, part ii, pp. 388 et seq. The Crown Prince calls von Valentini the Emperor's 'evil genius'; and says that von Lyncker was altogether out of touch with the army; that von Müller should also be dismissed, since he 'is hated throughout the Navy, where he is called "the German Rasputin".'—The Crown Prince continues: 'These three men are notorious pessimists and scaremongers; they act most depressingly on His Majesty's spirits.'

22. In 1887 a visit of the Tsar Alexander III to the Emperor William I was expected in Berlin. According to his usual custom Bismarck prepared certain notes for the Emperor's political conversation with the Tsar. Since the two monarchs spoke French together, Bismarck wrote his memoranda in French. See GP, v, pp. 320 et seq. Bismarck puts forward the idea he often expressed, namely, that the three Empires must preserve peace if only because in case of defeat there would be danger of revolution. Bismarck visualized this danger not only for Russia but also for Germany: 'Au temps où nous vivons plus qu'à une autre époque de l'histoire il est de l'intérêt des grandes monarchies d'éviter la guerre . . . même en

Allemagne—si contre toute attente nous venions à être vaincus—les chances de la république démocratique ou sociale gagneraient considérablement par notre défaite.' (It is in the interest of the Great Powers to avoid war in these days more than ever before . . . even in Germany—if contrary to all expectation we should come to be beaten—the chances of there being a Democratic or Socialist Republic would be considerably increased by our defeat.)

III

THE WORLD WAR AND THE *BURGFRIEDEN*

ON August 4, 1914, the Reichstag unanimously voted the necessary credits for War. The members then dispersed and left the task of government and the conduct of the war alike in the hands of William II and Bethmann-Hollweg without even making an attempt to establish a system of control. The various political Parties agreed not only to a truce as between themselves but also to abstain from all opposition to the Government. While the so-called *Burgfrieden*, as this political truce came to be called, was accepted as a matter of course, public opinion was astonished at the readiness displayed by the Social Democrats to defend their country. When the events of August 4 are to-day considered in the light of all that has happened since, a precisely opposite conclusion to that arrived at by their contemporaries must be drawn from the action of the Social Democrats. The decision of the Social Democrats to assist in the defence of Germany was in accord with Marxist Socialist tradition. The *Burgfrieden*, on the contrary, appears less easily understandable to-day than it was seventeen years ago.

The Social Democratic group in the Reichstag comprised one hundred and ten members, and this group decided in favour of supporting the vote of credit by ninety-six votes to fourteen. The fourteen dissentient voters nevertheless submitted to party discipline and voted in the Reichstag for the war credit. Karl Liebknecht himself approved the grant on August 4 of five milliards to the Imperial Government for war purposes. If the minority had looked upon the passing of the credit on August 4 as a sin against the Socialist gospel, it would have disregarded Party discipline; especially so self-willed and fearless a personality as Karl Liebknecht. It was only when the Social Democratic members of the Reichstag became convinced that the German Government was conducting a war of conquest instead of a war of defence that they refused for the first time to pass further credits. The attitude adopted on August 4 by the Social Democratic members of Parliament was primarily induced by the feeling animating the masses of the Socialist workmen who were not prepared to tolerate an invasion of Germany by the troops of the Russian Tsar. Moreover, as has already been said above, the action of the members was completely in accord with the Marxist doctrine.[1] Although Marx and Engels were of the opinion that a Socialist order of society would do away with war in the distant future, they held that under capitalism war was a political instrument with which statesmen— even proletarian statesmen—may reckon. Moreover, the Marxist theory accords every nation the right to its independent existence and, therefore, the right of self-defence, and judges every war from the standpoint of the interests of the international proletariate in the belief that the Socialist workmen in every land should take up a common attitude towards each war.

A classic example of the Marxist attitude to war is the standpoint taken up by Marx and Engels to the Franco-Prussian war of 1871. At the outbreak of the war these two leaders of International Socialism were of the opinion that the defeat of reactionary Bonapartism and the unification of Germany was in the interests of the proletariate. After Sedan, however, an altered situation arose. Marx and Engels called upon the French workmen to defend the new Republic with all their strength at the same time as they called upon the German workmen to use their influence in favour of moderate peace terms and, above all, to protest against the annexation of Alsace-Lorraine. For the annexation was contrary to the wishes of the Alsatians and Lorrainers, and therefore forced France into the arms of the Tsar. In the nineties of the last century Engels foresaw the Franco-Russian war against Germany and had formed the following opinion about it. Germany was not only the land of the Hohenzollerns but also the home of the strongest and best-organized Socialist workmen in the world. Hence an attack upon Germany was simultaneously an attack upon the Socialist German workman. Thus the interests of the Socialist International demanded a German victory. Obviously it was the duty of German workmen to take care that the war led to a Russian revolution and at the same time that France should not be ravaged by a victorious Germany. The war would have the effect of strengthening the power of the working class in Germany to an extraordinary degree and, if it ended successfully, would make clear the path for the victory of Socialism in Germany. Friedrich Engels also desired that in a European war the working class in each of the great States should work each in their own way for a common aim, i.e. the German workmen for a German victory, but with their own special war aims and not those of German capitalists; the Russian workmen for the

Russian revolution; the French workmen for a speedy conclusion
of peace with Germany without mutual financial or territorial
sacrifices.

The German working class was so permeated with the ideas of
the great Socialist thinkers that it seemed only natural to them
that they should share in the right and the duty of defending their
country in a war waged against the Russian Tsar and his allies.
These ideas exercised a decisive influence in deciding the Social
Democratic group in the Reichstag to vote as they did on August 4.
The *Burgfrieden*, however, was not a consequence of the teaching
of Marx and Engels, and even the middle-class political parties
could have advanced good reasons against its conclusion. When a
great nation is involved in a war for its very existence, it must
arouse all the forces that are latent within it, and no means must be
spared to stimulate the fighting spirit in the poorer classes in the
community. That, however, is not possible of accomplishment
under the battle-cry 'Order is the first duty of a citizen', but only
in the most complete and independent and individual activity of
the masses. The most famous instance of this as also of a national
war is the defence put up by revolutionary France in 1793–4
against monarchical Europe, while the Bolsheviks would never have
been victorious in 1917–20 were it not for the extraordinary energy
displayed by the Russian workmen and peasants. The English
Revolution of 1688 was followed by a long and exhausting war with
Louis XIV, from which England only emerged victorious because
the House of Commons aroused all the latent strength in the nation.
History, indeed, teaches us that a national war can only be conducted by the independent action of the people and not under
aristocratic leadership with a censorship and martial law. Is it,
moreover, desirable that Party differences should be stifled in a
great war and all criticism of the Government silenced? The lesson
of History is that this question must be answered in the negative.
The English House of Commons never dreamt in 1689–97 of
concluding a *Burgfrieden* with the Conservative Jacobites; it sent
them to the gallows. In 1792–4 in the middle of a great war the
Mountain destroyed the nobles as well as the middle class in
France, and the defence of France did not suffer in consequence.
It was through their ruthless conduct of the class war that the
Bolsheviks derived the strength that enabled them to defend them-
selves against the Entente. During the Turkish War of Liberation
Mustapha Kemal destroyed the old Turks with fire and sword,

while in order to be able to free his country from the French and
English he had first to overthrow the Sultan in Constantinople.
It is always the most determined party or class representative of
the feelings that are most deeply rooted in the masses that in a
national war achieve power, and by overthrowing their domestic
opponents derive the strength which enables them to conquer the
foreign foe. The course of events in England and France during
the World War proved this to be true. Middle-class democracy
was firmly established in both these countries. Workmen and
peasants alike placed themselves under the leadership of the
middle class who were thus enabled to mobilize the whole strength
of the nation. At the same time the political and military leadership
was ruthlessly criticized in both countries throughout the war, and
incapable Ministers and generals were overthrown by public
criticism. In England and in France alike the working class was
politically too weak to assume the reins of government. Nevertheless, as the situation became more and more acute, Lloyd George
became Prime Minister in England and Clemenceau in France.
Both these men were the representatives of the extreme Left Wing
of the middle class—the section which had the closest ties with the
poorer masses of the people. Before the war Lloyd George had
broken the power of the House of Lords, and in alliance with the
English working class had carried the famous budget which imposed
the heaviest burdens upon the rich. Clemenceau could look back
upon a career of forty years' warfare passed in the ranks of the
Radical movement from the days of Gambetta to those of Dreyfus.
It was thus that these two men were possessed of the authority
that enabled them to lead their nations to war. The German
Lloyd George and Clemenceau were Michaelis and Hertling.
Notwithstanding its unexampled self-sacrifices and endurance, the
German nation was forced to pay in the World War for its lack of
political education.

On August 4 all Parties represented in the Reichstag might have
agreed that the Anglo-Franco-Russo-Japanese coalition against
Germany revealed the complete bankruptcy of the foreign policy
pursued by William II and Bethmann-Hollweg. The outbreak of
war did not make an end of international politics, and the fate of
Germany depended at least as much upon the political cleverness
of its government as upon its army. If it were not desirable at this
moment to accomplish the downfall of Bethmann-Hollweg, or
even to compel the Emperor to abdicate, would it not at least have

been wise to ensure public criticism of the Government? Should not the freedon of the Press and the right of public speech have been defended? Should not the Reichstag have remained in session in order to be able to intervene in any crisis? Had the political Parties no anxiety as to the aim for which Germany was fighting? Politics are not made of general battle-crys, such as 'Defence', and 'Public Safety'. Yet not a single one of the Parties from the Conservatives to the Social Democrats raised any such questions on August 4. Instead they passed the war credits and permitted themselves to be sent home. Without any attempt being made to hinder them, the Government became possessed of a dictatorial right to decide all military, political and economic questions, and was in a position with the help of the censorship and martial law to suppress all public expression of political opinion. Such was the German *Burgfrieden* of 1914. How did it come about that such a state of things was possible?

It was in accordance with the ideas of the Prussian military aristocracy that the King should be given a free hand in time of war; thus the *Burgfrieden* fitted in with Conservative opinion and besides the Conservative leadership of the Centre had no desire to interfere with the constitutional rights of the Emperor. Opposition was more likely to come from the liberal middle class and the Social Democrats; but both these parties lacked the 'will to power' necessary to have enabled the Reichstag on the outbreak of war to acquire for itself new rights. The unprecedented authority of the German General Staff also contributed to this result. Since the *Daily Telegraph* affair, the Emperor had fallen in public esteem, and nobody reposed any great confidence in the ability of either the Imperial Chancellor or the German diplomats. The General Staff, on the other hand, was looked upon as the silent defender of the traditions of 1870, and, as it held itself entirely aloof from all controversies and disputes, it thus acquired for itself an unequalled silent authority. On August 4 the Reichstag met at a moment when mobilization was proceeding with an almost uncanny precision throughout the entire Empire and no Party dared to lift a hand or raise a voice against the General Staff. The Reichstag voted the necessary money and demonstrated the unity of the nation. It was a repetition of 1870. Then the politicians had kept silence and Moltke alone spoke.

It is the duty of an historian to point out the lack of political capacity in the Reichstag of 1914. It must be admitted that the

Reichstag was then under the influence of a mighty historical tradition from which it could not free itself. Friedrich Engels had indeed believed that the Social Democrats were possessed of a stronger feeling of independence, and he had advised the Party to demand on the outbreak of a war that the war should be conducted by revolutionary means. By this Engels meant above all else a general arming of the people and not merely the summoning to the Colours of all trained soldiers. He intended that all men of military age should at once be mobilized, armed, and given the necessary training. In this way every workman would at once have become possessed of a rifle, and the authority of the ruling aristocracy would thereby have disappeared without any revolution. Supported by the armed masses, the Social Democrats, in Engels's opinion, would have been able to secure the control over both the domestic and foreign policy of the Government. But no attempt was made to put Engels's teaching into practice. The liberal middle class remained equally passive. Naturally, the *Burgfrieden*, in the sense in which it was concluded on August 4, could only have been maintained throughout a short war. And when the German General Staff was unable to give the nation the speedy victory that had been hoped for the political and class warfare broke out anew.

The German army in 1914 united all the qualities that have enabled the German people to distinguish themselves in industry, craftsmanship, and organization. The greatest blemish upon the army was the extreme harshness of the discipline which was due to the Prussian aristocracy. Among the higher officers was to be found a large number of men who were thoroughly skilled in the complexities of modern military science and who were fully qualified to lead troops. The decisive question, however, was whether or not the right men occupied the right posts, and whether the technical skill and capacity for endurance which characterized the army were properly made use of. The filling of the highest military command is never a purely military concern, but also depends upon political conditions within the State. Moreover, it is never possible to tell with absolute certainty from his conduct of manœuvres how a general will behave in war. Even with the greatest care mistakes are bound to be made, and what is of chief importance is that such mistakes should be recognized and made good as quickly as possible. A certain public opinion exists in all armies with regard to the capacity of the better-known generals, and in middle-class democracies the responsible Ministers are accustomed to pay great heed to military opinion and to fill the higher posts in the military service accordingly; a manner of selection which proved itself a great success in France and England. Thus, at the outbreak of war, the French army was under command of the best possible leader in General Joffre. The English generals and officers, accustomed though they were to colonial warfare, took some time to adapt themselves to the conditions of a great European war. Nevertheless, it cannot be denied that throughout the World War the English G.H.Q. comprised all that was best in the way of military talent. In Germany, on the other hand, the appointment of the Chief of the General Staff rested, according to the Bismarckian Constitution, solely in the hands of the Emperor. When he was possessed of as fine a knowledge of men and was as experienced in military judgement as was William I, then in fact the best men were appointed. The Prussian General Staff was not indebted for its brilliant record of 1866–71 to any heaven-sent military capacity in the Prussians, but to the fact that William I discovered Moltke the Elder and entrusted him with the command of the army. Under William II, the commands were filled entirely by chance, and what was of decisive importance was the personal feeling of the Emperor, who, lacking any real technical knowledge and understanding of men, customarily formed his opinion purely upon externals. Moreover, the appointments were made as the result of proposals from the Military Secretariat which was affected by all kinds of personal and court influences. Thus it was that on the outbreak of the war the task of leading the German armies fell to the Chief of the General Staff, General von Moltke the Younger.

General von Moltke was an extremely cultivated man, with, for an officer of high rank, an exceptionally gentle and sensitive temperament. He suffered terribly through the outpouring of blood resulting from the battles which he planned. Moreover, his physical and nervous condition in 1914 was already so bad that he should have long since been put on the retired list. In any other country the Government would have noticed the condition of the Chief of the General Staff and would have deprived him of his post in an honourable manner. It is impossible to believe that in countries like France, England, America, Soviet Russia, a man like Moltke would have been permitted to command armies in war. William II, however, was completely unobservant of all this and left the conduct of the war in the hands of Moltke. Thus the

Bismarckian Constitution was responsible for the fact that the
control of German policy in 1914 was entrusted to Bethmann-
Hollweg and the command of the German armies to Moltke the
Younger.

As the basis of operations, General von Moltke adopted the
Schlieffen Plan.[2] A weak German army was stationed in east
Prussia to support the Austrians in their resistance to the Russians.
The mass of the German army marched westward through Belgium
in order to overthrow the enemy forces by means of an outflanking
movement from the north. In order that the German armies
should be able to resist the threatening Russian attack, it was necessary that the decisive battle in the west should be fought and won
within approximately six weeks. The opposing forces on the
Western Front were numerically about equal in strength, since in
the first weeks of the war the French were only supported by
one hundred thousand English soldiers and a few Belgian divisions.
Thus far Moltke proceeded in accordance with the Schlieffen Plan.
But he ruined any possible success that might have resulted from
its employment by leaving almost a third of the German army in
Alsace-Lorraine, where they could have no share in the decisive
combat. Hence the outflanking troops in Belgium were far too
weak. If Schlieffen's ideas had been followed out to the full, only
a handful of German troops would have been left in Alsace-Lorraine. If the French had effected a break-through in that sector,
and even if they had succeeded in crossing the Rhine, it would
have been so much the worse for them; for then the French troops
composing the Rhine Army of Invasion would have been lacking
at the very moment when the decisive battle of the war was being
fought between Lille and Paris. They would have been compelled
to withdraw across the Rhine and would have fallen into the hands
of the victorious German main army. It would seem that Moltke
allowed himself to be influenced by political considerations in
departing from the strict letter of the Schlieffen Plan. At all costs
he wished to save Germany from a great foreign invasion, and to
ensure that the prestige of army and Emperor alike should not
suffer by the presence of an enemy army upon German soil. On
this supposition is to be explained the military failure of holding
back masses of troops in Alsace-Lorraine as also the panic that
arose in the Great General Head-quarters on news being received
that the Russians had invaded East Prussia. The French Head-
quarters Staff was free from all such internal weaknesses. General

Joffre did not permit himself to be disturbed in the carrying-out of his plans by the German invasion.

After the advance in the west came to a standstill battles involving heavy losses were fought in Lorraine and before Verdun in which the Germany army covered itself with glory without achieving any real result. In the north, however, despite all alterations, the Schlieffen Plan revealed that it contained the germs of victory. The German armies advancing from Brussels and Liege turned the northern flank of the Entente armies, and the great battle at Charleroi ended in a German victory. The French and English armies swiftly retreated southwards in order to escape encirclement, and the survivors of the Belgian army retired behind the fortifications of Antwerp. If the strength of the German armies in Belgium had been that intended by the Schlieffen Plan, the encircling movement would have resulted as early as the end of August in a decisive victory. As it was the German armies were forced to content themselves by the pursuit of the enemy who retreated upon Paris.

General Joffre understood the situation completely, and perceived that the danger for the Entente armies lay in the steady encirclement of their left wing by the Germans. This danger must at all costs be countered and the Schlieffen Plan thereby brought to nought. Regardless of all sentimental considerations Joffre withdrew his troops far south of Paris. The German right wing, which was entrusted with the encircling movement, was numerically too weak to pass by Paris on both right and left and so was compelled to march past it in an easterly direction. Meanwhile Joffre brought as many army corps as possible from Alsace-Lorraine to Paris, for Joffre, unlike Moltke, knew where the decisive battle would be fought. The extreme right wing of the German army of encirclement consisted of the First Army under the command of General von Kluck, who had as his Chief of Staff, General von Kuhl. The extreme left wing of the Entente armies was formed by the English troops. At the beginning of September Kluck's army marched eastwards and southwards past Paris in pursuit of the English. At that moment a new French army coming from Paris attacked Kluck in the rear and thus destroyed the Schlieffen Plan. Instead of encircling their enemies the German armies were themselves surrounded. It was still possible for the Germans to prove victorious in the west, but the utmost result they could hope to achieve from a victory would be to free themselves from the grasp of their enemy and to throw him back in a frontal attack. The war was no longer to be won by the annihilation of the enemy. Meanwhile the German Great General Head-quarters remained in Luxemburg and daily lost touch with the Front. At such a distance General von Moltke hardly knew what was happening on the Front. In these first weeks of the war the communiqués issued by the Great General Head-quarters, and signed by Quarter-master-General von Stein, filled the German nation with en-thusiasm. There was little in common between them and the real course of events. Not that there was any deliberate intention to deceive on the part of the Great General Head-quarters, but it could not report more than it knew itself. When in the last days of August reports of victories flowed in from all sides, General von Moltke was filled with the greatest optimism: a fact that explains the celebrated communiqués of those days. At the same time the General in Command of the German troops in East Prussia, von Prittwitz, was compelled to report that two Russian armies, greatly outnumbering his forces, had invaded Prussia. The Great General Head-quarters in basing their tactics upon the Schlieffen Plan had to reckon with such an occurrence. Nevertheless, General von Prittwitz, although no negligence could be proved against him, was immediately deprived of his command, and was succeeded by General von Hindenburg with General Ludendorff as his Chief of Staff. Moltke also deemed it necessary to strengthen the troops in Prussia with two army corps drawn from the Western Front. He did not, however, withdraw these corps from Lorraine, where they could best have been spared, but from the main army of encirclement, with the result that the lack of these Corps seriously affected the issue of the Battle of the Marne. Apart from the general offensive carried out by the main German army by Paris, Moltke ordered the troops in Lorraine to take the offensive in the direction of Nancy—an offensive that miscarried with tremen-dous loss.

Meanwhile General Joffre in addition to turning the German West flank ordered a general offensive on the entire Front. Then came the battle of the Marne. Kluck's army found itself in a critical situation, between the British army and the French army advancing from Paris. Kluck and Kuhl took a bold decision. Calculating upon the undue cautiousness hitherto displayed by the English Head-quarters Staff, which was uncertain of the exact position of the German army, they broke off the engagement with the English and, turning round, forced the advancing French army to retreat after a battle that lasted many days. In the course of these operations Kluck's army became widely separated from the main body of the German army, which was engaged in repelling the French offensive from the Marne to Verdun.

All this time the invalid Moltke sat in Luxemburg—helpless and vacillating—and William II continued to repose confidence in him. Moltke instinctively felt that disaster was threatening the German armies in the west, but he lacked the strength to go himself to the Front and take charge of the operations. Instead he sent a young General Staff Officer, Lieutenant-Colonel Hentsch, armed with unlimited authority. Hentsch quickly perceived the situation in which Kluck's army found itself, and recognized that it was possible for the enemy to pour their troops into the gap which separated Kluck from the rest of the German army. He therefore gave the order for hostilities to be broken off and for the German army to retreat behind the Aisne. Thus the great offensive in the west came to an end. There was absolutely no justification for Hentsch's giving the order to retreat. All the German armies engaged in the battle had won tactical successes and, if there had been a clever Commander-in-Chief present in person on the Front, the danger which threatened from the English and the gap in the German Front could have been overcome.

Although a German victory on the Marne would have compelled the French armies to retreat still farther south, the German army would still have been threatened from the direction of Paris and the French armies would have continued the fight. Germany had no need in the west of an ordinary tactical success that would have given her armies freedom of movement. She needed a second and greater Sedan—the annihilation of the enemy—in order to set free her troops for the Eastern Front. All hope of such a victory was destroyed with the miscarriage of the Schlieffen Plan. The German army—thanks to faulty leadership—did not even gain the tactical victory it deserved from its fight on the Marne. While the German army proved itself at least the equal of its opponents in the battle of the Marne, the victory lay with the enemy owing to the intellectual superiority of the French over the German Head-quarters Staff. When the extent of the disaster became clear to him General von Moltke suffered a complete breakdown and had to be relieved of his command.

The Bismarckian Constitution was based on the supposition that the King of Prussia and his army were necessary to enable the German nation to establish its authority in the world. All moral justification for the old system finally disappeared in September 1914, since the King of Prussia had not only contributed by his mistaken foreign policy to involve the German nation in a forlorn war but he had also placed the Germany army, ready as it was for every sacrifice, under the most inefficient leadership of which it was possible to conceive. In the September days of 1914 there could be no question of a stab in the back. The German shells that were fired in the battle of the Marne were provided by the entire Reichstag, including not only those members who subsequently took up an independent attitude, but also including Liebknecht. No nation has ever given its ruler so great a proof of its trust as the German nation gave to William II on August 4, 1914. The thanks for that trust were the General Staff in Luxemburg and the defeat on the Marne. After Moltke's breakdown the army communiqués ceased for a time. Throughout the war the German nation was never told the truth about the battle of the Marne, and even leading members of the Reichstag only learnt much later, indirectly and incompletely, what really happened on the Western Front in September 1914.

General von Moltke was replaced by a new Chief of the General Staff. The German nation and the German Press had not the slightest voice in the decision to whom the fate of the German army and the German nation was to be entrusted. Of his own free will William II chose General von Falkenhayn, who had hitherto been Minister for War and who was at least physically fit for the task. Although he was capable of filling the post of an army commander with distinction, as was shown by his conduct of the Rumanian campaign in 1916 after he had retired from being Chief of the General Staff, he was as unfitted as was Moltke for the supreme responsibility. The German army in 1914 was certainly not wanting in first-rate generals; and in proof of that statement it is only necessary to mention the names of Ludendorff, Lossberg, Seeckt, Hoffmann, and Groener. Yet these men never came into power because William II never appointed them. For two long years the German army was inadequately led, and, when in the summer of 1916 a really first-rate General, Ludendorff, finally took over the command, all chance of attaining a military victory had passed away. Moreover, in their joy at having at last a real leader, the German nation entrusted General Ludendorff with absolute political authority and thus even what might have been saved was lost.

Throughout the winter of 1914–15 and the spring of 1915 Germany was unceasingly in danger of complete military defeat. The main German forces were held on the Western Front without having achieved any victory at the time when the Russian millions took the offensive in order to overthrow the Austrian and German troops in the East by sheer numerical superiority. If the Russians had achieved their object, the war would have been won for the Entente. But the German armies in the east under the command of Hindenburg and Ludendorff won a succession of important victories. The strategy of Ludendorff which led to the victory of Tannenberg, to the battle of the Masurian Lakes, to the advance on Warsaw in October 1914, to the battles by Lodz in November and December 1914, and to the winter battle among the Masurian Lakes, was a masterpiece of military skill. The less the achievements of the armies on the other fronts, so much the greater was the confidence of the army and the nation in Ludendorff and Hindenburg. On the battlefield of Tannenberg General Ludendorff laid the foundation-stone of the dictatorship which he exercised from 1916 to 1918. Meanwhile, the brilliant Chief of the Austrian General Staff, Conrad von Hötzendorf, had been successful in getting all that was possible out of the Austrian armies.

The situation was, nevertheless, not made any easier by these successes, for the strength of the Russian offensive could not be destroyed by local defeats, and in April 1915 it appeared highly probable that the Russians would be able to advance over the Carpathians towards Vienna and Budapest, destroy Austria, and then deal Germany a death blow. The whole war in the east from October 1914 onwards was conducted in direct opposition to the Schlieffen Plan. The Schlieffen Plan had been drawn up on the premise that within eight weeks of the outbreak of war the main German army in France would have accomplished its task and have been free to engage Russia. Of that there was no longer any question. Instead the German army fought until April 1915 a war on two fronts against numerically superior forces which any day might have ended in a complete defeat. How little the nation at home knew of the true state of affairs is revealed by the fact that in these very months a controversy broke out as to how much or how little territory Germany should annex on the conclusion of peace.

It was not until May 1915 that the situation became easier. The Great General Head-quarters took the risk of withdrawing a number of army corps from the Western Front in order to endeavour to obtain a decision on the Eastern Front. For the whole of 1915 the numerically weakened German army in the west held the Front from Flanders to Alsace against the renewed attacks of the French and English, and by so doing made possible the campaign in the east. Conrad von Hötzendorf had drawn up a plan by which the Russian Front was to be broken through in the neighbourhood of Cracow in order to fall upon the vast Russian army of the Carpathians in the rear and force it to retreat. Falkenhayn adopted Conrad's plan and placed a number of German army corps at his disposal. The Battle of Gorlitz in May 1915 brought about the collapse of the Russian Front in the Carpathians, and was the first of a long series of battles which resulted by the summer in the Russians being driven out of Poland and Galicia. The offensive strength of the Russians was broken at least for that year, and they had suffered untold losses. But the Russian army remained intact and the German army in the east had failed to win a decisive victory.

General Ludendorff perceived the weakness in Falkenhayn's conduct of operations, and he proposed a plan which in its essentials was an application of the Schlieffen Plan to the east, namely, a vast sweeping encirclement of the Russian army from the north through Courland and Vilna with the object of bringing about its destruction. Falkenhayn, however, refused to adopt Ludendorff's plan, and in consequence all the efforts and sacrifices of the German army in 1915 went for nothing. Although Germany had won battles and occupied territory, she had failed to come one step nearer towards achieving a decisive victory. In 1916 a new Russian army was ready to take the offensive; the French were not defeated; and England, adopting conscription, placed a million men on the Western Front. Hence the military situation for Germany in 1916 was even worse than it had been in 1915, inasmuch as she was called upon with her own unaided strength to fight simultaneously against three enemies whose armies numbered millions of men.

Before 1914 the General Staff in drawing up its plans had never conceived for a moment that such a situation was within the bounds of possibility. As a matter of fact, it was nothing less than a marvel, and a marvel that increased from month to month, that the German army maintained its position on the several Fronts. Meanwhile, in Germany, the controversy as to the annexations that should follow the peace grew fiercer. In 1915 Italy joined the Entente and a large part of the Austrian army became immobilized on the new Italian Front. The Central Powers, on the other hand, were joined by Bulgaria and Turkey, with the result that a number of English and French troops had to be diverted from the Western Front to the Balkans. An Austro-German-Bulgarian army overran Serbia, and, after the fall of Antwerp, virtually the whole of Belgium came into German occupation. But all this had no influence upon the main issue of the war. Falkenhayn never even planned any decisive operation for the spring of 1916, notwithstanding the fact that in view of the precarious military situation in which Germany found herself, an attempt should at the very least have been made—either in the east or in Italy—to achieve a decisive victory. For the Entente had an invaluable ally and Germany a deadly opponent—Time. Falkenhayn instead attacked Verdun without any real plan of operations and solely in the belief that he would destroy the French army by attrition. In truth, however, the ghastly battles in and round Verdun cost the German army at the very least as many casualties as the French.

The superiority of the Entente at sea was established from the very beginning of the war. The combined Fleets of the Entente outnumbered the German by three to one; and supremacy at sea depended upon great battleships and not upon submarines. The English cruisers did not need to provoke a fight; their very existence assured the mastery of the seas to the Entente, and enabled it to blockade Germany with the most terrible consequences to the German people. The attempt that was made by means of submarine warfare to destroy enemy transport at once involved Germany in grave disputes with the neutral states and especially with America. From the very outset the whole question of submarine warfare was in reality far more a political than a military problem.

The longer the war continued the more clearly did political and class differences manifest themselves within Germany itself. On August 4 an armistice had been concluded between the Hohenzollern Empire and the governing military aristocracy on the one hand and the Social Democratic working class on the other. Neither party had any very clear idea as to what the practical outcome of this truce was to be. And nobody came forward with a well-considered plan for organizing working and middle class alike within the frame of the Bismarckian Constitution. Bethmann-Hollweg promised as a concession to Social Democracy that Germany would be reorganized after the war. As to what form that reorganization was to take each and every individual could form his or her own idea.

The governing class in Prussia was under no illusion that after the war, if not indeed during the war, the working class would put forward very greatly increased political demands.[3] The millions of working-class soldiers on their return from the trenches would no longer permit themselves to be kept down by the old police methods. No matter how the war ended—*that* was quite certain. And before 1914 had elapsed the old Prussian suffrage question once more raised its head. The great Prussian landlords, however, were not as yet prepared to sacrifice any of their privileges, although memoranda and projects of all kinds were drawn up and conferences held.[4] The old-established majority in the Prussian Landtag saw no reason why it should reform itself to its own loss while the governing bureaucracy was also in no hurry to do so. It was only in 1917 that the suffrage question first became acute. The Prussian aristocrat felt his privileged position to be threatened by the emergence of a new era with possibilities of development which he could not forecast. Hence he looked round for means of defending himself and in doing so lighted upon the industrialists. The industrialists believed that this new era would at least result in a strengthening of the Trade Unions and in rendering their own position in the economic warfare of the future a more difficult one. If, however, the old Prussia once began to tremble, the strong Prussian governmental authority was endangered; a governmental authority that had hitherto been upheld by employers as against employees. Hence it was that Prussian National Liberals, acting under the influence of the Rhenish Westphalian industrialists, fought against the extension of the Imperial suffrage system to Prussia. In the years preceding the war industrialist circles had become more and more inimical to the policy of the agrarian Conservatives. At the time of Bülow's downfall, as in the Reichstag election of 1912 and the Zabern incident, the National Liberals were to be found in opposition to the Conservatives. On the outbreak of the war, however, a retrograde movement set in notwithstanding the fact that individual National Liberal leaders like Stresemann and von Richthofen recognized that the new era must bring with it the parliamentarization of Germany, and as a consequence the strengthening of the political influence of the middle class which would have resulted in a continuation of the National Liberal policy of 1912 and the strengthening of the Liberal middle-class coalition of the National Liberals and the Progressives.

From 1906 to 1914 the two great liberalizing influences, industry and trade, were almost invariably to be found working in collaboration. If this middle-class liberal coalition had strengthened its position during the war, it could have achieved very important results. Thus the middle class might have enlarged its rights at the cost of the conservative aristocrats and so rendered collaboration with the Social Democrats possible. In reality, however, the process was reversed. The policy pursued by the National Liberals during the war was not determined by men who desired to tread the path that led to parliamentary government, but by certain industrialists who wished, in alliance with the military aristocracy, to erect a barricade against the demands of the working class. In the days of its downfall the Bismarckian Empire thus beheld once more the resurrection of the old Bismarckian system of government by coalitions. The Fatherland Party of 1917 was nothing more than the coalition of 1887 in a form adapted to the conditions of the World War.

While an aristocratic industrialist defence against the working class thus came into life under cover of the *Burgfrieden*, the working class itself did not fail to pass in review the new situation. After August 4 the Social Democrats found themselves in a peculiarly difficult situation. The Social Democratic workmen readily offered themselves for the defence of their country, but they could not understand how it was that their old enemies, Prussian militarism and the great industrialists, were all of a sudden to be treated as friends. They knew that their representatives in the Reichstag voted for the Government and that the troops were permitted to read *Vorwärts*. But they knew also that the military and police régime in Prussia was the same as it had been before August 4, and that in the factories the preponderating authority of the employer had not been diminished by the *Burgfrieden*. In truth, nothing else could have been expected, for on August 4 neither a political nor a social revolution took place. Although the workman heard of the approaching change in the political organization of the Empire, yet he was under the impression that as a class the

proletariate had lost in influence since August 4. Before the War
Social Democratic newspapers and Social Democratic speakers
had openly voiced the grievances of the masses. Under martial
law and a military censorship the Press and public meetings alike
were silenced. Moreover, the feeling gained ground among the
workmen that while the employer had grown rich through the
war industries that had sprung up the workman had lost his old
weapon, the strike, for the *Burgfrieden* and military necessity
admitted of no strike.

A deep-seated discontent animated the masses of the population
throughout the first winter of the war. The depression which held
working men and women in its grasp could only have been removed by their being informed that they now shared in the
government of Germany and that they were actively and not
passively assisting in the prosecution of the war. In the middle-
class democracies the governing middle class was able to arouse
this feeling in the mass of the population. In England and in
France Labour leaders were to be found in the Cabinets and in
high administrative positions. It was possible in these countries
for the poorer classes to entertain the belief that they were the
governors of the State and that in a political sense they were free
from the authority of a ruling class. The result was a wholly
different attitude towards both the State and the War. But in
Germany the Bismarckian Constitution rendered the genesis of
any such mass-feeling impossible.

In the enthusiasm of the first weeks of war a feeling arose in
the subconsciousness of the working class that the torrent of
national fraternization would sweep away all the old differences.
But when the tide of enthusiasm ebbed the workmen naturally
saw that Army and Empire continued as before and that the
Prussian-German Civil Servants had not lost anything of their
love of authority. It is true that during the war the military and
civil authorities did not treat the broad mass of the people any
worse than they had done in peace. But the experience of war
awoke the masses to a consciousness that many things could no
longer be endured that had formerly been tolerated;[5] and thus
from the very first winter of the war the gulf separating the Social
Democratic working class and the ruling aristocratic-industrialist
class widened rather than narrowed. In addition to all this the
years 1915–16 brought an ever-increasing economic distress consequent upon the blockade. Foodstuffs became so scarce that

governmental control daily came more and more to take the place of ordinary trade. For the majority of the townspeople there began an era of famine of which the symbols were turnips and queues. Notwithstanding the increase in wages, especially in those of the munition workers, the large majority of wage-earners was unable to purchase enough to eat. A close observer could watch how profiteering grew up and how well-to-do families were in the position to enjoy many things that were out of the reach of the poor. So it came about that in Germany under cover of the *Burgfrieden* the worst of all known forms of class-warfare came to life —the fight for a piece of bread. Even if one believes that class-warfare is a typical and necessary phenomenon in modern society, one can only look back with horror to this time. A war of life and death was fought over five hundred grammes of bread, one hundred grammes of lard, and a single egg. The working class was filled with hunger and resentment. The feeling of hatred daily grew stronger for the factory owners, the rich shopkeepers, and business men who dealt in army supplies of all kinds, and for officers of the army and navy. The fight for food even made its appearance in the army where, under ordinary conditions, no one regarded it as anything but natural that officers should be better fed than the privates, and should have their separate mess. When, however, famine made its appearance and began to affect the rations of the men in the ranks, angry and envious glances were cast towards the officers' mess. This hatred was less common at the Front and in the submarines where a common danger united officers and men. It was most of all manifest in the reserve battalions, among the garrisons at home, and among the crews of the great battleships which were virtually inactive throughout the whole war and on whom a barrack routine was enforced. The student seeking for the causes of the revolution in the Germany army returns continually to the food-question[6] and to the embitterment of the soldiers and sailors who believed that they were less well-fed than their officers.

During the years 1915–16 two inimical forces gradually came into being in Germany. The one force was made up of the ruling class of officers, landlords, and industrialists, who occupied all positions of authority, who were represented in political life by the Conservative and National Liberal Parties, and of whom the masses believed that they 'lived better'. The other force was made up of the hungry working class, which was politically and economically deprived of all influence, and which was represented in political life by the Social Democratic Party. It is of interest to inquire how the remaining elements in the nation looked upon these two forces—the Centre and the Progressives, the non-Socialist workmen, the lower middle class, the shopkeepers, and, above all, the peasants.

It must first of all be noted that a great many of the middle-class and peasant voters, who had supported the Conservatives and National Liberals at the election of 1912, came in the course of the war to desert these parties. Although this process did not manifest itself in political life, it would be impossible to understand the causes of the revolution in 1918 without devoting some time to the study of this process.

The working-class members of the Centre suffered the same economic and political want as the Social Democratic workmen, with the result that the Socialist Independents and the Christian Trade Unions tended to draw together, as, for example, in the Prussian suffrage question. Over against these tendencies stood the old conservatively-minded leaders of the Centre who retained the upper hand within the Party until the spring of 1917. These high state officials and Catholic prelates sought support for conservatism in a political union with the Conservatives and National Liberals. The Bishops also endeavoured to prevent the Christian Trade Unions from raising the suffrage question in Prussia during the war.[7] In times of peace the leaders of the Centre had been able to maintain their authority over the Party by playing off the peasants against the workmen; but during the war the views of the German peasantry, Catholic and Protestant, underwent a radical change.[8]

Owing to their physical fitness the peasants were specially suitable for service at the Front and at first suffered the most severe losses. Work on the farms had to be done by women, children, and old people. The prices of manufactured goods increased rapidly during the war, yet the farm produce sold by the peasants remained below the maximum price. Then came the pressure exercised upon the peasants by a bureaucratic Food Control. The townspeople were angry with the peasants upon whom they laid the responsibility for their want of food. It is, indeed, indisputable that the mass of the peasantry, despite the Food Control, lived better than the factory workers, while the quantities of foodstuffs that were secretly passed from hand to

hand throughout Germany during the war must have ultimately
been produced somewhere. Nevertheless, the condition in which
the peasants found themselves during the war was sufficiently
severe to drive them into an ever-sharpening opposition to the
existing form of government. The German peasant in times of
peace had always been a conservative because the State guaranteed him his freehold property and protected him by means of the
tariff duties. Now, however, in the midst of the war and under
the blockade tariffs were of no value, while Civil Servants made
their appearance in the farmhouses to investigate whether a pound
of butter had been concealed anywhere. It seemed to the hard-
working peasants that the State grudged them enough to eat.
Thus war-time conditions resulted in the towns in the embitterment of the working man and in the country in that of the peasant.
It was in Bavaria, where the peasantry were very democratic and
not in any way under the influence of an aristocratic squirarchy,
and where every one was predisposed to put the blame for all mis-
fortunes on the Berlin officials, that the peasant opposition first
made its appearance and attained to its fiercest intensity. At the
same time it must not be forgotten that even in war time the
embittered German peasant was never a Social Democrat. For
he blamed the Social Democrats and above all the towns for the
oppression of the Food Control. What actually happened was that
the Radical movement among the peasantry resulted in 1917 in
a liberalizing of the Centre. A small local Peasant Party, the
Bavarian Peasant League, was forced more and more into the
ranks of the opposition. The discontent of the north German
Protestant peasantry did not find expression through any political
party. There was, however, a common meeting ground on which
the working class and peasant opposition could come together and
where their association could be most dangerous—the army.[9]

In the army there stood over against the great mass of the troops
the exclusive and aristocratic Corps of Officers. It is true that the
aristocratic officer who predominated in the old army had for the
most part fallen in the first months of the war. It was at the most
in the higher ranks that the officers of the armies from 1915 to
1918 bore any resemblance to the old type of Prussian officer.
The lower ranks of officers were almost entirely filled by officers
from the reserve and temporary lieutenants. For the most part
these were men who in their peace-time avocations as students,
shopkeepers, teachers, &c., would never have been reckoned among

the aristocratic ruling class and who were prepared on the conclusion of the war to return to their humble callings. But with the
officer's commission was bound up the aristocratic exclusiveness
that in Prussia separated an officer from his men. The German
officers as such showed themselves in the war to be no more and
no less immoral or inhuman than the French or the English, and
the bitter hatred that arose during the war in the broad masses
of the German population against the army officers is only to be
explained on the basis of the special social and constitutional
conditions then existing in Germany.

The great bulk of the nation did not feel that the State belonged
to them or that they possessed any authority over it. They felt
themselves to be governed from above—and very badly governed
in time of war. The authority of the State during the war was
everywhere represented by the officers, and thus it came about
that the officers, who as men were often wholly guiltless, acted as
a sort of lightning conductor for all the hatred and discontent
brewing in the masses. It has already been mentioned above that
these differences tended to disappear at the Front. For that very
reason they appeared all the more strongly among the nation at
home. The peasant soldiers found themselves joined in opposition
to the officers by soldiers who in civilian life were factory hands
and workmen. It is true that in 1918 the peasant soldiers did not
make the revolution; but they allowed it to take place and indeed
were mostly not unwilling that it should take place. The Bavarian
peasant who was the pride of the army in 1914 was among the
first in 1918 to place himself under the Red Flag.

From 1915 until the summer of 1918 the vast majority of the
nation, in spite of steadily increasing privation and of all disappointment and embitterment, looked upon the defence of the Fatherland
as a sacred duty. That did not prevent them from wishing that
the war should be ended as quickly as possible.

The economic situation of the urban shopkeepers during the
war varied very considerably. They felt less opposed to the
working class than to the peasantry. In accordance with their
traditions they desired a reformed Germany after the war. The
Progressives, for example, hailed with joy Bethmann-Hollweg's
announcement of this constitutional reform, and urged a reform
of the Prussian suffrage by all the means in their power. But
nothing was further from their thoughts than to disturb the
Burgfrieden and to place difficulties in the way of the Government.

It was not until the policy of the Centre underwent a change in 1917 that the Progressives also adopted a new attitude towards the course of events.

What was the attitude of the Imperial Government to the ever-widening political and social gulf within the nation? On the outbreak of the war William II retired from all political activities. The Emperor suffered more and more under the strain of the terrible responsibility which the German Constitution laid upon him in war-time, and nothing remained of the proud self-confidence which up to 1914 he had displayed in all questions and towards everybody. He looked upon it as his duty to take the advice of the Chief of the General Staff in military questions and that of the Imperial Chancellor in political issues. Hence first Moltke and then Falkenhayn led the armies without any real interference from the Emperor, while Bethmann-Hollweg gained for himself a political position that no Chancellor under William II had enjoyed since Bismarck was dismissed.

The two first Chiefs of the General Staff during the war were so preoccupied with military problems that they had no time in which to give any thought to political issues; while Bethmann-Hollweg for his part never interfered in the military conduct of the war. Hence in the first two years of the war no serious conflict of opinion arose between the Government and the Army authorities. In consequence of the proclamation of martial law the supreme executive authority in the Empire had passed into the hands of the Great General Head-quarters, and in every part of Germany the General in Command of the military district exercised the supreme executive authority. This came to be tantamount in the eyes of the people to a military dictatorship. As a matter of fact, while Bethmann-Hollweg was not always in agreement with every action of each individual general, the real decision in political matters still remained in the Chancellor's hands, as was unmistakably shown in 1916 in the discussions over unrestricted submarine warfare.[10] The Navy, whose head was the Secretary of State, von Tirpitz, pronounced itself in favour of a campaign of unrestricted submarine warfare, and the Chief of the General Staff, von Falkenhayn, supported the naval proposal on military grounds. Bethmann-Hollweg, however, was opposed to the proposed campaign out of regard for American feelings. William II decided the dispute in favour of the Chancellor and Tirpitz resigned. It was only when Hindenburg and Ludendorff took

over the Supreme Command that Bethmann-Hollweg's position
first began to be undermined.

Bethmann-Hollweg was convinced that the war could not be
waged without the assistance, and certainly not in opposition to
the wishes, of the working class. He therefore sought in the
Reichstag to secure the continued co-operation of the Social
Democrats. The leaders of the Social Democratic Party thereby
gained a confidential position in regard to the Imperial Chancellor
similar to that held by the leaders of the Centre before the war.
In order that the machinery of Government should function
without obvious friction it had been necessary before the war for
the Chancellor to secure the assent of Spahn to his proposals.
Now in a similar way he was compelled to turn to Scheidemann.[11]
But the Social Democrats never obtained from Bethmann-Hollweg
anything more than sympathetic expressions of goodwill and
of his intentions for the future. Yet even this was sufficient
to arouse the mistrust of the military aristocracy and the
industrialists who sensed that their position was imperilled with
every day that the war lasted. Directly after the outbreak of war
a distinct feeling of enmity towards Bethmann-Hollweg made its
appearance among the Conservatives and National Liberals; a feeling that turned into fierce hatred during the course of the
subsequent discussions on war aims.

All the class differences known to modern Europe—differences
that in Germany were intensified by the special circumstances of
the Constitution and the military situation—came to life in the
discussions over war aims. Thus the question of war aims became
the great problem of German domestic politics throughout the
war. William II and Bethmann-Hollweg had neither desired nor
prepared the war. They entered into it without any distinct
political object, and throughout the long years during which it
lasted they never achieved any clear idea as to the nature of
Germany's war aims. Nevertheless, their whole attitude to the
war and its aims depended upon the policy which Germany was
to follow in the future towards the three inimical Great Powers
in Europe.

In the eighties of the previous century Bismarck had declared
that any further weakening of France was not in the interests of
Germany, and that in the event of a Franco-German war he
(Bismarck), after the first German victory, would offer a peace to
the French on the model of the peace between Prussia and Austria

in 1866—namely, a peace without territorial acquisitions and which would not inflict any injury upon France. If Bethmann-Hollweg had been inspired by Bismarck's ideas, he would have offered the French on September 1, 1914, a peace on these lines. Obviously it is not possible to say whether the French would have accepted such a peace, yet it is certain that before the Battle of the Marne any such generous proposal on the part of Germany would have had good prospects of success. France was then under the depressing influence of her defeat, and the advance of the Germans on Paris, and the support of the little English army was of small importance in those days. Any chance of an independent Franco-German peace wellnigh disappeared with the alteration in the military situation brought about by the battle of the Marne and by the appearance in France of a million English troops. Henceforth France was forced to suit her war aims to English wishes.

Friedrich Engels advised the Social Democrats to use their influence to secure that after her first victory Germany offered peace to France, and to insist that this opportunity should be seized to make a final settlement with France by proposing a solution of the Alsace-Lorraine Question in either of two ways: the holding of plebiscites in Alsace and Lorraine; the return of Metz and the French-speaking districts surrounding it to France.[12] It is important to note that Engels did not suggest that these concessions should be made until after a German victory—that is to say, as a voluntary concession made in the interest of Germany's international position. Thus both Bismarck and Engels— the two greatest German statesmen since 1870—were at one in their ideas as to what should be Germany's war aims in regard to France. This fact gives these ideas a very considerable authority. United as they were in this respect, Bismarck and Engels were no less at issue with one another—or at least apparently so—as to what should be Germany's aim in a war with Russia. Bismarck was invariably of the opinion that not even the complete military annihilation of Russia would enable Germany to destroy the colossal Russian Empire, and that it would be absurd of Germany to demand territorial concessions from Russia. He also thought that Germany should seek to avoid awakening in Russia a desire for revenge similar to that which in 1871 she had aroused in France. It is certain that his experience in 1871 would have induced Bismarck to seek to end a Russo-German war as speedily as possible with a peace based on the *status quo*. Engels, on the contrary, advised the Social Democrats to turn a war with Russia into a revolutionary war with the object of bringing about a Russian revolution. In his opinion Germany should seek to reconstitute an independent Poland immediately after the declaration of war. This new Poland should include, in addition to Russian Poland, Galicia and a part of Prussian Poland. At the same time Germany should come forward as the champion of the liberation of all the peoples of west Russia who were oppressed by the Tsarist Government.[13] A wide gulf thus separated the ideas of Bismarck from those of Engels in this question. If an explanation of this divergence in opinion be sought, it is to be found in the diversity in the conceptions of Germany entertained by the two statesmen. The restoration of Poland would have been an irreparable mistake on the part of an Imperial Germany since it would have rendered impossible any friendship in the future with a Tsarist Russia. If, on the other hand, a revolutionary movement instigated by a Germany governed by the Socialist working class spread over the East and resulted in the separation of the Baltic provinces from Russia, a newly established Red Russia would be unable to reproach the German working class with the liberation of these provinces. In the World War a fantastical situation arose; Bethmann-Hollweg and William II actually sought to carry out Engels's revolutionary plan against the Tsardom.

The true interests of Germany from 1914 to 1916 demanded that peace on the basis of the *status quo* should be concluded as speedily as possible with both France and Russia. The conflict with England was of a more complicated nature. The English middle class had seized the opportunity afforded them by the war to extirpate German competition abroad. It was with this object that the German colonies and German property abroad were confiscated, the overseas interests of German firms liquidated, and every commercial link between Germany and the outer world severed. The destruction of German commercial competition was the common object uniting England with the great Dominions of the British Crown. It is only necessary to recall the part played by the Australian Prime Minister, Hughes, in the inception of an economic war against Germany. But in order to attain her object England had first to smash the military and political power of Germany. Hence the destruction of German militarism, i.e. of the German army and navy, became England's chief object in the war—an object in comparison with which territorial changes in the map of Europe were of little importance in the eyes of English statesmen. The only way in which England could have been brought to abandon this aim would have been by its finding itself opposed by the entire united force of Europe. But a European alliance could only have been attained were Germany to make good amidst the thunder of the cannon the mistakes of the Imperial policy since 1890. An understanding with France and Russia would have been necessary in order to force England to open the overseas markets to the European nations. It was in the interest of the German working class no less than in that of the middle class that Germany should be given her share in world commerce. The great masses of the German people looked upon England as their principal enemy throughout the war.

The German Government should never have permitted the childish and tactless ebullition of feeling symbolized in *Gott strafe England*. They should instead have aroused in the nation at large the conviction that a victory over England was only possible if Germany were to pursue a conciliatory policy towards France and Russia. The nation should from the outset have been given to understand that Germany, even after the conclusion of a separate peace with France and Russia, could never hope to bring the British Empire with its overwhelming sea-power to its knees, and that the utmost that was to be achieved was a compromise. If the Government, on the other hand, were of the opinion that Germany was too weak even to force England to accept a compromise, and that a reconciliation with England was at all costs necessary, then it should have conducted German foreign policy in a manner that was likely to result in the achievement of that end. It was the duty of the Government to have impressed the necessity of such a policy upon the German nation. William II and Bethmann-Hollweg followed neither of these courses and pursued no definite policy. The terrible stupidity and aimlessness that characterized German foreign policy from 1890 to 1914 survived the outbreak of the war. The declarations on the part of the German Government from time to time that it did not desire conquests, or that it wished to secure the future of Germany in the coming peace, were of little value for purposes of foreign policy. In confidential circles Bethmann-Hollweg often emphasized the necessity for a separate peace with France and Russia,[14] yet his public declarations and conduct of foreign policy resulted in rendering peace with Russia impossible.

The weakness of the Imperial Government could perhaps have been overcome by proposals or protests on the part of the nation. But for any such action the most important condition was lacking: the nation was ignorant of the true state of affairs. Not that the military communiqués were to blame for their ignorance. Enough has already been said above as to the extraordinary communiqués issued by Moltke and Stein. Under their successors, Falkenhayn and Ludendorff, from the end of September 1914 until the Armistice the communiqués were thoroughly accurate and reliable. These communiqués contained all that a report of this nature can be expected to contain, namely, indications as to where the Front lay and as to the most important events that had taken place. It is obvious that the really decisive factors in a military situation can never be made known in communiqués: the relative strengths of the opposing armies and of their reserves, and the whole strategical situation as it evolves from day to day. Neither the nation nor the members of the Reichstag learnt anything of the true strategical position[15] which was known only to the Court, to the Great General Staff, and always to the Imperial Chancellor. Outside that limited circle no one knew anything. The ignorance of the public as to the true state of affairs was increased by the circumstance that the German armies were everywhere fighting on enemy soil and were everywhere in occupation of important enemy territory. The objective in a war is the opposing army and not the enemy's territory. The victor is he who has overthrown his enemy. From a military standpoint it is a matter of little importance where the decisive battle takes place. The elder Moltke, for example, had prepared a plan for the eventuality of a Franco-German war by which the French were to be allowed to invade Germany and to be decisively beaten at Frankfurt-am-Main.[16] It was only the chance result of military operations in 1914 and 1915 that brought the German army into Belgium and Poland, and if an alteration had taken place in the extremely critical situation, the German troops might have found themselves compelled to evacuate these countries. The Imperial Government nevertheless did absolutely nothing to educate the German nation as to the highly precarious nature of the so-called 'conquests' made by the German troops. The bulk of the population was convinced that the occupied districts were at the disposal of Germany.

The deception thus practised on the nation arose from the patriarchal nature of the relationship between the Government and the people. The uttermost publicity as to the military situation obtained in England throughout the entire war. The nation and the Press were able to discuss openly and informedly both good and bad developments. It would have been as absurd for the governing English middle class to have secrets from itself as for a business man to be afraid to draw up a balance sheet. The German Government, on the contrary, held it to be necessary to keep up the spirit of its subjects by letting everything appear in the best light. They feared that any knowledge of unpleasant events might injure the authority of the State. The German Government behaved like an anxious father who hesitates to tell his wife and children when things are going badly in his business. Still more remarkable than the touching-up of the military situation is the fact that the German nation was not permitted to know anything whatever as to the state of its health throughout the war.[17] Silence was maintained as to the many thousand deaths that occurred among the civilian population in consequence of the blockade. The nation was officially assured that rationing was good for its health. A popular government which understood mass-psychology would have placarded every street corner with lists of those who died from famine in order to increase the bitter feeling against the enemy. It is only necessary to recall how England made use of the Zeppelin attacks on English towns in order to stimulate the fighting spirit of the nation.

The ignorance of the German people as to the true state of affairs showed itself in the way in which various sections of the populace regarded the war and the coming peace. The German industrialists hoped that a German victory would enable them to obtain their raw materials with greater ease. The mine-owners followed the German advance through Belgium and northern France with anxious eyes in the hope that the coal- and iron-mines in Luxembourg, Belgium, and Longwy-Briey would come into German hands. The industrialists in general demanded from the Government the annexation of Longwy-Briey, and also that of Belgium or at the very least its economic domination by Germany. They thus pursued the same tactics in war as in peace. Prior to 1914 certain great firms had compelled the German Government to lend the support of the Empire to their foreign undertakings. Now they demanded of it that it should realize as many as possible of their desires in the coming peace. If a middle-class industrialist party had itself been responsible for the government of Germany, it would also have been responsible for giving effect to the desires of its own members and would therefore have had to ask itself which, if any, of those desires were capable of realization. As it was, the Imperial Constitution afforded the industrialists the opportunity of presenting their demands without any consequent responsibility for their fulfilment. It was the business of the Government to put them into practice.

While the industrialists wished to augment their business opportunities in the west the Prussian landowners had similar plans for the furtherance of their own interests in the east. They hoped to acquire the thinly-populated agrarian districts of Courland and Lithuania for the settlement of the younger sons of German farmers, and for this purpose they sought to get into touch with the nobility of German origin in the Russian Baltic provinces. They hoped by means of an extension of Germany towards the north-east to strengthen the power of the aristocratic landed Prussian governing class within Germany itself. It is true that a number of the Prussian Conservatives preferred a separate peace with Imperial Russia to such projects.

It was of special importance in view of the distribution of political power in Germany to know what were the wishes of the General Staff and the Naval Staff for the strategic defence of the country. The leading generals were of the opinion that the industrial districts in western Germany bordered too nearly upon the existing German frontier; that a strip of French territory must be taken in order to safeguard the industrial districts in German Lorraine; and that for the defence of the Rhineland at least Liège should become German. It would be still better were Belgium to remain under the protection of Germany. In the east they desired a readjustment of the frontier that would afford better protection to Upper Silesia, east and west Prussia, involving a cession of Russo-Polish territory. It is clear that the war aims of the General Staff largely coincided with those of the industrialists; for Longwy-Briey lay within the territory which the generals demanded for the protection of Lorraine while soldiers and industrialists were at one in their views in regard to Belgium. The Navy also demanded that Germany should retain Belgium, for so long as Germany was in possession of the coast of Flanders she could hold England in check by means of submarines.

Out of all these different war aims there was created a unified programme for the so-called German 'peace of conquest' of which the vocal protagonists were the members of the Pan-German Association.[18] The enthusiasm with which the governing class in Germany took up this idea is not to be explained on the ground of personal interest alone. The political brains among the Prussian aristocracy and the industrialists recognized that in any event the war must result in a grave threat to their own power and to the old governmental system in Germany. In event of an unsuccessful conclusion to the war a terrible disaster was to be expected. If, on the other hand, the war ended with a peace on the *status quo ante* basis, the German nation would be compelled to pay thousands of millions in war expenses without having derived any advantage. These millions could only be raised by the imposition of heavy taxes. On their return from the Front the soldiers would find, after all their sacrifices, an impoverished country awaiting them and a Government which required from them the payment of huge taxes. All this would arouse such a feeling in the people that a revolution would be inevitable. According to the so-called 'Annexationists' the old system could only survive in Germany were the State in a position at the end of the war to offer the nation a definite compensation for its sacrifices: either reparations from the enemy, or land for colonization, or greater scope for industrial expansion, or, best of all, all these together.

Hence the Conservatives and the majority of the National Liberals saw in a German victory the last hope of salvation for the old Germany.[19] Although they did not know the real gravity of the situation, they must nevertheless have often said to themselves during 1915–16 that a complete military victory on the part of Germany over all her enemies was not very probable. At this juncture the Navy spread a rumour abroad that it was in possession of a weapon which would compel Germany's chief enemy, England, to listen to reason within six months. This weapon was a ruthless submarine campaign. An exaggerated regard for English and American susceptibilities made Bethmann-Hollweg reluctant to permit the use of this decisive instrument. The 'procrastinators' at Court, men like the chiefs of the Emperor's naval and military secretariats, von Valentini and von Müller, proved themselves Bethmann-Hollweg's most efficient allies in this regard. But the officers, Prussian *Junkers*, and industrialists argued as follows: 'war is permeating the country with its poison, eating away the roots of German power, and strengthening socialism and democracy; unrestricted submarine warfare must be brought into operation without regard for anybody's feelings ;[20] and Bethmann-Hollweg removed from his post. Thus, and thus only, can Germany prove herself victorious and achieve a victorious peace. Thus, and thus only, can the revolution be avoided and the traditional governmental system survive.'

The war aims of the Social Democratic workmen were utterly opposed to those of the governing class. For reasons already mentioned above the working class was filled with the deepest suspicion of its rulers and with the determination to end the war as speedily as possible. The masses of the populace gained the impression that the war was not unwelcome to the higher Staff Officers and the great industrialists. They learnt that their rulers were hatching great schemes of conquest, and they were indoctrinated with the official optimistic accounts of the situation on the several Fronts. The enemy offensives had been thrown back at all points and not an enemy foot stood upon German soil. Was it not possible, then, so the workmen thought to themselves, to conclude a peace by compromise and without conquests? Were not these schemes of conquest on the part of the governing class the real obstacle to peace? The Social Democratic workmen saw their suspicions[21] justified in the declarations of the Conservatives and Pan-Germans that Germany dare not content herself with a peace by compromise and must fight to the end for a victorious peace. It seemed to the workmen that the very men by whom they were held down in political and economic life and in the army alike were also responsible for the prolongation of the war. It was these men who had to be deprived of power in order to make an end to the general suffering. It was thus that the battle-cry 'Down with the Pan-Germans and Annexationists' awoke the spirit of class-warfare in the working man. With this battle-cry the proletariate burst the bonds of the *Burgfrieden* and began once more the fight for political power. In the eyes of the Social Democratic working class the Annexationists were synonymous with the governing class of Imperial Germany. The overthrow of the Annexationists thus meant the domination of the Social Democrats in Germany.

The passionate refusal of the workers to tolerate any form of annexation created a difficult problem for the leaders of the Social Democratic Party to solve. Although the Party had not taken up an independent political attitude in the sense desired by Engels, it had nevertheless held firmly to the tradition handed down to it from Marx and Engels that the chief aim of the war should be the

destruction of the Tsardom. The Party agreed that a German
victory in the east should be used to liberate all the peoples, and
especially the Poles, living under Russian tyranny. At the same
time it should have been perfectly clear to them that an Imperial
and aristocratic Germany could not play the role of liberator to
the nations subject to Russia. A Poland, Lithuania, and Courland
that had been 'liberated' through a victory of the Imperial armies
could never be anything else than the vasssals of the German
aristocrats and industrialists. In adopting for the west the formula
'no annexations and a peace on the basis of the *status quo*', the
Social Democrats must have been prepared to see the same
principle extended to the east. In order, however, to avoid the
abandonment of the war with Tsardom that had been one of their
proclaimed war aims on August 4, 1914, the Social Democrats
were forced to act in an illogical manner. They opposed all plans
for a public or secret policy of annexations in Belgium and northern
France, while at the same time they raised no serious objections to
the creation by Germany at the cost of Russia of new States out
of Courland, Poland, and Lithuania. It is true that the Social
Democrats demanded that in these 'liberated' countries the right
of self-determination should be put into practice;[22] a right that
was valueless from the standpoint of practical politics.

It is worthy of emphasis that the German working class pursued
with a special hatred any one who proclaimed himself to be in
favour of the annexation of Belgium, and especially of the Flanders
coast, while they made no opposition to proposals for annexations
in the east. The truth is that the mass of the population was not
indisposed to an extension of German territory and power, but
only to a policy of annexation that would prolong the war. This
attitude on their part appears quite natural if considered as a whole.
Why should the working class look upon the political frontiers of
Europe as they existed in July 1914 as sacrosanct? These frontiers
were only the result of a thousand diplomatic accidents. What the
working class did oppose with all their might was the prolongation
of the miseries attendant upon the war merely in order—as it
appeared to them—that a few industrialists might profit in Belgium.
The vast majority of the German populace looked upon Russia
as already defeated. The strongest and most dangerous enemies
of Germany seemed in their eyes to be England and France, to
whom concessions must be made in order to achieve a peace.
England had declared that she had entered the war in defence of

Belgium, and that the complete restoration of Belgium was her cardinal object in prosecuting the war. It was clear, therefore, that Germany must give up Belgium, and that the Annexationists who sought to hinder that being done must be deprived of their power. From a psychological standpoint this attitude on the part of the German working class is thoroughly comprehensible. Yet from an objective standpoint it was mistaken: the way to the speedy conclusion of peace lay not through concessions to England but in an understanding with Russia.

The question of war aims broke up the unity of the Centre. The Conservative leaders wished to unite with the Parties of the Right while the Christian Trade Unions were no less desirous than were the Social Democrats of a peace by understanding. Although the business communities in the great cities had no objection to an extension of German territory and influence, yet they desired it to be carried out along the line which was likely to arouse the least opposition, namely, by the creation of new States in the East and by the completion of the Berlin-Baghdad scheme.[23] They further hoped that the Quadruple Alliance of Germany, Austria-Hungary, Bulgaria and Turkey would result in a permanent politico-economic alliance in which their allies would follow the leadership of Germany. This scheme, of which the protagonist was the Progressive leader, Friedrich Neumann, was altogether Utopian, inasmuch as neither the Habsburg Monarchy nor the Balkan States nor Turkey were prepared to submit to the hegemony of Germany.

Such was the great scheme of annexation that came into being in Germany during the war. If it had been carried out, it would have resulted in the political and economic subjection of foreign States with almost a hundred million inhabitants to Germany. As such it was seen in its true light by English and American statesmen. Within Germany itself, however, it aroused less feeling than might have been expected, since the proletariate in thinking of annexations had in mind only the plans of the industrialists and the General Staff with regard to Belgium and northern France, while the commercial classes and the Progressives showed no interest whatever in the more particular war aims of the industrialists. The majority of the peasants, like the workmen, hoped for a speedy ending to the war without troubling to formulate any special conditions.

The controversy as to war aims which steadily intensified during 1915–16, was especially unwelcome to Bethmann-Hollweg, since it compelled the Government to abandon its reserve and to define its attitude towards the question at issue; and such a proceeding was regarded by Bethmann-Hollweg as an infringement of the *Burgfrieden*. He sought to make use of the censorship in order to divert the people from this controversy with the result that the evil he sought to prevent only became worse. For all classes in the population were at least united in the desire to know whither the war was leading them and for what object it was being fought. Bethmann-Hollweg's tactics only had the effect of driving the discussion beneath the surface with the result of making agreement between the controversialists still more difficult of attainment. The Chancellor himself regarded the situation in which Germany found herself as grave and almost hopeless. The Chief of the General Staff, von Falkenhayn, was in the main of his opinion. If Bethmann-Hollweg had only published an official and accurate statement, covered by the authority of the General Staff as to the nature of the military situation, he could have destroyed the annexationist propaganda in Germany at a single stroke. That he did not do so was due to his fear lest any such action might have the effect of weakening the endurance of the nation. Instead of coming before the nation with a clearly defined plan for the further conduct of the war, and with a precise programme of the terms on which Germany was prepared to conclude peace, Bethmann-Hollweg took refuge in evasions from a desire to avoid hurting the susceptibilities of the Conservatives and National Liberals. At the same time his speeches were of such a nature that the Social Democrats were able to interpret them in a sense favourable to their own plans. His programme came in the end to be a compound of the demands of both parties.[24] By conceding each a part of its demands the Chancellor thought he would be able to restore unity within the nation and to allay the domestic strife, and it was only in the East that he came forward with a pronounced policy.

As early as August 19, 1915, Bethmann-Hollweg announced in the Reichstag, in words that left little room for doubt in the minds of his hearers, that Germany would not restore Poland to Russia. His statement was the consequence of the German victories over the Russians in the spring and summer months of that year. On April 5, 1916, the Chancellor distinctly told the Reichstag that the 'liberated' Poles, Letts, Lithuanians, and Balts would never again be permitted to come under Russian rule. Bethmann-Hollweg thus thought to meet the demands of the Social Democrats at the same moment as he satisfied those of the General Staff and the Agrarians. Since her defeat in 1915 Russia had been virtually isolated from her allies, and she bore the chief burden of the war to the accompaniment of a steadily increasing threat of revolution. Since the German victories in the east had not proved decisive in a military sense, it was all the more important for Germany to derive what political benefit she could from those victories. It is probable that Germany could have concluded a separate peace with Russia on the basis of the *status quo* in the autumn of 1915 and throughout 1916. When, however, Bethmann-Hollweg announced to the Russian Government that Russia must be prepared in all circumstances to lose her Baltic provinces, the Tsar naturally preferred to remain loyal to his allies.

In the west Bethmann-Hollweg was determined upon the acquisition of Longwy-Briey, while at the same time he was prepared to compensate the French by a rectification of the frontier in other districts of Alsace-Lorraine. It was obvious that France would not surrender her valuable iron-mines before she had suffered a complete military defeat. Any proposal to compensate the French in other ways for the loss of these mines could not be taken seriously. Bethmann-Hollweg indeed made no public pronouncement on this subject. Instead he touched in his speech in the Reichstag on April 5, 1916, on the subject of the future of Belgium. He assured the Reichstag that the pre-war guarantee of Belgium's neutrality was a thing of the past, and that Germany must be given sufficient guarantees that Belgium would not in future become a vassal-State under Anglo-French domination. He added that it was the duty of Germany to protect the national traditions and language of the Flemish inhabitants of Belgium. This amounted in fact to an endorsement of the Pan-German programme for a German protectorate over Belgium. Bethmann-Hollweg even went so far as to intimate his agreement with the proposals in regard to Belgium which were based upon the support of the Flemings in opposition to the French-speaking Walloons. These proposals were founded upon a grave politico-historical misunderstanding. The two nationalities included within the Belgian State stood to one another in the same relationship as the French-speaking to the German-speaking Swiss. Here there could be no question of 'liberation'. At least ninety-nine per cent. of the Flemish people looked with hostility upon any interference on the part of Germany in Belgian affairs. If Germany had succeeded in calling into being an autonomous Flanders, she would have only been able to maintain it in existence by the exercise of military force.

Although it is easy to understand the fears entertained by the German Government lest England might make of Belgium a jumping-off ground for her continental schemes, yet nevertheless this danger was only to be met by means of an agreement between Germany, France, and Russia. If Germany had showed that she really had the defence of the European Continent at heart, then she could have demanded guarantees from Belgium (an entire Belgium and not the Utopian Flanders) that she would place herself in the ranks of a European coalition. When, however, Bethmann-Hollweg contemplated war aims whose attainment could only be possible after a complete defeat of France and Russia, how did he then propose to get his own way in the Belgian question against the opposition of England? Still more—how could he reconcile such a programme with his pessimistic outlook on the war?

It is quite clear that Bethmann-Hollweg drew up his programme without reference to the military and international situation in which Germany found herself, and that he intended it to serve as a compromise in domestic politics. Although in regard to German war aims in the west Bethmann-Hollweg was virtually in agreement with the views of the Conservatives and National Liberals, yet at the same time he chose his words so carefully that he avoided giving offence to the Social Democrats. It was even possible to interpret his words to mean that he desired no conquests but simply a peace by understanding. Yet his cautiousness only resulted in enraging the Conservatives and National Liberals. Although Bethmann-Hollweg actually offered the Annexationists all that they asked for, they were not content in that they desired that the German war aims should be publicly and resolutely announced to the nation as a test of the Government's authority within the country. Moreover, they wished to render it impossible for Scheidemann to say that he had placed the right interpretation upon the Chancellor's words.[25] The governing class in Germany was in truth not even willing to let it appear that the Social Democrats exerted any influence upon the conduct of the war. The whole question of war aims was primarily a domestic issue for both the Pan-Germans and the proletariate.

Bethmann-Hollweg was singularly unfortunate in the form in which he sought to effect a compromise between the war aims of the aristocrats and the industrialists and those of the Social

Democratic working class. He incorporated the Social Democratic
scheme for the liberation of the Baltic peoples with the Pan-
German plans of conquest, and thus drew up an utterly absurd
and impossible programme of war aims. As a result nobody was
satisfied with the Government's attitude. The opposition of the
Conservatives and National Liberals to the Chancellor's policy
grew daily more envenomed, while it became more and more
difficult for the leaders of the Social Democratic Party to defend
the policy of the Government against the attacks made on it by the
embittered working class.

Bethmann-Hollweg also sought for a solution to the economic
problems raised by the war along a similar path of compromise to
that which he pursued in the problem of Germany's war-aims. He
replied to the Social Democrats' continuous complaints of the poor
nourishment afforded the working class with an increasingly
rigorous application of the system of food control. Germany at
that time resembled a besieged fortress. It would have been
impossible for the Government to have avoided all interference
with the feeding of its garrison. Unfortunately the Civil Servants,
who in ordinary circumstances executed their duties with ability
and promptness, proved themselves unequal to this new and
tremendous task. The greater the organization created the more
completely did foodstuffs disappear from the market. To-day it
would only be possible to find out where the failure lay by means
of a searching investigation. For the Government, the Food
Control, which was finally extended to cover practically every
article of human consumption, resulted in a political set-back.
The food tickets which allotted the same rations to the poor and
to the rich were intended as a concession to the city proletariate.
But the increasing shortage only served to intensify the unrest
among the proletariate while at the same time the Government, as
has already been shown above, alienated the sympathies of the
peasants.

After two years of war and *Burgfrieden*, the Imperial Government had lost its authority with all classes in the nation. Nobody
trusted it and nobody hoped anything of it. A single misfortune
would suffice to overthrow it. This came with the new development in the military situation.

NOTES TO CHAPTER III

1. For Marx's and Engels's attitude to the War see Franz Mehring's *Karl Marx*, 2nd edition, 1919, p. 443: 'A great deal has been written about the attitude which Marx and Engels have taken up with regard to War, although actually there is very little to say. They saw in War a thing, not ordained by God, as Moltke saw it, but by the Devil; a phenomenon inseparable from class and particularly capitalist society. As historical thinkers, they did not, of course, maintain the totally unhistoric argument that "War is war and every war is to be judged from the same standpoint". For them every war had its definite premisses and conclusions upon which depended what attitude the working class should assume towards it. This was also Lassalle's conception, with whom they had quarrelled in 1859 about the actual conditions of the war that was in progress at the time, but all three argued from the definite point of view as to how this war might be best made to serve the cause of proletarian emancipation.' For Marx and Engels on the war of 1870 see Mehring, pp. 444 et seq.; on the war of 1859 see Mehring, pp. 273 et seq. Engels on the World War situation in 1892: *Politisches Vermächtnis*, p. 28.

2. On the subject of the military events of August and September 1914 see the authoritative publication of the State Archives: *Die Weltkrieg 1914–1918*, vols. i–iv, 1925–6. On the tragedy of General von Moltke, vol. iv, p. 526: 'The German Commander-in-Chief's nerves had been increasingly strained by the long waiting far back in Luxembourg, and the torturing uncertainty about the outcome of the battle.'—P. 531: 'In the early hours of September 9 the Chief of the German General Staff had absolutely collapsed spiritually under the weight of real and imagined tidings of evil. He had generally read only bad meanings into the sparse communications. . . . At his midday interview with the Supreme War Lord, at about the same time as the army had won a great victory, he suggested that the whole of the German front line in the West should be withdrawn.'—P. 533: 'How was such a breakdown on the part of the Chief of the German General Staff to be explained? Undoubtedly General von Moltke was hindered in his conduct of operations by his physical condition. In 1910 he had been seriously ill since when his physical freshness and nervous powers had been gradually falling off. The General finally felt that himself, and often told his more intimate friends during the months immediately preceding the outbreak of war of his serious intentions of retiring.'

3. The reports which von Loebell, the then Prussian Minister of the Interior, sent to the Imperial Chancellor during the first months of the War are typical. See REPORT, v, pp. 110 et seq. Thus we find in a report at the end of September 1914 (p. 111): 'It is already being unmistakably intimated by the Social Democrats and the Poles that the fulfilment of national duties has created a claim to special rights. Demands are unquestionably to be expected within a short time which it will be impossible for the Government to fulfil without injustice to other and more numerous sections of the nation, who have done their duty quietly and as a matter of course. It must not be concealed that serious apprehensions on this point

are felt and expressed in nationalist circles. Industry and agriculture are justified in their anxiety over the economic demands which the Social Democratic Press is already making.'

4. For the suffrage question during the war see Bergsträsser in REPORT, vii, part i, pp. 229 et seq.

5. For the psychological effect of the war see the fine observations of the Christian Trade Unionist, Joos, REPORT, v, pp. 207 et seq.

6. A typical document—Richard Stumpf: *Warum die Flotte zerbrach? Kriegstagebuch eines christlichen Arbeiters*, 1927. (This edition contains the diary with some unimportant omissions. A complete reproduction of the diary appears in REPORT, x.)

7. See Joos, REPORT, v, p. 213, on the attitude of the Cardinal Archbishop of Cologne, von Hartmann, on the subject of the suffrage question.— For the political views of the Cardinal Archbishop of Munich, von Bettinger, see Victor Naumann, *Dokumente und Argumente*, 1928, p. 118.

8. On the war-psychology of the peasants, especially in Bavaria, see Bergsträsser in REPORT, iv, pp. 126 et seq.

9. A very characteristic collection of letters from the Front published by Bergsträsser in REPORT, v, pp. 257 et seq.

10. Bethmann's victory over Tirpitz, see Bredt in REPORT, viii, p. 64.

11. Scheidemann on his relations with Bethmann-Hollweg, see REPORT, vii, part i, pp. 277 et seq.

12. Engels, *Politisches Vermächtnis*, p. 29: 'In any case we (i.e. the German Social Democrats) must explain that we have been ready to come to a friendly agreement with France ever since 1871; that as soon as our Party comes into power it will not be able to wield this power freely unless Alsace-Lorraine decides freely on its own future.' . . . 'If the French offensive is made innocuous, we may seize Poland as far as the Dwina and the Dnieper. . . . If that succeeds, there will probably be a revulsion in France. We must at the same time urge that the French should be offered at least Metz and Lorraine as a peace-offering.'

13. Engels, ibid.: 'This (the conquest of Poland) must be carried out by revolutionary means, and if necessary by ceding a part of Prussian Poland and the whole of Galicia to the future Polish State.'

14. Scheidemann on an interview with Bethmann-Hollweg in March 1915 (based on some notes of Scheidemann's of that date), see REPORT, vii, part i, p. 278: 'Bethmann-Hollweg even then spoke of his readiness to make a separate peace with Russia or France as soon as possible.'— Nevertheless, Bethmann allowed this readiness to come so little to the fore that even the best-informed men were of the opinion that the Imperial Chancellor only wanted peace with England. See the relevant opinion of Victor Naumann, who was then in continual touch with the Foreign Office; *Dokumente und Argumente*, p. 74.

15. On the subject of the inadequate information given to members of the Reichstag see Bell in REPORT, vii, part i, pp. 304 et seq.

16. See a memorandum of Moltke's of January 1880, quoted in the publication of the State-Archives, *Die Weltkrieg*, i, p. 50.

17. For the official glossing-over of the health-conditions in Germany during the War see Dr. Moses in REPORT, iv, pp. 200 et seq.

18. Detailed expert opinions by Hobohm and Volkmann on the German plans of annexation during the war appear in vol. xii of REPORT.

19. See the letter of von Gebsattel, one of the leading Pan-Germans, to Bethmann on May 5, 1915, in REPORT, vii, part ii, p. 350; as also the letter from Hindenburg to the Emperor on January 7, 1918, in REPORT, ii, p. 123.

20. On the submarine agitation see Bredt in REPORT, viii, pp. 67 and 71. Stresemann, ibid., vii, part ii, p. 307.

21. For the speech, for instance, of von Wedel-Piesdorf, the President of the Upper House, on March 15, 1915, and its effect on the workers, see Dittmann in REPORT, vii, part ii, p. 335.

22. See Scheidemann's speech in the Reichstag on April 6, 1916, as the official Social Democrat answer to Bethmann's declaration of war-aims on April 5: 'If we are successful in freeing those Poles who have been enslaved by Tsarism, the whole civilized world will rejoice.' In this connexion Scheidemann is also against the *status quo*, which he considered to derive from the 'diplomats of the Holy Alliance' and hence to be undeserving of any respect.

23. See the memorandum which Friedrich Naumann, together with Professor Jäckh, Dr. R. Bosch, and others, sent to Ludendorff on February 11, 1918, in REPORT, ii, p. 136. This contained among other things: 'What we have hitherto won in the War is the creation and welding together of Central Europe. It signifies our economic, military, and political enrolment as equals among the World Powers, a war aim which we can achieve quite apart from any alteration in the situation of our Eastern or Western frontiers. America and England are aiming at continuing the war in order to destroy this victory. They will prolong the war on this account.'

24. For Bethmann-Hollweg's real war aims see the confidential memorandum which he sent after his resignation to Count Hertling, the then Imperial Chancellor, on January 26, 1918, in REPORT, ii, p. 142: 'During the whole period of the War I have never laid before the Supreme Command, either the present or the earlier one, a general programme of war aims which must be achieved before the war can be brought to an end. On the contrary, I have always emphasized the necessity for seizing every possible opportunity to initiate peace negotiations, so as to be able to achieve during the course of such negotiations whatever was recognized in view of the military and political situation as possible and necessary for Germany. I have never for my part fixed any details, only suggested in outline: the regaining of our colonies; in the West—care lest Belgium should become an inlet for enemy invasion, if possible the acquisition of Longwy-Briey, perhaps by way of mutual rectification of frontiers; in the East—a kingdom of Poland and improvement of the strategic frontiers of Prussia at the cost of as few annexations as possible, also the creation of border states out of Courland and Lithuania. I have always opposed strenuously the annexation of any amount "worth mentioning" of Polish territory.'

25. Scheidemann on his 'interpretations' of Bethmann's speeches: REPORT, vii, part i, p. 277.

IV

THE DICTATORSHIP OF LUDENDORFF

THROUGHOUT the spring and summer of 1916 the German army was slaughtered in thousands at Verdun, where the Chief of the General Staff, von Falkenhayn, believed it to be possible to destroy the French army by a process of attrition. At the very moment when the battle of Verdun reached its height a million English troops took the offensive on the Somme. The German armies on the Western Front lived through the worst weeks they had experienced since the battle of the Marne. The English attacked in vastly superior numbers and with enormous reserves of ammunition. To fill the German cup of misery to overflowing the Russian armies under General Brusilow began a great offensive, in the course of which they broke through the Austrian Front, and compelled the Austrian armies to retreat after having inflicted upon them very severe casualties. The Russians once more occupied the passes of the Carpathians. The German army, which was faced with an almost superhuman task on the Western Front, found itself compelled in addition to give support to the entire Eastern Front from Riga to the Carpathians.

The Entente Powers had good reason for believing that victory would crown their efforts before the end of the year. Rumania had until now remained neutral. When, however, the situation was so profoundly altered in favour of the Entente, she also entered the war in August 1916 on their side. Her entry meant that some hundreds of thousands of fresh enemy troops suddenly fell upon the exposed southern flank of the Austro-German armies on the Eastern Front. It became impossible to say whether in these circumstances the Eastern Front could be held any longer. Events on the several Fronts between June and August, 1916, profoundly affected the morale of the German army and nation. All confidence in Falkenhayn's leadership disappeared. The authority of the army was broken, as was that of the Government, and therefore that of the Emperor disappeared.

Since the beginning of the war William II had lived in the strictest retirement. While in times of peace the German nation had heard only too much of its Emperor now, in time of war when, according to the Imperial Constitution, the Imperial will should be paramount, the Emperor was no longer to be seen or heard. It is not difficult to understand that William II in so acting was animated by a desire to avoid in any way complicating an already highly critical situation. The Emperor left the reins of government and the conduct of the war in the hands of his principal political and military advisers, and made no attempt to interfere in their decisions. William II, in fact, sought to play a role similar to that of the King of England, and by so doing did not enhance his authority. A discontented nation vented the hatred it already felt for the army officers in an increased degree upon their superiors, namely, the ruling German Princes, and, above all, upon the Emperor as Supreme War Lord. The Emperor was now called upon to pay for his autocratic behaviour before the war. The embittered workmen made him responsible for famine, misery, and war, regardless of the fact that since August 1914 he could hardly be said to have governed at all. Still worse for the Emperor was the fact that the upper classes in the nation day by day lost their feeling of loyalty to the Crown. The Prussian nobility, the officers, and the manufacturers were certainly not republicans—that would have been altogether contrary to their traditions. But they lost all confidence in the Emperor and felt that he had deserted them. The feeling grew in these influential circles that William II had been isolated from the nation by the heads of his Secretariats and by Bethmann-Hollweg; and that Bethmann-Hollweg and the Court put stumbling-blocks in the way of the pursuit of a purposeful domestic and foreign policy. It was these men who were opposed to the submarine campaign, and because of their opposition Germany was rushing headlong to destruction. Despite their complete lack of confidence in William II, Bethmann-Hollweg, and, since the military position had taken a turn for the worse in the summer of 1916, in Falkenhayn, these circles could not bring themselves to take the fate of Germany into their own hands. It would have been possible in the summer of 1916 to have formed a middle-class Conservative Government, for the Centre was still allied with the Conservatives and National Liberals, and the authority of the Emperor and the existing Government had so greatly waned that it could have been easily disregarded.

If a Spahn-Westarp-Stresemann Cabinet had been formed at that time, it would at least have been a step forward. The Annexationists would have been forced to bring their views into accord with the military situation and with the national interests. It is true that a few National Liberal members of the Reichstag foresaw that Germany was going along the path which led to parliamentary government, and that the middle class would play the decisive part in this development. In the eyes of the Prussian nobility, and also in those of the majority of the industrialists, the road to parliamentarism was identical with the road to democracy and to the rule of the working class. Consequently they would not hear of any such change. It is worthy of note that the National Liberal minority, led by von Richthofen,[1] who were resolute champions of a parliamentary system in Germany, also entertained pessimistic views upon the military situation and were opposed to the war aims of the Pan-Germans. These National Liberals stood in the political warfare of those days on 'the other side of the barricade', and their tactics resembled those of the Social Democrats. Although Stresemann sought to mediate between the Right and Left Wings of the National Liberals, the majority of the Party remained loyal to the Conservatives as the champions of a Pan-German programme.

If the upper classes in Germany recognized the bankruptcy of the Imperial Government and at the same time refused to have anything to do with a parliamentary system, what remained? Only the search for a strong man, a Dictator, who would win the war and prove himself the saviour of the old Germany. Some saw this man in Admiral von Tirpitz, who had been forced to resign his office as a scapegoat for the weakness of William II and Bethmann-Hollweg, while others placed all their hopes in Hindenburg and Ludendorff. The question was also asked in the summer of 1916 whether a Dictator would in fact be able to take the control over the army out of the Emperor's hands.

The German army of 1916 no longer bore any resemblance in a political sense to the old Regular army. The old army numbered at the most some three-quarters of a million men, of whom one-third were professional soldiers—officers, N.C.O.s, and men who had re-enlisted—who had been brought up in the most rigorous monarchical tradition. The old army was the impregnable fortress of the Hohenzollerns. But the army of 1916 was composed of four million men, and in it were reflected all the divergent political tendencies in the nation. Only a very small number of the officers belonged to the Prussian aristocracy. When, in May 1915, the Prussian Guards were again brought up to their full strength in readiness for the offensive in Galicia, there were already many middle-class officers in that famous Potsdam Regiment.[2] The nobility of Germany lay among the heaps of dead on the Marne or with shattered bodies in one or other of the field hospitals. The Prussian military aristocracy was not overthrown in November 1918. Its power in the army and the Empire was destroyed by the appalling sacrifice of life made in 1914 by the Prussian nobility in the great offensive on the Western Front. Not even their political opponents can fail to be inspired by the greatest admiration for the way in which in 1914 the Prussian officers went to their death. It is only fair to admit that the old Bismarckian Germany was destroyed on the battlefield of the Marne. *Requiescat in pace.*

Nevertheless, the officers as a body in 1916 were anything rather than democratic. The officers felt themselves to be the leaders of Society and would have been horrified at the idea of a German Republic. But they looked to Hindenburg and Ludendorff rather than to William II and the Crown Prince to rescue Germany from her plight. The existence of this attitude on their part is unquestionable; it sufficed to alter radically the relationship between the King of Prussia and the army. The upper classes in Germany and the army were ready in the summer of 1916 for a dictatorship. Was it likely that the Social Democratic working class would offer serious opposition?

The Social Democrats of those days were divided among themselves and incapable of any political action. The Party leaders were convinced that it lay in the interests of the German workmen to defend the country to the utmost. If the Party were publicly to go into opposition to the Government, the unity of the nation and the army would be shattered; [3] and the blame for a defeat would fall upon the Social Democrats. The Party leaders felt that their hands were tied by the *Burgfrieden*, and they did not publicly come forward with any programme of war aims or domestic policy. They contented themselves instead with emphasizing that Germany should not attempt any conquests and that the electoral system in Prussia must be reformed. Moreover, they invariably expressed their satisfaction with Bethmann-Hollweg's ambiguous speeches on the subject of war aims and German domestic policy. The official policy of the Party encountered increasing opposition not only from the side of the doctrinaires and leaders capable of forming an independent judgement but also from that of the workmen. This opposition ultimately crystallized into two tendencies: the Spartacus Association and the U.S.P.D. (Independent Social

Democratic Party of Germany). The former inherited the traditions of the pre-war Left Wing Radicals. The latter was composed
partly of former Revisionists and partly from the group that
centred round the Chairman of the Party. The leader of the Left
Wing Radicals, Rosa Luxemburg, was particularly exasperated by
the attitude of the Party on August 4, which resulted in the loss of
its independent political initiative. It is probable, however, that
Rosa Luxemburg would have given her consent to a revolutionary
war of self-defence along the lines laid down by Engels. In a
famous pamphlet which she published during the war under the
pseudonym of Junius, she laid down a similar programme for the
defence of Germany by the workmen with their assumption of
political power as its ultimate aim.[4] In this pamphlet she further
declared that, in voting for the war credits, the Social Democrats
had not only bowed the knee to capitalism but also to the Hohenzollerns and the Prussian militarists. Rosa Luxemburg saw in this
vote in favour of the war credits the subjection of the Socialists in
every country to the governing class and thereby the death-blow
to the Socialist International. Hence a new and independent action
on the part of the working class could in her opinion only begin
with a refusal to vote any further war credits.

In seeking to put her ideas into practice Rosa Luxemburg was
gradually brought into sympathy with the feelings animating the
most embittered and despairing of the working men, who in their
hatred for the middle class refused to participate in any national
undertaking, who saw in the war conducted by the middle class
no more than a means for the further enrichment of the capitalists,
and who therefore looked upon any voluntary support of such a
war as a betrayal of the working class. These were, in truth, the
ideas of a Utopian radicalism which manifested itself from the
beginning, in conjunction with the theories of Marx, in the Labour
movement, and which refused utterly to make use of the political
means at its disposal in a middle-class community. Since these
Utopian Radicals refused to recognize the existence of any national
question, they were invariably opposed to any participation in
parliamentary elections and to any collaboration with the Trade
Unions which in a middle-class State sought to improve the lot of
the working man. Marx and Engels, indeed, had no sympathy
with this type of Utopian radicalism, which found its chief supporters among the anarchists and syndicalists. On the contrary,
Marx and Engels believed that by the pursuit of such tactics the

working class would only put itself out of court and thereby play the game of the ruling classes.

This extreme radicalism was especially prevalent among the poorest workmen, while the famine resulting from the war stimulated its growth in the working-class quarters in the cities and in the manufacturing districts. The war appeared in the eyes of these men to be simply an affair of the rich, and they adopted as their war-cry 'Down with War—Peace at Once!' without any regard for the conditions on which peace was to be made. This attitude may be compared to that of the unfortunate victims of an earthquake who were subsequently to march beneath a banner bearing the inscription 'Down with Earthquakes'. For the World War was an event of world importance, which was not to be lightly dismissed by the refusal of a section of German workmen to recognize its existence. It was not such outbreaks of despair but only the pursuit of a clever policy which accorded with the political conditions of the day—a policy after the manner of Engels—that could have brought peace and political power to the working class. It was of tragic import that Rosa Luxemburg and her supporters, who pursued a Marxist policy, and looked upon the *Burgfrieden* as an act of hari-kiri on the part of Socialism, were forced to rely upon the extreme sections in order to gain any support with the masses. For, in the result, the leaders were at least as strongly influenced by their supporters as these were by the leaders. It is only when this fact is borne in mind that the tactics and the principles of the Spartacists—the name given to Rosa Luxemburg and her supporters during the war—became comprehensible. Rosa Luxemburg was at pains to bring the 'Down with War' cry into some sort of relation with Marxist theories. Hence in her Junius pamphlet she argued that in an age of imperialism like the twentieth century every war was the result of differences between the great financiers, and was to be interpreted as the rivalry between different trusts; and that therefore a national war was an impossibility. The working class must refuse to have anything to do with the war since, whether the war ended in the victory or defeat of Germany, it would be equally disastrous for the working class. For the working class there existed only one road to power—revolution. It is worthy of note that Rosa Luxemburg's refusal to recognize the possibility of a nationalist war appeared side by side in the Junius pamphlet with her plan for a nationalist revolutionary defence of Germany. When, in 1916, this pamphlet came into the hands of Lenin in Switzerland, he pointed out and criticized her inconsistency in a famous review.

The Spartacists proclaimed a revolutionary war on the ruling system in Germany. The Government endeavoured to suppress the Spartacists by confiscating their publications and arresting their leaders whenever they could lay hands on them. The Spartacist movement became an illegal movement. Karl Liebknecht was the sole member of the Reichstag who announced himself to be a supporter of Rosa Luxemburg. He refused in December 1914 to vote for the war credit which was demanded of the Reichstag, and so finally broke with the Social Democratic Party. Liebknecht looked upon it as his duty to protest publicly at the risk of his life against the *Burgfrieden*. He was mobilized and joined the army. Nevertheless, on May 1, 1916, he took part in a street demonstration in the Potsdam Square in Berlin. He was arrested, court-martialled, and sentenced to a long term of imprisonment. He thus became the martyr of the Socialist peace movement. In 1916 the Spartacists were still numerically weak,[5] they had not succeeded in capturing a single important Social Democratic organization, and their numbers did not greatly increase until the revolution in 1918. The sympathy extended to Karl Liebknecht by vast numbers of the populace was not given to him as a revolutionary Socialist, but as the champion of peace. In the later days of the war, however, when strikes and demonstrations on the part of the half-starved workmen became frequent, it seemed as if they were animated by Spartacist ideas. As a matter of fact the crowds who took part in these demonstrations were not in the least under the domination of Spartacism. Another extreme group, which differed in many respects from the Spartacists, was organized in Bremen, and enjoyed only a local importance.

Far more important than the Spartacist movement was that which subsequently led to the establishment of the U.S.P.D.[6] The great majority of the working class, in contradistinction to the Spartacists, firmly believed in the necessity for defending Germany. But they demanded that the war should be confined to defence and that Germany should not embark upon any schemes of conquest. The workmen themselves were far more desirous of opposing the aims of the Annexationists than were the leaders of the Social Democratic Party; and in this desire, behind which was concealed a wish to renew class warfare, they were supported by a minority of their representatives in the Reichstag. It is true that this group differed from Liebknecht in that they were opposed to any revolutionary action. All that they desired was that the Party should regain its freedom of action. Since no enemy stood on the frontiers of Germany, the question at issue was no longer one of national defence, but rather that of a Pan-German war of conquest. Notwithstanding Bethmann-Hollweg's polite phrases, the Government was dominated by the Annexationists. Hence, in order to avoid sharing in the responsibility for the Government's policy, it became necessary for the Social Democratic Party to refuse war credits. In December 1915 twenty Social Democratic members of the Reichstag, inspired by this belief, separated themselves from their Party colleagues and voted against a proposed credit. Thus the Social Democratic Party in the Reichstag was split into two sections. This division was carried into the Party organization throughout the country, until the Opposition was formally expelled and in 1917 formed itself into a separate Party known as the U.S.P.D.

The Majority Social Democrats, who were known by that title in order to distinguish them from the U.S.P.D., carried on in the main the policy pursued by the Party leaders in pre-War days. The Spartacists were the heirs of the old Left Wing Radicals. The U.S.P.D., on the other hand, was composed of a number of Revisionists to whom were added the dissentient members of the Central Committee of the old Social Democratic Party. The U.S.P.D. was joined by outstanding Revisionists like Bernstein and Eisner, whose action was prompted by a desire to show that in their opinion the *Burgfrieden* was inconsistent with the interests of Labour. In the U.S.P.D. Bernstein found himself united with his old opponent Kautsky, who had been regarded by the Party for many years as a sort of official theoretician, as also with Hasse and Dittmann from the Central Committee of the old Party. During the war the old-time Revisionists found themselves split into three groups; the first remained faithful to the Central Committee; the second joined the U.S.P.D.; and the third, whose views found expression in the *Socialist Monthly*, although they remained within the ranks of the old Party, dissociated themselves from the foreign policy pursued by the Central Committee and demanded a separate peace with Russia in place of the general condemnation of a policy of conquest.[7]

The U.S.P.D. was the product of a temporary war-time situation. Primarily it was composed of the Social Democrats who were opposed to the *Burgfrieden* and who desired to refuse the war credits in order to free themselves from all connexion with the Government. Apart from this aim, however, the U.S.P.D. was divided into a number of groups each of which differed from the other in its views on Labour policy. These differences of opinion were still further accentuated by the fact that the Spartacists made use of the legally constituted U.S.P.D. as a blind behind which they continued to pursue their own particular aims. The U.S.P.D., unlike the Spartacists, refused to take part in illegal activities, and did not in any way seek to interfere with the defence of the country. It contented itself with carrying on a lively propaganda with the object of ending the war by a peace by agreement, and was successful in capturing the organization of the old Social Democratic Party in Greater Berlin, Leipzig, Halle, Bremen, Brunswick and other towns which it made use of for its own purposes.

The Majority Party found its chief support in the Independent Trade Unions. Nevertheless, in the course of 1916, the Central Committee found itself in an increasingly difficult situation, and, even within the group in the Reichstag, the opposition steadily grew to the passing of war credits. Party discipline was nevertheless maintained, and the disaffected members did not formally separate themselves from the Party organization. Under pressure from the U.S.P.D. and the refractory members within their own ranks, the Majority Socialists gradually came to dissociate themselves more and more from the *Burgfrieden*. They entered more fiercely into the campaign against the Annexationists, and made themselves the champions of the peace by mutual agreement, which was so popular among the masses of the people, and also of a constitutional reform of Germany. Throughout the years 1917–18 the gulf between the two Social Democratic Parties was still a narrow one, and revealed itself only in their respective attitudes towards the passing of war credits. The historical importance of the U.S.P.D. lies in the fact that they once more turned the whole Socialist movement in Germany against the existing governmental system. In the summer of 1916, however, the Central Committee of the Social Democratic Party was still preoccupied with its own domestic warfare against the refractory elements in the Party organization, and it was averse to making any attack upon the Government in the Reichstag for the purpose of altering the political situation in Germany. The Centre and the Progressives showed themselves equally indisposed to overthrow the Government and to take power into their own hands. Hence, despite the increasing discontent among the populace, power remained in the hands of the officers, landed proprietors, and industrialists. The Emperor and the Imperial Chancellor were set aside by the military dictatorship of General Ludendorff. It has been said that the World War was for Germany militarily a war of lost opportunities, and politically that is equally true. In the summer of 1916 political power in Germany lay at the mercy of whoever liked to seize it. If, in those days, there had existed a determined majority in the Reichstag, akin to that which came into being in 1917, it could without much difficulty have carried through the parliamentarization of Germany. The opportunity was allowed to go past unused. When in 1917 the Reichstag finally did make an attempt to assert its authority, it found itself no longer opposed by a helpless Emperor and Chancellor, but by General Ludendorff, and was incapable of attaining its object.

On August 29, 1916, under pressure of the feeling in the nation and the army, the Emperor was forced to relieve von Falkenhayn of his command. This day marked the downfall of the Bismarckian Empire and the beginning of the German Revolution. Nobody else could be appointed to Falkenhayn's vacant post except Field Marshal von Hindenburg. He brought with him to the Great General Head-quarters, General Ludendorff, who had been his Chief of Staff in the east. The change in personnel at once brought about a complete change in the authority of the army commands. The Supreme Army Command, which was famous throughout the whole world during the later years of the war, came into being. According to the Bismarckian Constitution, however, the Supreme Command of the German army rested solely in the hands of the Emperor, who in giving his commands could avail himself of the advice of the Chief of the General Staff. The Chief of the General Staff was responsible to the Emperor for the exact execution of the Imperial commands and for the proper administration of the army, in the same way as a regimental commander is responsible to a general or, in civil life, a cashier to his employer. If the Emperor was not satisfied with the conduct of the Chief of the General Staff, he either deprived him of his post or through a public manifestation of his displeasure induced him to proffer his resignation. The Chief of the General Staff had under him a number of assistant staff officers of whom one—by no means the most important—was the

Quartermaster-General. Such was the organization as it existed in accordance with the German Constitution in the German Great General Head-quarters until August 1916.

The first sign of an alteration in the organization of the Great General Head-quarters was the creation of an extraordinary dual command. It was common knowledge that the victory won by General von Hindenburg in the east had been planned by General Ludendorff. The nation and the army alike demanded that the entire conduct of the war should be placed in the hands of Hindenburg and Ludendorff. Hence Ludendorff accompanied the Field Marshal to the Great General Head-quarters, where, as Chief Quarter-Master-General,[8] he was given a new and unprecedented post. In this capacity General Ludendorff shared with Hindenburg the full responsibility for the conduct of operations. Thus the Emperor came to have two Chiefs of the General Staff. As a matter of fact, however, the division of work resulted in Hindenburg's taking into his own hands the Supreme Command with, as his Chief of the General Staff, Ludendorff who, as he had done formerly in the east, drew up the plans to which Hindenburg lent his authority. In assenting to this reorganization of the Great General Staff the Emperor in reality abandoned the Supreme Command which he had until then at least formally retained in his own hands. After August 1916 the Emperor's authority over the German army became an empty formality.

The basis of Ludendorff's dictatorship was the entirely new interpretation—an interpretation entirely foreign to all the traditions of the German army—which he put upon his 'responsibility'. It was not merely that Ludendorff understood by 'responsibility' the duty of a subordinate towards his superior, but rather that he interpreted his position as though it were that of a Minister responsible to Parliament. Thus, for example, when the Imperial Chancellor pursued a policy that, in the opinion of Ludendorff, was mistaken and even injurious to the conduct of the war, Ludendorff declared that he could not assume the 'responsibility' for such a policy and proffered his resignation. The result was that it was the Imperial Chancellor who resigned and not Ludendorff. By a skilful use of this form of blackmail, which he called his 'responsibility' or his 'dislike of assuming the responsibility', Ludendorff not only forced the Emperor to give way to him in military matters but also in all decisive political questions.

General Ludendorff enjoyed the complete confidence of Field

Marshal von Hindenburg. If Ludendorff proffered his resignation, Hindenburg did likewise. It was, however, impossible for the Emperor to relieve Hindenburg and Ludendorff of their commands. The Imperial authority had sunk so far, and that of the two Generals had risen so high, that William II was helpless as against Ludendorff. If in 1917 the Emperor had attempted to get rid of Ludendorff, a 'Ludendorff' crisis would very quickly have become an 'Emperor' crisis. It was only in October 1918, when the Quarter-master-General himself formally admitted that he had lost the war, and thereby in a sense announced his abdication as dictator, that it became possible to deprive him of his post. The fact that Field Marshal von Hindenburg did not resign in October 1918 but continued in the service, first of the constitutional monarchy under Max von Baden and then under the Republic, only serves to show that Hindenburg never thought of himself as being a dictator. It was the man who in October 1918 was forced to resign in conse-quence of the military and political collapse of Germany who had been the real ruler of the country ever since August 1916.

In military affairs Ludendorff's authority was so great that he never permitted a single subordinate officer (and who was not subordinate to the Supreme Command?) to express to the Emperor any opinion that was not in agreement with his own views. This was clearly shown, for example, in January 1918 in a discussion which took place over the future of Poland. In a conference on January 2 the Emperor expressed himself in the question of the future demarcation of the German-Polish frontier in favour of the views of General Hoffmann. Thereupon, on January 7, 1918, Hindenburg wrote a letter to William II in which among other things he said:[9]

'In the Polish Question Your Majesty has chosen to place greater reliance upon the judgement of General Hoffmann than upon that of General Ludendorff and myself. General Hoffmann is my subordinate, and bears no responsibility whatsoever in the Polish Question. The events of January 2 have been the cause of pain to General Ludendorff and myself, and have shown us that Your Majesty disregards our opinion in a matter of vital importance for the existence of the German Father-land.'

It is clear that this was a purely political issue, and, in accordance with the Constitution, the Chief of the General Staff had neither the right to interfere nor any responsibility for the decisions that might be taken. At the same time it was open to the Emperor to ask the advice of a military authority in a political question. In January 1918, however, the balance of power had been so completely altered that Ludendorff interpreted his 'responsibility' to cover every question that could remotely affect 'the existence of the German Fatherland', that is to say, over all political issues, and he regarded it as outrageous that the Emperor should ask for the advice of any other officer in a political issue: 'for General Hoffmann is my subordinate, and bears no responsibility whatsoever in the Polish Question.' If this standpoint were to be accepted, the authority of the King of Prussia over the army would be destroyed and the army would acquire a single commander in the person of the Chief Quartermaster-General. The issue was speedily decided in favour of General Ludendorff. The Imperial Chancellor informed the Supreme Command that it was clear that a misunderstanding had arisen. The Emperor on January 2 had taken no final decision in regard to Poland.

Ludendorff even claimed the right to name the Imperial Chancellor. Bethmann-Hollweg was dismissed because Hindenburg and Ludendorff refused to work in collaboration with him; and the events leading up to the appointment of his successor, Michaelis, were almost grotesque. The Emperor instructed the Chief of his Civil Secretariat, von Valentini, to ask Hindenburg whom he wished to have as Chancellor. Valentini, who was somewhat disturbed by the Imperial command, betook himself first to his colleague, von Lyncker, the Chief of the Military Secretariat, with whom he found the Emperor's aide-de-camp, General von Plessen. In the course of conversation the name of the Prussian Food Controller, Dr. Michaelis, was suddenly mentioned by Plessen. Subsequently the three men went off to Hindenburg and Ludendorff with whom they took counsel as to who was to be the new Chancellor. Ludendorff declared that he strongly approved of Michaelis, who had recently visited the Great General Headquarters and left behind him the impression that as Chancellor he would be the right man in the right place. Hence they agreed upon Michaelis; Valentini returned with their proposal to the Emperor, who immediately accepted it, although he was forced to confess that he did not know Michaelis.

The nation was no better acquainted with Michaelis than was the Emperor. The whole world was astonished that the fate of Germany in this critical hour should be entrusted to a man who had played little or no part in politics. The mystery of Michaelis's appointment to the Chancellorship can be unravelled by means of a communication made by von Valentini to Bethmann-Hollweg, and written down by the latter on July 14, 1917, immediately after the interview. Bethmann-Hollweg's remarkable memorandum is preserved among the documents of the Imperial Chancellery.[10] On reading this memorandum it is easy to see that Ludendorff's will was decisive and that William II immediately assented to the General's proposals. It is no less clear that in political affairs Ludendorff took decisions carelessly, and that a chance proposal and a no less chance personal impression sufficed to cause the General to adopt a point of view. Such was the haphazard fashion in which the German nation was governed during the war.

After a very few months it became clear that Michaelis was wholly unequal to his task, and the Supreme Command sacrificed him ruthlessly to the Reichstag. His successor, Hertling, felt himself to be primarily the representative of the Supreme Command, and as such he devoted all his energies to endeavouring to put its political views into action. It is true that the personal opinions of the experienced old Chancellor in vital questions were very different from those of General Ludendorff. Nevertheless, Count Hertling did not feel equal to embarking on a controversy with Ludendorff.

Ludendorff not only refused to suffer any Imperial Chancellor who was not welcome to him, but he extended his dictatorial supervision to Ministers and Secretaries of State. When von Kühlmann, who was Secretary of State for Foreign Affairs, delivered in June 1918 a speech in the Reichstag with which the Supreme Command was dissatisfied, he was dismissed at Ludendorff's desire. Moreover, the Supreme Command reserved to itself the right to define Germany's war aims. When the peace negotiations between Germany, Russia, the Ukraine and Rumania were initiated, Ludendorff insisted that the Emperor should formally permit the participation of the Supreme Command notwithstanding the fact that, according to the Constitution, the Imperial Chancellor alone was responsible for the conclusion of peace. The rivalry between the Supreme Command and the Imperial Chancellor brought into being a situation that was contrary to the Constitution. Nevertheless, the attitude of Germany in the peace negotiations at Brest-Litovsk, and with Rumania, was determined by General Ludendorff.

The Supreme Command also interfered in all questions of domestic policy in so far as it was interested in them. At that time in Germany hardly anything happened that could not in some form or other be traced back to the Supreme Command. Its excuse for interference in Labour questions, food supplies, Trade Unions, raw materials, &c., was the fact that these all came under the heading of war industries. If no direct ground for interference was present, Ludendorff declared that his reason for interfering in a domestic issue was 'that it had an unfavourable effect upon the morale of the army'. The pressure brought to bear on the Emperor by the Supreme Command far exceeded anything in the nature of authoritative advice in military and political questions. William II was even forced to propose to General Ludendorff the names of those whom he wished to appoint to positions at Court.

In January 1918 the Supreme Command demanded of the Emperor that he should dismiss the Chief of his Civil Secretariat, von Valentini,[11] who had for years enjoyed his complete confidence. The Emperor did not dare to refuse, although he insisted that the Supreme Command should make known to him the ground on which they based their demand. On January 16, 1918, in agreement with Ludendorff, Hindenburg replied to William II that von Valentini had borne a large share of the responsibility for the dangerous policy pursued by Bethmann-Hollweg. Hindenburg further declared that he had frequently begged of the Emperor to replace Valentini, since, as Chief of the General Staff, the trend of public opinion could not be a matter of indifference to him. He went on to say that he hoped the Emperor would summon to his councils a man who 'viewed the situation clearly and impartially, and who would openly and manfully inform His Majesty as to the state of affairs and restore the confidence of the nation, which was eagerly waiting for such an appointment'.

It is easy to see that the Supreme Command did not hesitate to identify its own personal views with those of the army and the nation. In view of the unprecedented authority which Hindenburg and Ludendorff then wielded this was not so mistaken as it might appear. For were the Supreme Command to declare that any measure was necessary in order to win the war it could be sure until the autumn of 1918 of being supported in its wishes by the majority of the nation. In obedience to the Supreme Command the Emperor dismissed von Valentini. It is quite clear that in such a state of affairs it was no longer possible to talk of a monarchical government in Germany. The Constitution of 1871 had been in fact thrown aside. Nevertheless, General Ludendorff quite sincerely looked upon himself as loyal to the Emperor. At the same time he demanded of the Emperor that he should only do that which was right and necessary, and only retain in his service suitable and competent men. But it was General Ludendorff himself who decided what was to be done and in whom confidence was to be placed; and he demanded of William II that he should assent to these decisions. It was thus that the Carolingian Mayors of the Palace treated the Merovingian Kings.

William II was not ignorant as to the state of affairs, and looked upon Ludendorff's dictatorship as a grave personal humiliation. As in the past so now William II poured out his heart in marginal comments on the documents that were laid before him.[12] Yet what a difference existed between the pre-war Imperial marginal comments with their proud and harsh expressions characteristic of an autocratic ruler and the depressed, embittered observations in 1917 and 1918! In January 1918, for example, a report from Field Marshal von Mackensen in Rumania, in which he set forth his views on the situation in the Balkans and on Austro-German relations, was laid before the Emperor. William II wrote in the margin that Mackensen's views 'wholly coincide with my own. Up to the present, however, I have been unable to gain a hearing for them from the Chief of the General Staff.'

On January 9, 1918, an article appeared in the *Berliner Börsenzeitung*, which was clearly inspired by Kühlmann, in which the differences between Kühlmann and Ludendorff were dealt with in a very cautious manner. Kühlmann, indeed, sought to undermine Ludendorff's dictatorial authority. He emphasized in memoranda that the preponderating authority of the Supreme Command was in contradiction to the German Constitution, and he also endeavoured in as far as was then possible to influence public opinion in this sense. But Kühlmann's opinions were known to the Supreme Command, which secured his dismissal a few months later. The very cleverly worded article in the *Börsenzeitung* was covered with marginal comments from the Emperor's pen. All places in which the writer attacked Ludendorff, naturally without mentioning the name of the much-feared Quartermaster-General, were marked by the Emperor with 'Yes'—'Quite right'—'Very true', &c. In truth William II himself was in all questions of foreign policy and war aims a supporter of the moderate policy of Bethmann-Hollweg and Kühlmann and an opponent of that of Ludendorff. Yet he saw no possibility either of retaining in power the politicians with whom he sympathized or of insisting upon Ludendorff's adopting their policy.

The article in question contained the following sentence: 'Again and again comes a cry from the German public for a statesman to lead us. Unhappily the present conditions are little calculated to permit of a statesman's attaining to greatness.' On which the Emperor made the following comment: 'Very true. Either he does not please the Reichstag or Kreuznach or both.' At that time the Supreme Command had its Head-quarters at Kreuznach. The Emperor did not ask himself the question as to whether the chances for a statesman were any better in the pre-War Germany than they were in 1918. The article went on to point out that in the opinion of the writer the relations between the military and civil authorities left much to be desired. On this William II, not without reason, commented: 'Because the Emperor is ignored by both.'

In those days William II judged the political situation in Germany somewhat as follows: 'On the one side stands the all-powerful Supreme Command. On the other the majority of the Reichstag and certain Ministers who, relying on the support of the Reichstag, seek to overcome the authority of the Supreme Command. Neither party bothers about the Emperor, who himself can do nothing to improve matters.' And that was the same William II who in 1890 could dismiss a Bismarck from office, and who had formerly wished to trample underfoot everything that stood in his path! In Ludendorff he had found his master. The Emperor was 'ignored' by every one. Bismarck was revenged.

Now and again throughout 1917 and 1918 William II sought to make it appear as if he were still the old autocratic Emperor. He delivered fierce speeches against Democracy in general and against the Social Democrats in particular. In Kreuznach, however, the Emperor was estimated at his true worth. The events that took place in 1918 at the Great General Head-quarters can only rightly be understood when it is recalled that William II had there been looked upon for years as a powerless and indeed superfluous individual.

It is true that General Ludendorff never sought to make himself the ruler of Germany. When in August 1916 he found himself placed in the Supreme Command by the desire of the army and the nation, he ruthlessly interfered whenever he deemed it to be necessary without worrying himself very much about his fitness to do so; and when he found that his will had become all-powerful he accustomed himself to govern. If Ludendorff had been an English or French General, or even a Prussian General under William I, he would never even have dreamt of interfering in politics. Fate, however, brought General Ludendorff to power at the very moment at which the Imperial Government, in the sense of the Constitution of 1871, had ceased to exist, and a new form of government had not yet come into being. Ludendorff the Politician is the stopgap between two periods in German history and, from a moral standpoint, it would be wrong to condemn him for having played this role. That Ludendorff was a strategist of the first order is unquestionable. Great soldiers, however, are seldom statesmen. As a politician Napoleon was as great a failure as Caesar. Hannibal, by his—from a political standpoint—mistaken invasion of Italy, largely helped to bring about the downfall of Carthage. Moltke the Elder never attempted to interfere in politics.

In August 1916 Ludendorff possessed neither political capacity nor experience. Hence in non-military questions he allowed himself to be influenced with the greatest ease if only the person or the measure proposed fitted in in general with his train of ideas. He seized upon the advice given him by clever individuals and proceeded to put it into practice with his own peculiar tenacity and his immense authority. Ludendorff indeed defended himself from the charge of being a reactionary by pointing to his work for the wounded soldiers and for the promotion of building and the creation of settlements. At the same time it was incomprehensible to him that a workman could possess an independent judgement in politics. Nor could he understand why it was that the working class was influenced by the appalling want of the later years of the war to adopt views on the subject of war aims which did not coincide with his own. He was prepared to adopt the most ruthless measures against strikers. In no circumstances was any concession to be made to any wish put forward by a striker. In a letter to the Minister for War on February 18, 1918,[13] Ludendorff voiced his belief that it would be possible in the future to settle disputes 'in general without the employment of force'. 'Nevertheless it is necessary', he added, 'to be prepared for all eventualities, and it is for this reason that I have consented to leave the desired troops in Germany.' In the same letter Ludendorff advised the Minister for War to place all factories under military control. 'Military control is naturally only a temporary expedient. It appears, however, to be specially effective in that the workmen once more gain the impression of an over-riding authority which has power over them and is prepared to afford the utmost protection to those who desire to work—these are always by far the greater majority among the workmen.' Strikes in time of war were high treason. The guilty should be tried by court martial to avoid their being given mild sentences. It followed that suitable Judge-Advocates-General should participate in such trials as Presidents of the Courts and Crown Prosecutors. If the Ministry of War had not sufficient energetic officers for this purpose, Ludendorff declared his readiness to come to its assistance with suitable officers withdrawn from the army at the Front. Moreover, Ludendorff was of the opinion that the leaders of the Social Democrats should be forced to declare whether or not they approved of strikes in war time. If they pronounced themselves against strikes, and if the workmen nevertheless again went on strike, then the leaders would be compelled to take action against the strikers. Their inability to prevent strikes would reveal publicly their helplessness, whereas at present they could always threaten to use their power over the working man. If, however, the Social Democrats were to refuse on principle to condemn the use of the strike, they could at once be branded as traitors. Ludendorff advised the formation of a bloc composed of all the peaceful Labour organizations to act as a counterpoise to the Social Democratic Trade Unions. In the letter from which we have already quoted Ludendorff emphatically warned his correspondent against any further increase in wages for which in his opinion there was no justification. In explanation of his attitude towards the question of wages Ludendorff referred significantly to a report which he had received on the mining industry in the Ruhr. Instead of increases, he advised the reduction of the 'high' wages and, as he invariably did, also that of the high profits accruing to the employers.

Ludendorff sought to give effect to his politico-social ideas by securing that the Minister for War issued instructions in this sense to the Generals commanding the various Home Commands, who would on their part issue similar instructions to the Presidents of the Industrial Tribunals. Ludendorff sought through the Home Commands and the existence of martial law to create an executive authority that would be wholly independent of the Imperial Government. Since the beginning of the war the General commanding a Home Command had exercised supreme authority over the civilians within his command. He censored the Press, forbade meetings, made preventive arrests, &c., &c. These Generals were subordinate to the Minister for War, who, up to August 1916, received his instructions in political questions from the Imperial Chancellor. Until August 1916, Bethmann-Hollweg was in full control of the governmental apparatus. All this was changed with Ludendorff's appointment as Quartermaster-General. Henceforward the Minister for War felt that his first duty was to carry out the wishes of the Supreme Command under which were also the Home Commands. Hence a pure military dictatorship came into being. From the Chief of the General Staff down to the smallest village official this overwhelming authority was directed above all towards the suppression of the Social Democrats. Ludendorff was not in the least troubled by any regard for the *Burgfrieden*. It is obvious that the Commander-in-Chief of an army in time of war cannot look with complaisance upon strikes in munition factories, and that he must seek for some means by which to prevent their occurrence. But Ludendorff went far beyond this in his ideas. It is significant that he wished to impress the working men with the feeling that there existed an 'overriding authority' with power over them. Social Democracy, alike in its political and industrial manifestations, was *the* enemy in Ludendorff's eyes, and he made no distinction between the various tendencies within the Social Democratic Party. It was his wish to utilize the strikes in order to be able to place the Social Democratic leaders in such a position that they would either be rendered politically powerless or be able to be treated as traitors.

Any one who could in 1918 share in Ludendorff's views on the wage question was not only ignorant of industrial conditions but was an avowed enemy of the working class. Although the wages then paid to the munition workers were on paper high, yet in relation to the price of food-stuffs they were extremely low. For if the workman desired to obtain food beyond the rations legally permitted to him he was compelled to purchase smuggled goods. Hence any reduction in wages would have resulted in the then existing situation in Germany in an increased famine amongst the masses of the populace; whereas the lowering of the employers' margin of profit would at the most have reduced the dividends paid by the great companies.

Thanks to his military training Ludendorff in social questions was an even more die-hard Conservative than Bismarck. The army, the landed proprietors, and the industrialists were in his eyes the chief elements in the nation. He was always open to proposals coming from industrial circles. He shared completely in Bismarck's ideas on the subject of a forcible suppression of Social Democracy —that is to say, of an independent political public opinion in the working class. The difference between them was that Bismarck, in order to be able to hold down the workers, sought by every means in his power to prevent Germany from being involved in war. Ludendorff, on the other hand, developed his plan of campaign against the Social Democrats in the midst of the most frightful war in which the German nation had ever participated—a war which demanded the most tremendous sacrifices from the working class that comprised the majority of the German people. Such a policy could only lead to a catastrophe. The political and economic subjection of the working class could only result in an embitterment so great that an explosion would be unavoidable the moment the military authority of the Supreme Command ceased to exist.

The industrialists and the landed proprietors perceived that in vital social issues they had the support of the most powerful man in Germany. Bethmann-Hollweg had never shown any desire to deprive the ruling classes in Germany of their power. But he had looked upon it as a necessity that the working class should not be provoked during the war, and he wanted to make it easy for the Social Democrats to remain at least outwardly loyal to the *Burgfrieden*. This attitude on the part of Bethmann-Hollweg earned for him the distrust of the ruling classes, who placed their confidence all the more readily in Ludendorff in the hope that he would bring about the fall of Bethmann-Hollweg himself, his supporters in the Government and at Court, and his whole system. Hence it was that until the summer of 1917 Ludendorff could rely upon the support of the majority in the Reichstag. Among his supporters were the Conservatives and the National Liberals as well as the old leaders of the Centre, who still retained their authority over the Party. His sole determined opponent was the small group of the U.S.P.D. It is true that the Majority Socialists and the Progressives did not sympathize with the views of the Pan-Germans, yet they were not then disposed to go into opposition. The majority in the Reichstag publicly displayed its confidence in Ludendorff in the question of unrestricted submarine warfare.

Ludendorff not only shared in the views of the industrialists and the landed proprietors in all vital political and social questions. He was also a believer in their war aims.[14] He was a convinced supporter of the so-called peace by conquest. Moreover, he was also greatly preoccupied with the question of the military security of Germany, and he devoted much thought to envisaging the position of Germany in a future war. His attitude to these problems was purely that of a strategist. It was necessary for Germany to possess as much coal and iron, wheat and potatoes, as possible within her own frontiers, or at least within the frontiers of districts directly under her influence, in order to be virtually independent of foreign countries for her supplies. In order to protect the important industrial areas from attack by enemy aircraft it was advisable that the frontiers should be drawn as far as possible away from these districts. But what Ludendorff could not or would not see was that a clever domestic and foreign policy affords a State better protection than the finest strategical frontiers. It has already been mentioned above that the strategical plans for Germany's security were practically identical with the plans of conquest put forward by the industrialists.

In the sphere of foreign policy Ludendorff was in favour of a future alliance with Japan, which was in itself a feasible idea. Only in order to achieve such an object Germany would have had to be certain of the friendship of Russia, and Ludendorff's eastern policy was framed on the basis that Russia was the natural enemy of Germany. For the safeguarding of the food-situation in Germany in a future war Ludendorff demanded that Courland and Lithuania should become German protectorates, while on strategic grounds east and west Prussia would have to be 'somewhat enlarged'. Ludendorff considered an adjustment of the frontiers necessary to protect Posen and, above all, Upper Silesia must be protected by an accession of territory. 'The liquidation of the factories there at present in enemy possession, and their transference to German owners would render this more easy,' wrote Ludendorff in a memorandum dated September 14, 1917, which reveals his complete agreement with the war aims of the German industrialists. In the west—here again his views coincided with those of the industrialists—Ludendorff demanded a westward extension of the frontier of German Lorraine and the annexation of Longwy-Briey, for the purpose of placing Germany in possession of a greater supply of iron ore in the event of another war. Belgium must be brought into such close economic dependence upon Germany that she would of her own accord seek a political union with Germany. This would afford the only real protection for the Rhenish-Westphalian industrial district. In order, however, to compel Belgium to seek union with Germany it would be necessary to exercise military pressure by the seizure of Liége and a long occupation of the country.

Ludendorff was convinced that an economically unfavourable peace for Germany, which involved the imposition of overwhelming taxes upon the nation, would be a tremendous disappointment to the demobilized troops and would carry in it the seeds of revolution. Thus a victorious peace became identified for Ludendorff with the continued political domination of the ruling class in Germany. It is true that there was a vast difference between the demands for annexation put forward by manufacturers, who lacked a full knowledge of the military situation, and the same demands made by General Ludendorff as the head of the German army. The Pan-Germans were without any political responsibility and were incapable of achieving such aims by themselves. It was expected of Ludendorff, however, that he would win the victory which was the indispensable preliminary to the fulfilment of his war aims. It was not against Scheidemann and Bethmann-Hollweg that such a victory had to be won. It was against England, France, and Russia. Only the complete defeat of these three Great Powers could have opened the road to the peace desired by Ludendorff and the industrialists.

The military situation in which Germany found herself in August 1916, at the time when Hindenburg and Ludendorff assumed the Supreme Command, was exceedingly critical. It was feared that Rumania's participation in the war on the side of the Entente would speedily result in the defeat of Germany. Notwithstanding the unfavourable situation Ludendorff was successful in reorganizing the German Fronts from the Somme to Verdun and from Riga to the Carpathians. The offensives undertaken by the English, French, and Russian troops only resulted in small local successes. The German defence proved impregnable on all Fronts. Ludendorff further managed to collect together a German army which, in co-operation with the forces of Germany's allies, invaded Rumania, decisively defeated the Rumanian army in several battles, and overran the greater part of the country. The danger which threatened the German Eastern Front was thus brilliantly overcome.

The Rumanian campaign, which was carried out in a sense before the eyes of the Russian, French, and English armies, was from a strategical standpoint no less remarkable than Tannenberg. Yet a peace of conquest was still very far from being achieved. The campaign of 1916 had failed to bring any more decisive result than that of the previous year. The German army by enormous efforts had saved itself from defeat and restored a balance of strength on the Fronts. But victory had in no wise been achieved and—worst of all for Germany—it was no longer to be expected. Since more than a million English troops had joined the Russian and French millions, the Entente armies so greatly exceeded the German in numerical strength that a German victory on either of the two Fronts was out of the question. The assembling of the German divisions for the Rumanian campaign was a feat of extraordinary military daring. In order to have waged a decisive campaign against Russia, for example, it would have been necessary to have transferred far greater masses of troops from the Western Front than could possibly have been spared there. The English and the French would have broken through and the war would have been ended. On the assumption of the Supreme Command by Hindenburg and Ludendorff, the military situation in which Germany found herself was so bad that not even the cleverest generalship could have availed to alter it. The most that Germany could do was to postpone defeat by a clever defensive strategy. Here again Time worked in favour of the Entente and against the blockaded Germany.

Ludendorff himself was under no illusions as to the true facts of the situation. He proved this not only by his neglect to plan any great offensive for the year 1917, but also by the fact that he wished to confine himself to the defensive both on the Western and Eastern Fronts throughout the coming year. The German public, however, who did not know how serious the situation was and who were not informed as to the relative strengths of the opposing forces, awaited from Hindenburg and Ludendorff a victory in the west on the scale of Tannenberg. Ludendorff would never have permitted himself to take the risk of an offensive which could only result in certain disaster. But Ludendorff was not only the matter of fact soldier who confined the military operations of his armies within the range of possibilities. He was also the politician who was pledged to a victorious peace. Nevertheless, Ludendorff the Soldier could not give victory to Ludendorff the Politician. Hence Ludendorff was forced to look round for another way in which to make certain of a German victory. He thought he had found it in submarine warfare. The supporters of a victorious peace were also clutching at this last straw.

Thus Germany once again missed an opportunity of emerging from the war without loss. The political outcome of the 1916 campaign was that Germany at last endeavoured to make peace with Russia. In view of the critical situation in which Germany found herself Bethmann-Hollweg determined, admittedly at the eleventh hour, to initiate serious negotiations with Russia for the conclusion of a separate peace.[15] He dispatched the famous industrial magnate, Stinnes, to Sweden, where he met the Vice-President of the Duma, Protopopoff. At that moment the Tsarist Government was disposed to make peace on account of the general political situation in Russia and the increasing difficulties it was experiencing. The Tsar appointed Stürmer, who was not indisposed to conclude a separate peace, to the Premiership, and Protopopoff to the Ministry of the Interior. It is clear that in order to achieve a peace with Russia Germany would have had to abandon the plans for territorial acquisitions at Russia's expense to which Bethmann-Hollweg had frequently pledged himself in the Reichstag. The parliamentary orations of an Imperial Chancellor, however, could not be looked upon as binding in international law. The negotiations, which were carried on in secret between Germany and Russia, progressed favourably up to the point at which they were interrupted by one of the worst political mistakes made by Germany throughout the war—the proclamation of the kingdom of Poland on November 5, 1916.[16] This action was in accordance with the eastern policy which Bethmann-Hollweg had pursued since the outbreak of the war. It was nevertheless contrary to the wishes of Austria. The Habsburgs and the Austrian aristocrats were not at all content that Austria should owe its continued existence as a State to the armed support of Germany and to her *Niebelungentreue*; and they sought instead to make dynastic conquests on their own. The kingdom of Poland was to be resurrected under the sceptre of the Habsburgs. This 'Austro-Polish' solution of the Polish problem ran counter to certain German plans by which a greater or lesser portion of Russian Poland was to be united to Prussia in order to effect a rectification of the frontier. At the same time Austria no less than Germany was at pains to seek to detach Poland from Russia.

The proclamation of the Kingdom of Poland took place in

accordance with the plans and advice of the German military authorities. The German Governor of Warsaw, General von Beseler, was of the opinion that the Central Powers should at first only proclaim the independence of Poland, since by doing so a strong Polish volunteer army could at once be raised. Beseler believed that three Polish divisions could be raised immediately and that others would subsequently be formed. This plan was vehemently supported by General Ludendorff, who in a letter to the Under-Secretary of State for Foreign Affairs, Zimmermann, on July 17, 1916, declared that the Austrian army daily failed more and more in its role of ally; and that therefore it was all the more necessary for Germany to seek for support in Poland. 'Let us create a Grand Duchy of Poland, including Warsaw and Lublin, and raise a Polish army officered by German officers. The Polish army will come into being in any case, but if it does so now it will be of use to us.' Ludendorff admitted that there were political objections to this course; yet he argued that they must give way to military necessity. Bethmann-Hollweg agreed to the demands of the military authorities, which in truth coincided with his own views. Nevertheless, it is General Ludendorff who bears the chief responsibility for the resurrection of Poland, since his opposition would have been sufficient to have brought the project to naught. It would appear that Bethmann-Hollweg and the Foreign Office, despite the secret negotiations in Sweden, did not place any confidence in Russia's pacific intentions. If they had done so, the attitude of the German Government in the Polish Question would be utterly incomprehensible.

The proposal for a restoration of Poland was strongly opposed by the Conservatives and National Liberals, who did not wish to see all possibility destroyed of a separate peace with Russia. It was now that the Parties of the Right in Germany paid the penalty for their failure to assume the reins of government themselves. A military dictatorship was preferable to them than parliamentarism and democracy. Hence they were forced to let things take their course. Under pressure from the Supreme Command, which was only interested in the troops to be raised in Poland, and after having reached an understanding with Austria, Bethmann-Hollweg took action. The German Emperor and the Emperor of Austria issued simultaneous proclamations announcing the independence of Poland. The Polish volunteers were, nevertheless, not forthcoming. Until the end of the war, Poland continued to be an apple of discord between Berlin and Vienna. The Imperial proclamations did not prevent the Nationalist Party in Poland from entering into negotiations with the Entente that subsequently resulted in Poland's receiving her independence from the hands of the victors at Versailles. On November 5, 1916, any hopes that might have existed that Russia would desert the ranks of the Entente in the course of the winter were annihilated. Indeed, instead of Russia's defection, the Entente received the addition of the economically, and potentially also militarily, most powerful State in the world— the United States of America.

The domination of the seas by the Entente was assured from the first day of the war. The battleships of England, France, and Russia outnumbered those of Germany by three to one, while the Italian fleet sufficed to keep the Austrian fleet in check. Hence the position of the German fleet throughout the war resembled that of an army shut up in a besieged fortress. It is true that it was able to make a number of attacks on the English coast and the Channel; but these failed to result in any decisive engagement. One of these attacks in 1916 led to the Battle of Jutland, which ended in a technical German victory. Many English cruisers were sunk, yet the English mastery of the seas was not in the least affected by the issue of the battle. Owing to their mastery of the seas the Entente Powers were able to blockade Germany, seize the German colonies, and to transport troops and supplies of all kinds from England and America to Europe without any serious loss. The Entente did not need to attempt any direct naval attack upon the German coast. The German cruisers nevertheless rendered valuable service in that they enabled Germany to retain her mastery over the Baltic and prevented the enemy from landing troops on her northern coast. If it had not been for the German cruisers, the Entente would have been able to invade Schleswig-Holstein and Pomerania, and a Northern Front would have been added to the already existing Eastern and Western Fronts. If that had come to pass, and if the Allies had attacked simultaneously on the three Fronts, it is probable that as early as 1915 Germany's defence would have been broken.

Since the dawn of history the weakest side in a naval war has always had resort to privateering. Privateers, commanded by clever and daring captains, slipped through the numerically superior battle fleets of the enemy and inflicted enormous damage. Thus, for example, the French in the eighteenth century and in the

Napoleonic Wars were able to inflict severe losses upon the English. In 1914, however, the possibility of making use of her cruisers in such a manner was hardly open to Germany. The latest inventions at the disposal of a naval Intelligence Service enabled the commander of the fleet that had the mastery of the seas to receive speedy and accurate information as to the movements of privateers. Hence he could order their pursuit with cruisers developing a far greater turn of speed. It is only necessary to recall the fate meted out in 1914 to the German cruisers operating in far-distant waters. The German navy was thus compelled to rely upon the submarine to attack enemy transports.

Submarine warfare proved itself to be an extraordinarily effective weapon against the enemy's mercantile marine. It is obvious that a submarine can only prove effective when it is able to torpedo the enemy's merchant craft without warning. If a cruiser were to challenge a merchant vessel, it would be impossible for the latter to offer any resistance. If, on the other hand, the tiny submarine were to come to the surface, an energetic merchant captain could simply ram it and, if his vessel were armed, could seriously damage and even sink the submarine. The risk naturally occurs in the extreme form of submarine warfare that the crew of a merchant vessel or the passengers on a liner may be killed.

The submarine campaign gave rise to a fierce controversy among international lawyers; for the law relating to naval warfare had only contemplated privateering operations by cruisers and the actual blockade of a coast by warships. The Entente accused Germany of endangering the lives of peaceful voyagers and of accomplishing the deaths of neutrals through the submarine campaign. Germany answered that the blockade caused equal suffering to her civilian population. Millions of women and children were starving in Germany, and the only proper answer to the blockade was submarine warfare. It is impossible to discuss here the question as to whether or not there was a justification for the submarine campaign.

From the outset the neutrals protested against the injury inflicted on them by the submarine campaign, and the most powerful of them all, America, was specially loud in her protests. The history of the United States teaches that in accordance with American traditions American policy has never been particularly friendly to England. The relations between America and Germany in 1914 were correct. American industry nevertheless believed itself to be justified in selling materials of all kinds to the belligerents. If the grouping of Powers in the war had been different, and if Germany, for example, had been able to maintain direct communication with America through Russia and Japan, then the Americans would undoubtedly have been just as ready to supply Germany as they were to supply England with munitions, raw materials, and food. But Germany was cut off from America and American supplies went to the Entente in enormous quantities. American industry looked upon the interruption of this commercial traffic by the German submarines, and the menace thereby arising to the lives of American citizens, as illegal and unjustifiable. The United States announced that they were prepared if necessary to assist in putting an end to submarine warfare by declaring war on Germany. As has already been mentioned above, von Tirpitz was nevertheless in favour of embarking on a campaign of ruthless submarine warfare; but Bethmann-Hollweg was opposed to it and Tirpitz was forced to resign. The question came up anew on the assumption by Hindenburg and Ludendorff of the Supreme Command.

The supporters of ruthless submarine warfare were of the opinion that this was the sole means by which Germany could inflict serious injury upon British commerce. The naval authorities calculated that within the space of six months a ruthless submarine campaign would destroy so many English ships that England would be compelled through lack of food and raw materials to sue for peace.[17] The intervention of America involved Germany in no real danger, since American industry was already at the service of the Entente, and the Entente fleets were already so superior to the German in cruiser strength that the addition of the American fleet was a matter of indifference. It would take from one to two years before America would have mobilized and trained an army capable of intervening in Europe. The submarine campaign would in the meanwhile have brought England to her knees, and the war in Europe would have been ended. Moreover, there were no longer any ships available to bring millions of American troops with all their necessary equipment to Europe, and even if such transports became available, they would be an easy prey for submarines.

Such arguments were not difficult to confute. It is indeed speculative to think that one can win a war at sea without possessing the supremacy of the seas. If the belligerent Power attacked by submarines is capable of making good use of its mastery of the seas, it will be able to protect its mercantile marine in a hundred different ways. Although submarines may cause it great loss, yet the supremacy of the seas cannot be won by privateering. That is an elementary principle of naval strategy that is incapable of being changed by any new technical invention. The notion was still more absurd that a successful submarine campaign would result in the defeat of an enemy who possessed a numerical superiority such as that possessed by the Entente in the winter of 1916–17 on land as well as on the sea. The chief naval experts in Germany until 1914 were wholly of this opinion. It was for this reason that they laid the chief emphasis in their building programme on battleships, and rejected the proposals of the theorists who wished instead for a greater number of submarines and cruisers. Whoever bases a naval programme on capital ships, as did Tirpitz and his school before 1914, is inspired by the sound strategic point of view that a naval war is fought for the mastery of the seas; and that without the mastery of the seas no naval victory is possible. If that were true before 1914, it was also true in 1916. Any hopes of winning the war by means of submarines were from a strategical standpoint utterly unfounded. It cannot at the same time be denied that it was quite otherwise with the question as to whether Germany in her submarines did not possess a remarkably effective weapon for use in an economic warfare; and one which might enable her to compensate herself for the damage inflicted by the blockade. In event of the initiation of peace negotiations England could renounce the blockade and Germany her submarine campaign—the one would counterbalance the other. It could with good reason be expected that a ruthless submarine campaign would inflict enormous loss upon the enemy, and this belief proved itself later to be well founded. In the winter of 1916–17 the question before both the military and civil authorities in Germany was in truth as follows: Will a ruthless submarine campaign prove so effective as a counterpoise to the English blockade that Germany can afford to risk the danger of America's entering the war?

It is only fair to concede to the supporters of submarine warfare that America was already in an economic sense at war with Germany, and that it was a matter of indifference whether or not the American Fleet joined that of the Entente. What was of decisive importance was the danger threatening from the active participation of an American army in the battle in France. Moreover, it was exceedingly questionable whether the Entente, with its command of the seas, would not be able to transport an army from

America to France. At least a year, however, must elapse before
the United States would be capable of transforming its tiny peace-
time army into an army of millions, and of transporting these to
Europe. Hence in 1917 there was no question of having to reckon
seriously with the military participation of the United States in the
war. The conclusion must be drawn that a ruthless submarine
campaign could only cease to have for Germany the character of
a highly questionable adventure if the German Government knew
for certain that the war on land against France and Russia would
be ended in 1917 either by a military victory or by a peace by
mutual agreement. If France and Russia had ceased to carry on
the war, and if England had been forced to withdraw her armies
from France, the Americans would never have attempted to land
troops in Europe or, if they had, Germany at least would not have
had to fear them. Such were the views of the small group of
Revisionists who, within the Social Democratic Party, were in
favour of a ruthless submarine campaign. They were also in favour
of a separate peace with Russia and of an attempt being made to
bring about an agreement between Germany and France.

That Germany should have pursued a ruthless submarine campaign without regard for France and Russia, and without any
prospect that the war would end in 1917, thereby bringing America
into the enemy's camp, was a foolhardy action. Why was it that the
greatest soldier in Germany, General Ludendorff, did not recognize this? If Ludendorff, not as Quartermaster-General but as a
lecturer in the Staff College and in one or other of the 'war-games',
had had to deal with a situation akin to that in which Germany
found herself, and had he had to consider the arguments for and
against a submarine campaign from a purely technical standpoint,
his decision would certainly have been other than it was. It was
not Ludendorff the Soldier but Ludendorff the Politician who
insisted upon the initiation of a ruthless submarine campaign in
the hope that thereby he would achieve the victorious peace which
was necessary to him for political reasons.

The attitude of the naval authorities during 1916 and 1917 in
carrying out the submarine campaign is only comprehensible on
political grounds. The leading admirals failed to show themselves
to be level-headed, and one misses the technical skill and clearness
of vision displayed by the commanding officers in the Battle of
Jutland. The naval authorities assured any one who would listen to
them that England would probably have to sue for peace within six

months from the inception of the campaign. At times the word 'probably' was even altered to 'certainly' in this prophecy. The admirals took it upon themselves to declare on their word of honour as naval officers that the soil of Europe would never be disturbed by the foot of a single American soldier, and that the Americans would play absolutely no part in future military operations. These are the words of political agitators who seek to gain credence for their views by every means that lies in their power rather than those of technical experts delivering a sober opinion. Every one of these men, and all the officers subordinate to them, the high Civil Servants, the industrialists, landed proprietors, and the intelligentsia, were convinced that the Germany which they loved, and in the form in which it alone was conceivable to them, would be destroyed by the abandonment of the submarine campaign. Submarine warfare was the way that led to a victorious peace, to the salvation of Germany, and to the survival of the order of society which in their eyes seemed to be the only possible order. It was as if a political intoxication had overcome the governing class in Germany and for the time being destroyed their capacity for clear thinking.

It is easy to believe that the majority of the working class held other views as to a ruthless submarine campaign. They desired a speedy conclusion of peace above all else, and if such a peace were to be achieved through a German victory, it would have been warmly welcomed by the great majority of the working class. The masses, however, were convinced that such a victory was very far from being realized, and that if only those above were willing a reasonable peace without annexations was easily to be obtained. The belief was obviously deceptive that an unmistakable declaration on the part of Germany of her willingness to negotiate a peace on the basis of mutual concessions would bring the much-desired cessation of hostilities; for the masses of the population had in mind not merely diplomatic negotiations with Russia and France but the conclusion of a general peace which would have foundered on the military ardour no less than the war aims of the British middle class. A peace within six months, even though achieved by a submarine campaign, would have been greatly welcomed by the working class, although they did not identify their existence as a class with the achievement of such a peace in the same way as did the upper classes. Hence the working class was filled with anxiety lest the submarine campaign should also miscarry after the fashion in which all former promises of a speedy end to the war had revealed themselves to be illusive.

The opponents of the Pan-Germans were filled with anxiety at the prospect of America's joining the Entente. The great majority of the Majority Socialists and the whole U.S.P.D. therefore opposed the initiation of a ruthless submarine campaign. Since, however, General Ludendorff had already determined upon such a campaign, the matter was once and for all decided, especially as Bethmann-Hollweg had neither the power nor the inclination to fight with the new heads of the army. The Imperial Chancellor toed the line. The Emperor had no further say in the matter. But the attitude of the Reichstag in this controversy is worthy of note.

On October 16, 1916, a remarkable declaration was delivered by the Centre in a Committee of the Reichstag:

'The Imperial Chancellor is solely responsible to the *Reichstag* for all political decisions in connexion with the war. In taking his decisions the Imperial Chancellor must rely upon the views of the Supreme Command. If it is decided to initiate a ruthless submarine campaign, the Imperial Chancellor can be certain of the agreement of the *Reichstag*.'[18]

This declaration was, in effect, the public announcement that Ludendorff had assumed dictatorial powers. It was further an attempt on the part of the lawyers of the Centre to bring the new state of affairs at least outwardly into conformity with the Constitution. The declaration states that the Imperial Chancellor is responsible for political decisions. Nevertheless, he must only do that which the Supreme Command desires. The Chancellor thus becomes a sort of agent for the Supreme Command which, owing no responsibility to the Reichstag, remains the supreme irresponsible authority. If the Imperial Chancellor were to refuse to play the role thus assigned to him, he could only resign and leave his place free for some one else who would prove more submissive. The declaration of October 16 sought to express the constitutional situation as it existed at that date. Hence it is all the more remarkable that the Emperor is not even mentioned—not even as a sort of intermediary between the Imperial Chancellor and the Supreme Command. Yet it is indisputable that the members of the Centre who drew up this resolution regarded themselves as loyal monarchists. It was only the irresistible logic of events, and not republican sympathies, which caused the Emperor to be looked upon as politically powerless.

The Conservatives and the National Liberals were equally in

favour of the submarine campaign. The Progressives were loath to separate themselves from the other middle class parties. Hence Ludendorff had the Reichstag at his mercy. The Social Democrats were alone in their opposition to the submarine campaign. Nevertheless, Ludendorff did not let himself be hampered by the considerations which had formerly led Bethmann-Hollweg to be unwilling to take important decisions against the will of the Social Democrats. On January 9, 1917, the Government decided to embark on a ruthless submarine campaign. There followed the rupture of diplomatic relations with the United States and the American declaration of war on Germany.

The first six months of Ludendorff's dictatorship brought great military victories without achieving the defeat of the enemy. Two momentous political mistakes were made which spelt for Germany defeat in the war. The proclamation of the Kingdom of Poland destroyed all hope of a separate peace with Russia and the ruthless submarine campaign drove America into the arms of the Entente. It is naturally impossible to avoid asking the question whether the United States would not in any case have entered the war, since their economic interests were so bound up with those of England that they could not have afforded to permit an English defeat. It is true that America would certainly have entered the war at the moment when England's existence was endangered. In the winter of 1916–17, however, the 'danger' of a German victory did not exist. The Entente was stronger than Germany both on sea and on land. Hence, apart from the submarine campaign, there was no imperative reason to induce President Wilson at the beginning of 1917 to declare war on Germany. As a matter of fact at this very time Wilson had made an attempt to mediate between the belligerents.

The entry of America into the war strengthened the alliance of the Western Powers to such an extent that notwithstanding the collapse of Russia it was capable of beating Germany. Until the close of 1916 Germany could have saved herself by means of a separate peace with Russia. Now it was too late. The chief responsibility for this failure lay far more in the political situation that had arisen within Germany in consequence of the Bismarckian era and of William II's government than in the mistakes of individuals. The authority of the Emperor and the Prussian military aristocracy disappeared during the war. Since, however, neither the middle nor working class had the strength and insight to seize the reins of government themselves, the government of Germany passed into the hands of a brilliant but politically narrow-minded and short-sighted general—Ludendorff.

A nation experienced in politics would have recognized the problems arising out of war and would have solved them as, for example, England did in the World War. In Germany, however, a clear apprehension of war problems was prevented by the feelings and desires lying in the subconsciousness of the different classes in the nation. The broad masses of the populace were in favour of a peace by mutual consent which spelt in their eyes—Democracy. The governing upper class wanted a victorious peace in which they saw a security for their privileges. Although the decisive factor in the war was the difference in the opposing strengths of Germany and the Entente, the two contending classes in Germany persuaded themselves that it was within the nation itself that the decision lay. The party warfare throughout the war was of so peculiar a character that it almost gave the appearance as if a German victory depended on Bethmann-Hollweg and Scheidemann being driven from power, and as if a peace by mutual consent depended upon the dissolution of the Pan-German Association.

Only a very few men in these two opposing groups were able to free themselves from the mastery of these set formulas. A few National Liberals like Stresemann were at one and the same time in favour of a peace of conquest and parliamentary government in Germany, while a few Social Democrats from the circle of the *Socialist Monthly* were in favour both of the ruthless submarine campaign and a Labour government in Germany. Any unity in conception between the domestic party warfare and the object for which the war was being fought was not of itself necessary. It is possible for a statesman in his domestic policy to stand forth as the champion of a propertied upper class and at the same time to conduct a conciliatory foreign policy. The conduct of Bismarck after 1871 and the attitude of the Hungarian Prime Minister, Count Tisza, in July 1914 witness to this truth. A political party can in the same way base its domestic power upon the will of the people and, after the manner of the French Jacobins and the Russian Bolsheviks, pursue a ruthless foreign policy.

The identification of war aims with domestic political ideals, which sprang from the confusion of thought and want of political experience obtaining in Germany since 1871, resulted in nothing being achieved in either sphere. A separate peace with Russia was rendered impossible, despite the support it found in all quarters, owing to the fact that it came into conflict with the two formulas. Again, in 1917, the vitally necessary introduction of parliamentary government into Germany came to nothing because the majority in the Reichstag thought that their success would be sufficient if they achieved a peace by mutual consent. Parliamentary government—so they argued—would in that case follow as a matter of course. The political parties further believed that a victory in the domestic political warfare could only be signalized by forcing their opponents to accept their own peace-programme. Hence it was that the Left Wing of the majority in the Reichstag played its hand badly both in domestic and foreign policy.

After centuries of political impotence the German middle and working classes were called upon to take their fate in their hands in the midst of a catastrophic world crisis, and under the impression of the wholesale slaughter on the Fronts and the famine at home. It is only natural that they should have clung to formulas that promised them a speedy and successful conclusion to the war in accordance with their individual aspirations. The miseries of the Ludendorff-Peace Resolution period are only understandable as an outcome of the Bismarckian constitutional system and the incapacity displayed by William II and his advisers. The German nation paid heavily for not having itself achieved its own unity instead of receiving it as a gift from the hands of the King of Prussia.

NOTES TO CHAPTER IV

1. For the different currents within the National Liberal Party during the war see Stresemann in REPORT, vii, part ii, p. 300; and von Richthofen, ibid., pp. 214 et seq.

2. For the comparative numbers of officers on the active list and on the reserve during the war, and the losses among the former, see General von Altrock's monograph, *Vom Sterben des deutschen Offizierkorps* (1921).

3. On the 'war constraint' of the Majority Socialists see David in REPORT, vii, part i, p. 145.

4. Cf. *Die Krise der Sozialdemokratie (Junius-Broschüre)* by Rosa Luxemburg, 1919 edition, p. 81: 'Yes, the Social Democrats are pledged to defend their country in a great historical crisis. And therein a burden of guilt lies on the Social Democrat group in the Reichstag. In their declaration of August 4, 1914, they announced solemnly: "We shall not desert our Fatherland in the hour of need," but at the same moment they belied their words. In the hour of greatest need they deserted their country. For the chief duty to the country at that time was to demonstrate the true background of this imperialist war; to tear asunder the tissue of patriotic and diplomatic lies in which this attack against the Fatherland

was veiled; to indicate clearly that victory or defeat were equally fateful for the German nation in 'this war; to withstand to the uttermost the gagging of the country by martial law; to proclaim the immediate necessity for arming the nation, and for giving the people the chance to decide for peace or war; to demand with the utmost firmness the permanent session of the representatives of the people for the duration of the war, so as to assure that the Government should be vigilantly supervised by the representatives of the people, and they in turn by the people themselves; to demand the immediate abolition of all political inequalities, since none but a free people can effectively defend their native land; finally, to substitute for the imperialist programme of the war which is designed for the preservation of Austria and Turkey, and means a reaction in Europe and in Germany, the old truly nationalist programme of the patriots and democrats of 1848, the programme of Marx, Engels, and Lassalle, whose solution is a great united German Republic. This was the banner which should have been borne before the country, and which would have been truly national, truly liberal, and in accord with the best traditions of Germany as with the international class-policy of the proletariat.' This programme of how 'a free people can effectively defend its country,' is, as Rosa Luxemburg rightly emphasises, in perfect accord with Friedrich Engels. But in the daily discussion of the Spartacus Society it was driven into the background by an utopian radicalism. Rosa Luxemburg wrote the Junius pamphlet in a Berlin prison in April 1915. Lenin's review of the Junius Pamphlet (1916) may be found in Lenin-Sinoviev: *Gegen den Strom*, 1921, p. 415. The illegal Spartacus letters of the war period have been re-issued by the German Communist Party (two vols., 1920 and 1921).

5. For the real strength of the Spartacus Association see Rosenberg in REPORT, v, p. 220.

6. For the U.S.P.D. during the war cf. two important articles by Dittmann in the *Leipziger Volkszeitung* of June 15 and 16, 1917, reprinted in REPORT, vii, part ii, pp. 325 et seq.

7. See especially the essay by Max Cohen and Quessel in the *Sozialistische Monatshefte* for 1916 and 1917.

8. On the subject of Ludendorff's constitutional position see Bredt in REPORT, vii, pp. 31 et seq.

9. On the subject of Ludendorff and Hoffmann in January 1918 cf. Hindenburg's letter to the Emperor on January 7, 1918, in REPORT, ii, p. 124.

10. Bethmann's memorandum is reprinted in REPORT, ii, p. 155: 'From Valentini's remarks I gathered the following: after the Emperor had refused to accept Bernstorff he commissioned Valentini to ask Hindenburg whom he would like as Chancellor. Valentini, who did not wish to have personal dealings with Hindenburg, addressed himself, with the Emperor's permission, to Lyncker, to induce him to carry out the mission. General von Plessen, who was with Lyncker, seems to have mentioned Michaelis's name. Thereupon Valentini, Lyncker, and Plessen conferred with Hindenburg and Ludendorff, and Ludendorff said that he could only recommend Michaelis most warmly; that the

latter had been in the Great Headquarters recently and had given the impression that he was the right man. As soon as Valentini had laid his suggestion before the Emperor, William had immediately agreed to Michaelis, although he did not know him; and Michaelis had accepted the post after short reflection.'

11. On the subject of Valentini's dismissal see Schwertfeger in REPORT, ii, p. 174; also Prince Max of Baden's *Erinnerungen und Dokumente* (1927), p. 379.

12. William II's marginal notes on the subject of Ludendorff in REPORT, ii, pp. 169 et seq.

13. For the records of Ludendorff's relations with the Labour movement see REPORT, ii, pp. 125, 149, 151.

14. Ludendorff's war aims: memorandum of September 14, 1917, in REPORT, ii, p. 102.

15. The description in the text is based on the sworn statement which Stinnes made to the second Sub-committee of the Committee of Inquiry of the Reichstag. The second Sub-committee is investigating the question of the possibilities of peace during the World War, but has not yet published its results. Nevertheless, Dr. Quessel, a Social Democrat member of the Reichstag, discussed these facts in the transactions of the fourth Sub-committee and thus made them accessible to the public. Cf. REPORT, vii, part ii, p. 244. Von Richthofen confirms that these events were personally known to him, owing to his relationship with the Foreign Office (ibid., p. 245). On the other hand, in 1916 neither the Social Democrat nor the National Liberal groups in the Reichstag were informed on these possibilities of peace. (Cf. Quessel and von Richthofen, loc. cit.) The same would therefore obviously be true of the other Parties too. The Russian emigrants in Switzerland were also not conversant with the prospects of peace at the beginning of November 1916. Thus on November 6 Lenin wrote an article (*Über Separatfrieden*, reprinted in *Gegen den Strom*, p. 355), which begins with the words: 'Negotiations for a separate peace are already being carried on between Russia and Germany. These negotiations are official, and both Powers are already agreed on the most important items.' Lenin gives details as to what reasons can be given for such a separate peace, and why the official contradiction by the Russian Legation in Bern of the Russo-German negotiations does not deserve credence. The Entente, by way of a counter-blast, spread about the rumour that Russia was prepared to give up Poland on her own initiative. Then the Entente would make an alliance with Poland and would promise her Posen, Galicia, &c. (cf. Naumann, *Dokumente und Argumente*, p. 145). This was an endeavour to scare Bethmann-Hollweg and force him into hasty measures in favour of the Poles in order to destroy the possibilities of a Russo-German peace. The manœuvre of the Entente was completely successful. See Bredt in REPORT, viii, p. 318.

16. Records of the history of events leading up to the Polish proclamation: REPORT, vii, part i, pp. 363 et seq.

17. Stresemann (REPORT, vii, part ii, p. 307) relates of a meeting of the chief committee of the Reichstag in which the submarine question was discussed: 'The Secretary of State for the Admiralty, Herr von Capelle, ...

said that he considered that the danger of America's sending any troops to Europe was non-existent. Herr von Capelle had a habit of repeating the last words of his sentences, and this time, as I remember clearly, he repeated the word three times, "non-existent, non-existent, non-existent . . .". His description of plans for hindering the transport of troops, which he ended with these words: "If the Americans should really come, my submarines are already looking forward to the prey which they will have," was definitely the attitude of his group.'—For the six months period see Capelle's speech to the Chief Committee of the Reichstag on July 7, 1917, reprinted in Report, viii, p. 112. Also cf. Bredt, ibid., viii, p. 71.

18. The Centre and the Supreme Command; see Bredt in REPORT, viii, p. 68.

V

THE PEACE RESOLUTION OF 1917

THROUGHOUT the winter of 1916–17 and the spring of 1917 the German army remained on the defensive. A great Entente offensive was repulsed in the spring of 1917 with tremendous loss to the enemy. The Supreme Command nevertheless showed no signs of taking steps to bring the war to a conclusion. All hope was concentrated on the submarine. The number of enemy ships sunk was extraordinarily high and England found herself in an increasingly difficult economic situation. There was, however, no sign of any peace movement on the part of England or the other Entente Powers as a result of the submarine campaign —not even as the end of the six months period drew near within which England was to sue for peace. Moreover, if England suffered under the submarines, the German nation only suffered all the more under the blockade. Famine and resentment steadily increased from month to month among the broad masses of the working class. The assumption of power by Ludendorff and the decision to embark on a ruthless submarine campaign had only served to augment the self-confidence of the Conservative elements in the nation, and render them less willing than ever to make the smallest concession to the working class; and much less to pay any regard to the views of the Social Democrats.

Bethmann-Hollweg found himself in a painful situation. He neither wished to nor was capable of opposing the Supreme Command, and at the same time he did not want to offend the Social Democrats. This indecisive attitude on the part of the Imperial Chancellor only served to increase Ludendorff's mistrust of him. Some among the Prussian Ministers were in favour of holding a stronger language and made difficulties for him. It is symptomatic of the conditions then prevailing that in January 1917 the Prussian Government introduced into the Landtag a new law for the regulation of the *Fideikommiss*.[1] It seemed as if in the third year of the war the high Prussian officials had nothing else to preoccupy them than the legal regulation and protection of the great indivisible feudal estates. The eagerly expected suffrage reform in Prussia showed no signs of making its appearance. The aristocrats in the Prussian Upper House took the opportunity

afforded them in March by a bill for the reform of the allowances
made to members of the Landtag to make a fierce attack upon
democracy and parliamentary government. It was obvious that the
Prussian nobles, relying on the support of the Supreme Command,
would offer the uttermost resistance to any reform. The working
class, and even the middle-class Liberals, looked upon this attack
as a challenge. On March 14 a heated debate took place in the
Prussian Lower House. Bethmann-Hollweg sought to throw oil
on troubled waters by emphasizing once more the necessity for
constitutional reform and a new suffrage system in Prussia. On
the same afternoon the Imperial Chancellor learnt over the wireless
that a revolution had broken out in Petrograd.

The Tsardom collapsed in the course of a single night to be
succeeded by a democratic republic in which at first the middle
class held the reins of power. The impression made upon the
masses of the German population by events in Russia was overwhelming. A mighty military empire had been simply flung aside
by the revolution, and the Cossacks and the Guards were powerless
before the fraternizing soldiers and workmen. The wish for peace
animating the workman, peasant, and soldier became identified
with their general resentment at their political subjection. The
revolution in the army found outward expression in Soldiers'
Councils, which were joined by Workmen's Councils formed in
the great factories. Thus there came into being a democratic
army opposed to the Tsar, his officers, and the police.

For generations the German nation had never beheld a revolution
that could in any way be looked upon as a model for what might
come in Germany. The experience of the Turkish, Chinese,
Serbian, and Portuguese revolutions was worthless for German
purposes. And 1848 had become a legend for the mass of the
population. Now the nation suddenly learnt from Russia how
a revolution became possible and in what way it could be made.
The Spartacists hailed with enthusiasm the example offered to
the world by Russia. For events in Russia showed that the
Spartacists had rightly judged the international situation. The
World War was beginning to turn into the World Revolution. The
German workman must follow in the footsteps of the Russian
proletariat. The illegal literature distributed by the Spartacists
incited the masses to revolution. This propaganda nevertheless
showed small results in view of the Spartacist lack of organization.
The two Social Democratic Parties believed that a revolution

after the Russian pattern was not possible in Germany. At the same time they now began to press with increased energy for domestic reforms and a peace by mutual agreement. The middle-class Liberals thought that the moment had also come for a reform of the German Constitution; and every speaker in favour of reform was at last able to introduce into his speech a monitory reference to Russia. Bethmann-Hollweg thought that he could keep matters in check by giving added prominence in his speeches to the question of constitutional reform and by renewed promises of a suffrage reform in Prussia.

The Supreme Command looked upon any and every concession as a mistake. Together with the supporters of a peace by conquest the Supreme Command saw in the events in Russia the consequence of Russia's defeat by Germany. They looked upon the revolution as the beginning of the end of Russia's military power. They further believed that if the war ended in their favour, and if the German Government remained firm, there would be no question of Germany's being infected by the revolutionary spirit in Russia.

It was at first impossible to foresee the effect of the Russian revolution upon the course of the war. In the March revolution the Russian middle class came into power; and they were far from wishing to desert the alliance with England, France, and America. They were inspired by desires of conquest and by the hope of securing Constantinople. Indeed, in the last days of the Tsarist Government, reactionary circles in Russia were far more favourable to a separate peace than were the middle-class Liberals. It was clear that if the Liberals remained in power Germany would not be the gainer by the Russian Revolution. The Russian proletariat, on the other hand, was opposed to these plans of conquest, and desired a speedy conclusion of peace 'without annexations and reparations'. The Russian proletariat believed as implicitly as the German in this formula, which gained international importance when put forward by the Workers' and Soldiers' Councils in Petrograd. But the Russian proletariat was itself divided on the question of a separate peace. The Right Wing of the Russian Socialist Party, which was also in favour of collaborating with the middle class, only wished to make peace in common with its allies. It was opposed to a separate peace which might enable Germany to place her entire military force on the Western Front, win a great victory, and establish her military domination throughout Europe.

For that reason they believed it to be necessary to carry on the war.

The Left Wing of the Russian Social Democrats, who were known as Bolsheviks, were opposed to any collaboration with the middle class and wished for the immediate conclusion of peace. The Bolsheviks were not in the least afraid of the military power of Germany. A temporary increase of strength due to the conclusion of a separate peace with Russia would not be of any assistance to the German Empire since Germany would soon be swept by the World Revolution. Hence the Bolsheviks and the German Supreme Command each thought they could play a game with the other. Ludendorff permitted Lenin, who was then living in Switzerland, to return through Germany to Russia in order to complete the revolution and initiate negotiations for peace. The future was to show that Ludendorff was less far-seeing than Lenin.

The question of peace and war in Russia was bound up with the class warfare between the middle class and the proletariat. The victory in this warfare must inevitably go to the side which was supported by the hundreds of millions of Russian peasants. Until the summer of 1917 the middle-class parties and the Right Wing of the Social Democrats retained power, and in July the Kerenski Government was even able to order a great offensive on the part of the Russian armies which met with initial successes like those of the 1916 offensive in Galicia. It is true that immediately after the revolution the longing for peace animating the Russian peasant-soldier manifested itself throughout the entire army. The measures taken to restore discipline and morale nevertheless proved themselves in the July offensive to have been successful. Moreover, the military situation in the east was so involved that the German Supreme Command dare not remove its troops from the Eastern Front, although at the same time it was not possessed of sufficient reserves to make use of the opportunity afforded by the disorganization of the Russian army to take the offensive for the purpose of forcing a decision in the east.

The U.S.P.D. introduced a resolution into the Reichstag in March in which they demanded peace without annexations and the introduction of parliamentary government into Germany. The Majority Socialists proposed the appointment of a Commission for the purpose of preparing a new constitution. Still more amazing—the National Liberals also came forward with a proposal of a like nature.[2] The Progressives demanded the introduction of universal suffrage in all the Federal States and also the oft-promised reform of the Prussian suffrage system. The Russian Revolution had accomplished what could not be accomplished in Germany in three years of war. The reform of the German Constitution suddenly became the question of the day.

The political parties, however, omitted to pay sufficient attention to the existence of an indisputable fact. A political reorganization of the Empire had already been accomplished. It is true that this had not resulted in a parliamentarization of Germany—rather since August 1916 it had been brought about by the dictatorship of the Supreme Command. When in March 1917 the Reichstag began its fight for power, its attack was in reality directed neither against the higher Civil Servants, who sat peacefully in their offices, nor against the Emperor, but against General Ludendorff. If the hope ever existed within the National Liberal Party that Ludendorff's co-operation could be secured for a constitutional reform, such a hope was doomed to disappointment. Until September 1918 General Ludendorff brutally rejected every proposal for the introduction of parliamentary and democratic government into Germany. He was also no less opposed to a reform of the Prussian suffrage system.

The fact that the National Liberals made common cause with the Social Democrats was symptomatic of the division of opinion and the conflict of interests among the propertied middle class. On the one hand there were those who desired to retain the existing constitution through fear of the proletariat. On the other hand, there were those who desired to destroy the power of the Prussian aristocracy, and who, in order to secure this object, were not afraid to ally themselves with the Social Democrats. The Right Wing of the National Liberals was chiefly represented among the National Liberal members of the Prussian Landtag, while the Left Wing possessed certain active representatives in the Reichstag. The proposal for the appointment of a Commission charged with the reform of the Constitution was due to the initiative of the Left Wing National Liberals; and in taking this initiative the National Liberals temporarily returned to the tactics they had pursued in 1912. Since the Centre also supported the proposal for a reform of the Constitution, the isolation of the Conservatives was complete. The Conservatives thereupon declared that the whole problem arose in the first place out of the question of a reform of the Prussian suffrage system; and that, as this was a purely Prussian matter, the Reichstag had better not interfere in it. Supported by the Supreme Command, the Prussian aristo-cracy took up the challenge. The Reichstag adopted the proposal for the Commission by an overwhelming majority. The Commis-sion met on May 2 and elected Scheidemann as its Chairman.

The problem at once became actual. The Centre, the Progres-sives, and the National Liberals demanded that the Imperial Chancellor and the Secretaries of State should be made responsible for their actions to the Reichstag. This proposal amounted to a substitution of a parliamentary Imperial Cabinet for the Bis-marckian Imperial Chancellor. The three parties further demanded that in the future all army commissions should be counter-signed by the Minister of War. Such a proposal amounted to the destruc-tion of the Emperor's absolute power of command; for the power of the King of Prussia over the army had been hitherto manifested in his complete freedom of choice in the appointment of officers. The proposal that the Minister for War should countersign com-missions meant that he should assume the responsibility for such appointments in Parliament. If the Parliament were able to bring about the resignation of the Minister for War by a vote of want of confidence, the Minister would certainly be careful not to counter-sign any commission that was likely to bring him into conflict with the Parliament. This was virtually a replica of the constitu-tional situation in England, where the army while formally under the command of the King is in reality the servant of the House of Commons.

The Commission speedily discovered that the vital issue was far less the Emperor's power of command than that of Ludendorff. Thereupon the Commission invited the Prussian Minister for War to take part in their discussions. He took no notice of the invitation, and in so acting doubtless did so with the approval of the Supreme Command. It was clear that if the Commission had not the power to compel the attendance of the Minister for War, it certainly could not alter the command over the army. When the Reichstag was prorogued in May nothing had been achieved by the Commission.

It would, however, be wrong to blame the Reichstag for its failure. Things had gone so far in Germany that not only the Social Democrats, but also the great middle-class parties were discussing the abolition of the Bismarckian Constitution—and that was no small advance. It is true that for the moment the Supreme Command was still more powerful than the Reichstag. A fact to be explained by the military situation, for, notwithstanding outward appearances, the authority of the Supreme Command was a moral rather than a physical authority. The autocratic power wielded in peace by the King of Prussia with the help of the Regular army existed no longer. The nation and the army alike only obeyed the Supreme Command because Hindenburg and Ludendorff were looked upon as the last hope of Germany in the war. The political authority of the Supreme Command ceased at the very moment in September 1918 in which it was forced to admit that the war was lost.

If Bethmann-Hollweg had really wished for a reform of the German Constitution he would have furthered the work of the Commission by all the means in his power. He sought instead to control the Commission through fear lest it should give rise to new differences of opinion with the Supreme Command; and he used his influence with Scheidemann in this sense. As a compensation he was prepared to promise that the Imperial suffrage system should be introduced into Prussia after the war.[3] At the beginning of April 1917 Bethmann-Hollweg proposed to the Emperor that he should issue a proclamation to the German nation in which he should promise the carrying-out of a wide programme of reform including that of the Prussian suffrage and of the Upper House after the war. It was known at Court that Ludendorff was an irreconcilable enemy of any reform of the Prussian electoral system. Hence the Emperor declared that, although he was in agreement on principle with the proposed proclamation, he rejected the introduction of the Imperial suffrage system into Prussia. It is worthy of note that the Emperor was restored to his old energy by finding that he was in agreement with General Ludendorff. Negotiations were set in motion within the Prussian Government, which resulted on April 7, 1917, in the publication of the Emperor's Easter proclamation which promised the reform of the Upper House and of the Prussian electoral system after the war. The suffrage reform was to be along lines which would result in doing away with the three classes and in introducing a direct and secret method of voting, but not universal suffrage. The Conservatives could only be won over to agree to any suffrage reform on the understanding that the propertied classes would be accorded a plurality of votes. Bethmann-Hollweg himself would have preferred to promise the introduction of the Imperial suffrage system, but he did not think himself strong enough to carry this through in face of all opposition.

The refusal to introduce the Imperial suffrage system into

Prussia both before and during the war aroused the bitterest resentment in the poorer classes of the population. It seemed to them intolerable that the poor soldier at the Front should not have the same electoral rights as the more fortunate arm-chair soldier who never saw the trenches. It has often been said that the refusal to introduce universal suffrage into Prussia was one of the principal causes of the revolution. That is true in so far as the Prussian suffrage question was one of the first magnitude in domestic politics, and also in that it gave rise to the sharpest class distinctions. Nevertheless, it was not of decisive import for the balance of political power in Germany.

It is true that the governing aristocracy in Prussia found it to be in their interest to dominate the Lower House in addition to the King and the Upper House. The real strength of the old Prussian system nevertheless did not rest in the Conservative members of the Landtag, but in the autocratic authority wielded by the King over the army and the administration. So long as the King of Prussia could appoint and dismiss Ministers at his pleasure, the constitution of the majority in the Landtag was a matter of indifference to him. It is true that, under Bülow, it would have been easy to introduce universal suffrage into Prussia. In those days it would not have amounted to a revolution, and would only have resulted in the Landtag becoming a replica of the Reichstag. The Government majority in the Landtag would not have been composed solely of Conservatives and National Liberals, but would have included members of the Centre, which, in any case, generally made common cause in Prussia with the Conservatives. At the worst a few more Catholic Conservatives could have been introduced into the Landtag.

In these circumstances it was narrow-minded as well as short-sighted on the part of the governing class in Prussia to refuse a reform of the suffrage. The decision lay between the Imperial Government, i.e. the system which the Imperial Government covered with its authority, and a form of Parliamentary Government; and not with the suffrage. The fall of the old system in October 1918 was due to the assumption of power by the majority in the Reichstag and not to the Prussian suffrage question. The reform of the Prussian suffrage thereupon followed as a matter of course—as an accompaniment of the revolution and not as its cause. The Imperial Government in the spring of 1917 thus made no serious attempt to achieve a reform of the domestic political situation in Germany. It contented itself with empty promises while famine steadily grew worse in the great cities, and the workmen became more and more enamoured of the Russian Revolution. A feeling of opposition steadily increased among the Socialist workers, and the Social Democratic Party leaders became doubtful whether they could assume the responsibility, in face of the feeling among their supporters, of assenting to a new war credit on the reassemblage of the Reichstag at the beginning of July. In any case they wished to make any further financial supplies dependent upon a distinct declaration on the part of the Government that no conquests would be sought for. The hopes that had been set on the submarine campaign had been disappointed. It became clear that neither in July nor in August would England sue for peace. Ludendorff and Hindenburg had failed to win any great victories in the past six months. The Russian Revolution resulted in July in a new Russian offensive instead of in a separate peace. All that was certain was that the slaughter increased from day to day and that the economic situation in Germany became steadily worse. Hence in the summer of 1917 there occurred the second great test of the confidence reposed by the German nation in its political and military leaders. It is true that the masses did not recognize that Germany was confronted with the possibility of defeat. It is also true that they saw no way in which to end the war. All that they did demand was that in some way or other peace should be concluded—a peace that the Emperor, the Government, and the Supreme Command were obviously incapable of achieving. All the classes in the nation suffering under the economic and social distress were animated by this desire. The feeling was common to all classes of workmen from the Social Democrats to the Clericals, to the peasants, and to the middle-class. The Centre set the match to the powder.

Erzberger became the mouthpiece of the Catholic workmen and peasants, who no longer placed any confidence in the Government and who desired peace.[4] Throughout the first two years of the war Erzberger had worked in common with the Government and the military chiefs as well as with the conservatively minded leaders of the Centre. It was he who had drafted the programme of a victorious peace, and probably also the remarkable resolution of October 1916 in which the Centre pronounced itself in favour of a political dictatorship of the Supreme Command. His views underwent a change in the spring of 1917 when he perceived with great clarity the critical nature of the military situation in which Germany found herself.

A journey which Erzberger, in company with a National Liberal member of the Reichstag, von Richthofen, made to the Eastern Head-quarters was of importance in this connexion. Since Hindenburg and Ludendorff had assumed the Supreme Command, the Eastern Command had been placed in the hands of Prince Leopold of Bavaria, whose Chief of Staff, General Hoffmann, was not only one of the outstanding officers in the German army, but also one who retained his independence of judgement as against the Supreme Command. General Hoffmann revealed the true state of affairs to Erzberger and von Richthofen. Erzberger resolved to seek to induce the Reichstag to bring the war to a conclusion as quickly as possible before it was too late and a catastrophe overwhelmed Germany. This decision on the part of Erzberger was supported by the vast mass of the populace, especially of the Socialist workmen, and this gave to his action an especial significance and force. If, however, the Reichstag were to succeed in imposing its will in the matter of peace upon the Government and the Supreme Command, it was essential that a strong and active majority should be formed in the Reichstag and that the power of the Reichstag should be greatly increased. Erzberger's action in July 1917 was bound up with the existing situation in Vienna, and with the preparations that were being made by the Papal diplomats for the inauguration of a Papal intervention in favour of peace. Austro-Hungarian policy had altered completely with the death of the Emperor Francis Joseph and the accession of the Emperor Karl.[5] Only those ignorant of politics could look upon the Habsburg Monarchy as a sort of federal State, and persuade themselves that Austrian policy was formulated by the citizens of Vienna or the Tyrolese peasants. The natural sympathy of the German Austrian for the German Empire scarcely influenced the Viennese Government.

Since the so-called *Ausgleich* of 1870 Austro-Hungarian policy was the outcome of the conflict between two forces; the Magyar aristocracy, working in collaboration with the wealthier Hungarian townsfolk, with its seat in Budapest; the cosmopolitan 'black-yellow' aristocracy, with its centre in Vienna, from whom sprang the higher civil servants and the officers. The so-called *Ausgleich* between Austria and Hungary was the compromise between these two forces.

In order to retain power in their own hands the ruling class in Hungary had to hold down the Magyar workmen, peasants, and small townsfolk as well as to suppress the nationalist movements among the Germans, Croats, Serbs, Rumanians, Slovaks, and Ruthenians, who were subjects of the Crown of St. Stephen. In like manner, in the Austrian half of the Dual Monarchy, the ruling aristocracy had to curb the nationalist aspirations of the Emperor's Czech, Polish, Italian, and Southern Slav subjects and, in truth, also those of the German middle class; as well as to hold in check the peasantry and the working class in all the different nationalities. Finally, the southern Slav inhabitants of Bosnia, which was a common possession of Austria and Hungary, had the happiness of carrying out at one and the same time the orders of their Viennese and their Budapest overlords.

The Habsburg Monarchy in the twentieth century presented a picture of appalling inefficiency. It is true that Austria-Hungary could have continued to exist as an economic and geographical entity, and that the many nationalities included within her frontiers did not present an insuperable bar to the establishment of a well-organized federation. The cause of the misery that obtained in Austria-Hungary is to be found in the power wielded in both halves of the Monarchy by the aristocracy, who were forced to refuse the national and economic claims of ninety per cent. of the population. The underlying cause of all, and that which prevented the achievement of a German-Czech *Ausgleich*, lay in the fact that the governing aristocracy, among whom the great Bohemian nobles played the leading part, refused to accord political power to either nation.

The foreign policy of William II had united the fate of Germany to that of this ramshackle Empire. Austria naturally suffered in the war from the effects of these profound internal dissensions. The Czech regiments proved themselves to a large extent unreliable, while the long duration of the war affected the fighting spirit and morale of the Austrian armies far more than that of the German. It is indeed astonishing that the Austrian army managed to hold together until the end of the war. It has been said by Austrians that the German Revolution was made by the German army, whereas the Austrian army held together until it was demobilized by the Imperial Government. The century-old tradition of the military and political power of the Habsburgs managed to maintain itself against all disruptive tendencies until the end. Since the chief agricultural lands of the Dual Monarchy lay in Hungary, which retained its agricultural products for its own use, the Austrian cities, especially Vienna, suffered from the most terrible want. The famine of the years 1917 and 1918 had the effect of driving the Viennese workpeople into the arms of Socialism.

As long as Francis Joseph lived Austrian policy was based on the alliance with Germany, not, indeed, out of any special love for Prussia, but because of a very comprehensible national egotism. Any one who judges the situation impartially must admit that in a German victory lay the only salvation for Austria-Hungary. In Vienna, however, it was hoped that the Habsburg Monarchy would not only be saved by the war but that it would actually be possible to add to its dynastic possessions in Poland and elsewhere.

The accession of the Emperor Karl placed power in the hands of quite a different political school among the Austrian aristocrats— a school that desired to see Austrian policy based on an alliance with France directed against Prussia. This was the school that in 1870 had sought to bring Austria into the Franco-German War on the side of Napoleon III and that in the years immediately succeeding to 1871 had been the supporter of an *entente* with France. The long-standing connexions between the Catholic nobility of Austria and the Catholic nobility of France contributed towards this end. Moreover, the men around the Emperor Karl were of the opinion that Germany was in a critical situation, and that it would be better for the Habsburgs to desert the sinking ship in time in order to seek to achieve an understanding with France and England at Germany's expense. Austria's chief enemy, the Russian Tsardom, no longer existed, and it was hoped that it would prove possible, despite the promises which the Western Powers had made to Italy, Rumania, Serbia, and the Czech National Revolutionary Party, to come to an understanding with France and England. It is true that if these promises were kept the dissolution of the Dual Monarchy was inevitable. Was it not possible, however, that the Entente might go back on its promises in return for a speedier conclusion of peace with the help of the Habsburgs? These plans of the Emperor Karl were Austria's gratitude for Germany's *Niebelungentreue*! The German Government should have been aware even before the war that the Habsburg Monarchy was not a vassal of William II, but an independent Power pursuing a traditional policy, and that the interests of the

Habsburgs were by no means wholly identical with those of Germany. The German Government might also have remembered that gratitude is not a factor in international politics. The events of the years 1917–18 justified Bismarck's judgement of Habsburg policy up to the hilt.

It was, however, not so easy for Karl to transfer his allegiance to the Entente. In the first place, so long as Germany dominated Central Europe it could send its troops to occupy Vienna. In the second place, any such action on Karl's part would have been productive of serious results within the Empire. The German Austrians would have revolted, and the Hungarian aristocracy would have refused to have any hand in such a game, since an anti-German policy in Austria was identical with a Slavophil policy which was diametrically opposed to the interests of Hungary. Hence Court circles in Vienna had to proceed with great care. They justified their tactics on the ground that they desired peace, and thereby sought to gain the support of the poorer classes in the populace who were suffering most from the effects of the war. There seemed to them to be a possibility that with the support of the workmen and the Czechs they could hold down the German-Austrian middle class in Austria, while in Hungary they played off the Democratic Parties against the aristocrats. Court circles in Vienna thus embarked on a dangerous game. In order to free themselves from the alliance with Germany they played with revolution. Yet who was prepared to guarantee that the Czechs, Hungarian Democrats, Austrian Socialists, &c., would really be willing to pull the chestnuts out of the fire for the sake of the Houses of Habsburg and Parma. In March 1848 the Court in Vienna coquetted in a like manner with revolution in order to get rid of the great Prince Metternich, who had become unwelcome to it, and in 1918 as in 1848 the waves of revolution swept away the Habsburg wire-pullers. Only in 1918 the armies of the Russian Tsar, which in 1848 had proved themselves the saviours of the House of Habsburg, were no longer in existence.

Throughout 1917 the Court Party in Vienna systematically removed the supporters of the German alliance from their posts. The dismissal of the brilliant Chief of the General Staff, Conrad von Hötzendorf, started the disintegration of the army, while the dismissal of the Hungarian Prime Minister, Count Tisza, resulted in the disorganization of the Hungarian State apparatus. It is true that in appointing Count Czernin as Minister for Foreign

Affairs the Emperor's choice fell upon a man who did not allow himself to be influenced by the Court clique. Czernin's position, however, was one of extraordinary difficulty. He recognized the unfavourable military and economic situation in which the Central Powers found themselves, and he considered that the Supreme Command in Germany did not pay sufficient respect to the facts of the political situation. Moreover, Czernin was confronted at home with revolution and was attacked from the rear by the Court, which was prepared to make a separate peace at any moment. The only salvation for the Central Powers in Czernin's opinion lay in the speedy conclusion of a tolerable peace before it was too late. Thus Czernin sought in every way to emphasize to political circles in Germany that, unless peace was speedily concluded, Austria was faced with a collapse. He also informed Erzberger of the true state of affairs in Austria. At the same time Czernin could not tell German politicians that the real danger lay not in the starving masses but in the Viennese Court.

Erzberger was forced to take into his calculations the information he received from Austria, since if Austria were to desert the alliance all was lost. An Entente army would invade Germany by way of Tirol and Bohemia, and the war would be at an end. Czernin himself was unquestionably loyal to the Alliance, and resigned in 1918 on the publication by Clemenceau of the letter which the Emperor Karl addressed to Prince Sixtus of Parma for communication to the French Government. One of the most important factors in the World War was the knowledge possessed by Germany since 1917 that she could no longer rely on her Austrian ally, and that the Austrian Court was resolved to take the first opportunity to leave her in the lurch. Next to the entry of America into the war, and Bethmann-Hollweg's mistaken Eastern policy, the attitude of Austria contributed above all else to decide the fate of the German Empire. The knowledge which since June he possessed of a coming attempt on the part of the Pope to mediate between the belligerents was the final contributory cause prompting Erzberger's action.[6] The papal diplomats were truly informed as to the state of the war. They knew of the serious developments that had taken place in Vienna, and that the Entente was stronger than Germany. Notwithstanding the political neutrality imposed upon him by the international character of the Catholic Church, the Pope wished to prevent the defeat of the Central Powers; for Austria-Hungary was the sole remaining Catholic Great Power, and the Catholic minority in Germany was exceptionally well treated. The Pope wished at least to make an attempt to save Germany, and for this purpose to seek to mediate between Germany and England. He wished Germany to declare her readiness to restore Belgium, and to assent to moderate terms of peace, in the hope that this would enable the peace party in England to gain the upper hand. It is true that the majority of the English middle class, following the lead of Lloyd George, was resolved to destroy German competition. At the same time a few statesmen of Lord Lansdowne's type held the view that, while England would certainly win in the end, she would do so at enormous cost and in the knowledge that the economic hegemony of the world would pass into the hands of America. It was for this reason that men of Lansdowne's type were willing to compromise with Germany. But their influence was slight, and the papal proposals were subsequently roughly rejected by France and England. From the beginning the Pope did not set too great hopes on the success of his action. But he wished to make the attempt; and it was for this reason that he desired that the German Government should announce their consent to moderate conditions of peace. And this was what Erzberger hoped to get them to do.

On July 6 Erzberger delivered a speech in the Reichstag that was destined to be of historic importance.[7] He demonstrated to the Reichstag that since the Government had been completely mistaken in the question of submarine warfare they could no longer expect to enjoy the confidence of the Reichstag. A conclusion to the war was not in sight. In order to restore unity within the nation it was necessary to return to the policy of August 4, that is to say, a war of defence. The Reichstag must give the Government to understand that it desired a peace based on compromise without any forcible subjection of peoples or annexations. Such a declaration on the part of the Reichstag would prove to be the surest and quickest way to peace.

As early as 1914 Karl Liebknecht had delivered a fierce attack upon the Government. But he spoke only on behalf of a small and uninfluential minority in the nation. If, on the other hand, Erzberger was the attacker, it was clear that he would be supported by the Centre and the Social Democrats, i.e. by the majority of the Reichstag and the nation. Through the mouth of Erzberger this majority informed the Imperial Government that it no longer enjoyed their confidence, and that from now onwards they would seek independently to bring about peace. This declaration amounted to a revolutionary action. The foundation stone was laid on July 6, 1917, of the middle-class German Republic.

By a skilful use of the feeling prevalent among the Catholic workmen and peasants, Erzberger wrested the power from the reactionary leaders of the Centre and with his intimate friends laid down the policy of the Party. The Centre together with the Social Democrats went into opposition against the ruling class in Germany, and were joined by a third group, the Progressives, as representatives of the commercial classes and especially the upper middle class. Thus the anti-Bismarck block was resuscitated, and the miseries induced by the war gave it the support of the overwhelming majority of the nation. The embitterment, the desire for peace, and for power on the part of the workmen, the poor peasants, and the middle class had thus finally found political expression. Although Erzberger's speech on July 6 expressed the views of the Reichstag and the majority of the nation, it nevertheless revealed the weakness inherent in the movement. Against whom did Erzberger direct his attack? Certainly not against the Emperor of whom Erzberger himself said that during the war he had completely disappeared into the background, from whence he only emerged to address the troops in speeches which, if they stimulated the soldiers, were none the less unfortunate in their effect upon the nation at large. It was obviously necessary that the Emperor should be made aware of the state of public opinion. Events in Russia had shown what happened to a monarchy when it was cut off from all contact with the people. Although Erzberger spoke thus of William II, neither he nor any of his hearers looked upon the Emperor as a decisive factor in German politics. In a formal sense Erzberger's attack was directed against the Imperial Government, that is to say, against Bethmann-Hollweg and the Secretary of State, Helfferich, but he was in reality attacking the actual ruler of Germany, General Ludendorff, and, above all, the Supreme Command.

Every one knew that Ludendorff and not Bethmann-Hollweg was responsible for the ruthless submarine campaign. The Centre itself had assisted in gaining the victory for the Supreme Command over Bethmann-Hollweg in the submarine question by its declaration in October 1916. If Erzberger had been prepared to draw the obvious conclusions from the general disappointment at the result of the submarine campaign, then he must have proclaimed his want of confidence in the Supreme Command rather than in the Imperial Chancellor. He must have further demanded that in future Ludendorff should cease to meddle in political questions, and that the final decision in all questions of national importance should be with the Reichstag. Perhaps the greatest mistake made by Erzberger was that in his speech on July 6 he contented himself with a few veiled references to the Supreme Command and did not come out into the open against it. Erzberger believed that he could undermine Ludendorff's position by circuitous means such as the formation of a determined majority in the Reichstag, and also by the substitution of another and stronger personality than that of Bethmann-Hollweg in the office of Imperial Chancellor. The man he had in mind was Prince Bülow. General Ludendorff, however, was not to be dismissed so lightly. For Ludendorff was not in the least afraid of an opponent who never came out into the open against him. Thus Erzberger's action in July 1917 was very speedily rendered null and void by a counter-action on the part of Ludendorff. The victory went to the Supreme Command.

The second mistake made by Erzberger lay in his failure to convert the newly formed majority in the Reichstag into a parliamentary government. A National Liberal, von Richthofen, did indeed attempt to force Erzberger along this path. The formation of such a government would have materially furthered the cause of peace. The knowledge that the Emperor and the Supreme Command had been replaced by a government of the people would at once have bridged the gulf separating Germany from the Russian Republic, and would also have materially altered the attitude of France towards Germany. The fact that the Reichstag proclaimed itself in favour of a peace without annexations failed to impress the world at large so long as the old forces remained in power in Germany. For the phrase 'without annexations and reparations' could be interpreted by each man to mean what he himself desired. It is possible for one State to subject another to the severest economic and political oppression without formally annexing it or even exacting the payment of reparations from it. Hence Erzberger's formula, which was later embodied in the Peace Resolution passed by the Reichstag, was valueless from the standpoint of foreign policy and certainly failed of effect abroad. The Peace Resolution was looked upon in enemy countries either as a manœuvre on the part of the German Government in conjunction with the Supreme Command to throw dust into the eyes of the Entente nations or it was thought that the Reichstag, even though it were acting in good faith, was powerless and that the final decision lay with the Supreme Command. A resolution couched in such general terms was utterly useless as a basis for negotiations with a foreign power. The Pope and Count Czernin would undoubtedly have greatly preferred a definite statement of Germany's war aims, especially in regard to Belgium, to the Peace Resolution as passed by the Reichstag.

Nevertheless, in domestic politics, the resolution was in every respect a success. It gave voice to the desire for peace animating the populace who, indeed, knew nothing of diplomacy, but were determined not to pursue a war of conquest. The Resolution came as a severe blow for the Pan-Germans and the supporters of a victorious peace. It was couched in terms that could be understood by the working class, although unwelcome to the rulers of Germany, and thus was a moral victory for the classes in the nation which were conscious of being oppressed. It was this that made it of such value and importance in the eyes of the masses. It was the strength no less than the weakness of Erzberger that he went with the crowd. The crowd wanted to see a door opened before them that would lead to peace. They wanted by means of a reasonable peace to hit back at their oppressors. It would, however, be wrong to think that the idea of parliamentary government was then popular in Germany. Erzberger himself thought that the first thing to do was to fulfil the demands of the masses and that what seemed less important in their eyes must be postponed. Erzberger's weakness was perceived by Ludendorff, who immediately proceeded to turn it to his own advantage.

The inactivity displayed in these days by the Social Democrats must always be a matter for wonder. It is true that by the mouth of Scheidemann they gave real support to Erzberger on July 7, and that they demanded a peace without annexations and a reform of the Prussian suffrage. But they failed to make good the mistakes made by Erzberger in his attack on the Supreme Command no less than his failure to insist more strongly on the formation of a parliamentary government. The Social Democrats, in truth, felt themselves, even more than the middle-class parties, the prisoners of the *Burgfrieden*. The Party leaders feared that if they took up a determined attitude in opposition to the Government, the entire working class would rise in rebellion, and the German defence collapse in consequence. If, however, the middle-class

Parties were to go into opposition, the Majority Socialists would be forced to join them, and by so doing they would be identifying themselves with the policy of the U.S.P.D. and fulfilling the wishes of the working class.

A great deal depended on the attitude which Bethmann-Hollweg would take up in the situation created by Erzberger. The Imperial Chancellor knew that the Supreme Command would gladly see him removed from office. He was, moreover, not responsible for the ruthless submarine campaign, and he should have put himself at the head of the newly formed majority in the Reichstag and led it in its campaign against Ludendorff. But Bethmann-Hollweg was incapable of a cool and calculating policy. It ran counter to his conservative Prussian principles to become the servant of a majority in the Reichstag. The difference between Bethmann-Hollweg and the Militarists and Pan-Germans was a matter of form rather than of principle. Bethmann-Hollweg never seriously attacked the Supreme Command. Moreover, in contrast to Erzberger, he was not a realist in politics. He never, for example, perceived whither the crisis in the Reichstag was leading, and thought that it meant nothing more than that Erzberger wished to force the Government to make a new peace proposal to the Entente—a proceeding that Bethmann-Hollweg held to be useless, since in the previous December the Entente had rejected such a proposal. Bethmann-Hollweg never saw that the real motivating force behind Erzberger's action was the desire to form a strong majority in the Reichstag, and not the drafting of a resolution in favour of peace. Hence Bethmann-Hollweg opposed Erzberger's motion, and, by so doing, fell between quite a number of stools. His action failed to conciliate the Supreme Command, while, on the other hand, it encouraged Erzberger in his determination to force Bethmann-Hollweg's resignation; and Erzberger at that time was supported by the Centre. Moreover, the Progressives and the Social Democrats did not feel disposed to support Bethmann-Hollweg, since he had refused his consent to the resolution in favour of peace.

It was Bethmann-Hollweg's hope that he would be able to ride out the storm in his old fashion by promising still further reforms. He published an Imperial decree promising equal suffrage in Prussia, which, however, did not by any means imply that equal suffrage became an accomplished fact. Before that could happen the Government had to introduce a Bill for the purpose into the Prussian Landtag. If the Landtag refused the Bill, what would be the Government's next step? What form of force could the Government employ against a majority in the Landtag which was only defending its privileges? Thus the promises of the Emperor and the Chancellor afforded no guarantee that even after the war equal suffrage would be introduced into Prussia. Hence this manœuvre on the part of Bethmann-Hollweg proved unsuccessful. Meanwhile the Supreme Command had begun its counter-offensive. General Ludendorff determined to make use of the domestic political crisis in order to overthrow the Chancellor who was personally distasteful to him.[8] A determined supporter of a victorious peace was to replace the indecisive Bethmann-Hollweg whom the Supreme Command mistrusted. Since Erzberger and the other Opposition members of the Reichstag had not dared to make an open attack on Ludendorff, the Supreme Command found itself in a favourable tactical situation. If it was not openly attacked, the Supreme Command did not need to feel that it had been attacked. Hence Ludendorff entered into communication with the Parties in the Reichstag in order to discuss the matter with them in a friendly way for the purpose of uniting the Reichstag to the Supreme Command against the inefficient Chancellor. In the debate in the Reichstag on July 9 Stresemann, in agreement with Ludendorff, gave a new turn to the situation. He announced in an extremely clever speech his agreement with Erzberger without at the same time committing himself to the support of the peace tactics of the newly formed majority. He demanded a reform of the Prussian franchise, and, in a far more decisive manner than the Centre and the Social Democrats, the introduction of parliamentary government into Germany. At the same time he made a fierce attack upon Bethmann-Hollweg's domestic and foreign policy which he characterized as a complete failure. He declared that through the policy he had pursued throughout three years of war, and especially by his declarations in regard to Russia, the Chancellor was so deeply engaged that his continuance in office stood in the way of a conclusion of peace. Thus Stresemann publicly made Bethmann-Hollweg's continued tenure of the Chancellorship into the question of the day. It is clear that Stresemann held the mistaken view that parliamentary government could be introduced into Germany with the help of the Supreme Command—a mistaken view in that Ludendorff only wished to overthrow Bethmann-Hollweg and not to strengthen the power of the Reichstag.

A second offensive on the part of the Supreme Command

followed Stresemann's attack. On July 12 the Crown Prince summoned the leaders of the political Parties in the Reichstag to meet him, and inquired of them whether they considered a change of Chancellors to be necessary. The Crown Prince in those days was the tool of the Supreme Command. The situation that arose was wholly unconstitutional. The Crown Prince had no place or part whatever in the government of the Empire. During his Chancellorship Bismarck had strongly resisted every attempt made by the then Crown Prince Frederick to interfere in political affairs. In 1917 the Crown Prince had no authority whatever to inquire of members of the Reichstag whether the Chancellor appointed by his father should remain in office or not. One can imagine what would have happened if in 1880 the Crown Prince Frederick had attempted to negotiate with Windthorst, Richter, and Bebel to achieve the dismissal of Bismarck. In the summer of 1917, however, Germany from a constitutional standpoint was in a state of absolute chaos. On the one hand was the power wielded by the Supreme Command in a wholly unconstitutional manner; on the other were the demands of the majority in the Reichstag which were no less irreconcilable with the existing Constitution. In the midst of this chaos nobody took exception to the fact that the Crown Prince offered his services as a mediator between Ludendorff and the Reichstag and William II.

At the conference with the Crown Prince, the Conservatives, the National Liberals, and the Centre demanded through their spokesman Erzberger the resignation of Bethmann-Hollweg. The Social Democrats and the Progressives, while they did not demand his resignation, displayed no great willingness to fight in his defence. The Supreme Command now embarked on a third and final offensive. Hindenburg and Ludendorff informed the Emperor that they were no longer able to work in collaboration with Bethmann-Hollweg, and that they would resign if he remained in office. It thus became impossible for the Emperor to retain Bethmann-Hollweg in office. The Chancellor accordingly resigned.

Throughout the war Bethmann-Hollweg displayed the same utter unfitness for his office that he had displayed in peace. It was he who prevented the German nation from forming an independent judgement on the situation, and from playing their part independently of the Government in the defence of Germany, by the narrow bureaucratic *Burgfrieden*. In foreign affairs Bethmann-Hollweg let pass every opportunity of obtaining for Germany the peace with one or other of her enemies that would subsequently have led to a general pacification. From August 1914 to August 1916 Bethmann-Hollweg was the most powerful man in Germany. Nevertheless he made no use of his power to effect any serious reform. Up to the day before his resignation, he continually spoke of reform without ever attempting to put his words into effect. Opposed by the stronger personality of General Ludendorff, he was at first rendered powerless and then dismissed from office.

The Supreme Command and Erzberger, who had insisted passionately upon the dismissal of Bethmann-Hollweg, had thus obtained their desire. It very quickly became apparent that the victory lay with Ludendorff and not with the Reichstag. Erzberger wished to replace Bethmann-Hollweg by Prince Bülow. Yet the Parties composing the majority in the Reichstag took no formal step in order to secure the appointment of Bülow or of any other candidate. Nemesis now overtook them for not having placed the introduction of parliamentary government into Germany at the head of their demands. Bülow was utterly unwelcome to the Emperor owing to his part in the *Daily Telegraph* affair. Neither Erzberger nor Stresemann was powerful enough to compel the Emperor to accept Bülow. The one man who could have done so was General Ludendorff, and he displayed no interest whatever in Bülow's candidature. It has already been mentioned that at that time the appointment of the Prussian Food Controller, Dr. Michaelis, was suddenly proposed in Court circles, approved by Ludendorff, and given effect to by the Emperor. This appointment was a blow in the face for the Reichstag. The Supreme Command, ignoring the Reichstag, appointed the new Imperial Chancellor in collaboration with the Emperor, and thereby brought to nought in an almost laughable manner the attempt to introduce parliamentary government into Germany.

The Parties composing the majority in the Reichstag contented themselves with the drafting of the so-called Peace Resolution and with the demand that the new Chancellor should make this Resolution the basis of his policy. The Centre, the Social Democrats, and the Progressives collaborated in the work of drafting the Resolution. The National Liberals, who had worked with the majority as long as the question was one of overthrowing Bethmann-Hollweg, now refused to participate in the work of drafting the Resolution and once more resumed relations with the Conservatives. It is true that the small Richthofen group within the National

Liberal Party was in agreement with the terms of the Resolution, but it was powerless to make its influence felt over the majority of the Party who remained true to the Supreme Command. In a series of personal interviews Ludendorff sought to induce the Parties composing the majority in the Reichstag to abandon the Resolution. When he saw that the Social Democrats, Centre, and Progressives were not to be shaken in their determination, Ludendorff withdrew his opposition to the Resolution in order to avoid provoking an acute conflict. The general terms in which the Resolution was drafted were entirely harmless 9 and a mere repetition of the feelings expressed on August 4, 1914, which were voiced in the phrase, 'We are not animated by any desire for conquest.' The Resolution demanded a peace by 'mutual agreement and reconciliation', and protested against all possible 'acquisition of territory' and all 'political, economic and financial oppression'. Every political and diplomatic action is capable of the most widely differing interpretations. It is purely a question of opinion, and one in which might has the last word, whether territorial acquisitions have been forcibly obtained or not. The German Government with the Peace Resolution in their hands might have conquered half the world. It was even subsequently said that the Peace of Brest-Litovsk accorded with the terms of the Resolution!

Ludendorff did not need to fear that in any future peace negotiations he would be in any way hampered by the phraseology of the Resolution. Nevertheless the Resolution was unwelcome to him for reasons connected with his domestic policy. In the political warfare within Germany as great importance was attached to phrases as to deeds. Now the Resolution was drafted in the sense of Bethmann-Hollweg's promises and not in the phraseology of the Pan-Germans. Hence the adoption of the Resolution by the Reichstag was a moral defeat for Ludendorff, and brought an increase of strength to his opponents. Notwithstanding the Supreme Command's feeling of strength, it did not wish to engage in an open war with the Reichstag. The balance of power within the nation had been profoundly altered since the outbreak of the war. Although the opinions of members of the Reichstag were not of much concern to the Supreme Command, the millions of supporters of the Social Democratic Party and the Centre, who stood in the trenches and before the benches in the munition factories, constituted a tremendous force to which Ludendorff was afraid openly to throw down the gauntlet. For a long time it would seem that he feared lest Bethmann-Hollweg would appeal to the Reichstag as against the Supreme Command, and he therefore did all that lay in his power to estrange the Reichstag and Bethmann-Hollweg. It was for similar reasons that the Supreme Command assented to the Resolution. Moreover, Ludendorff was convinced that at the first favourable opportunity he could bring about the withdrawal of the objectionable Resolution.

The new Chancellor, Michaelis, looked upon himself as the representative of the Supreme Command, and adopted all Ludendorff's views without question. In the debate in the Reichstag on July 19, 1917, on the Resolution, Michaelis supported the Resolution with a reservation that has since become proverbial—'as I interpret it'.[10] This was a severe blow for the Reichstag and not wholly undeserved. For, in truth, each man could interpret the Resolution as he liked. Michaelis's reservation made it clear to the world at large—and in making the reservation he emphasized that he did so on behalf of the Supreme Command—that he interpreted the Resolution very differently from the interpretation placed upon it by Scheidemann and Erzberger.

The leaders of the majority felt themselves to be so powerless on July 19 that they could only make the best of a bad job. Hence they acted as if they had either not heard Michaelis's reservation or attached no importance to it. They sought to make it appear as if the Reichstag, the Chancellor, and the Supreme Command were at one. The Resolution was passed by the votes of the three parties composing the majority, fresh war credits were granted, and the Reichstag was prorogued. On July 25 Michaelis triumphantly reported to the Crown Prince: 'the hateful Resolution has been passed by two hundred and twelve votes to one hundred and twenty-six with seventeen abstainers. I have deprived it of its greatest danger by my "interpretation". One can, in fact, make any peace one likes, and still be in accord with the Resolution.'

The Reichstag had in truth been completely defeated by the Supreme Command. All that the majority had been able to achieve, after the great hopes that had been set on constitutional reform in Germany and the conclusion of peace, was a piece of paper which the rulers of Germany could contemptuously tear up before their eyes. Nevertheless, Erzberger's Peace Resolution is a notable milestone on the political path of Germany. For the moment what the Reichstag achieved was of less importance than the fact that the Parties forming the majority existed at all. The coalition formed in July 1917 by the Social Democrats, the Progressives, and the Centre continued to exist. It was a coalition of the working and middle class directed against the Prussian nobility and the great industrialists. If the Peace Resolution was of little actual value, it was nevertheless the standard round which the coalition rallied. The 'internal enemy' of the Hohenzollern Empire, whose appearance Bismarck had feared at a critical moment in time of war, had become a reality.

It is not difficult to understand that the ruling classes, who were the supporters of the Supreme Command, closed their ranks to present a united front to their opponents. Thus the Fatherland Party, which comprised the Conservatives and the Right Wing of the National Liberals, in short, the so-called Pan-Germans, and was led by Tirpitz and Kapp, came into being. The Fatherland Party denoted an attempt to renew the Bismarckian Coalition, with the difference that after the election of 1887 the Coalition was in the majority in the Reichstag, whereas the Fatherland Party of 1917–18 only represented a small and much-hated minority in the nation. The leaders of the Fatherland Party were convinced that the German nation could only survive by displaying an iron endurance and a determination to win the war at all costs. They further believed that they could create a movement in Germany similar to that aroused by Lloyd George in England and Clemenceau in France. Their task, however, was impossible of achievement by reason of the class distinctions which had arisen in Germany since 1871, and which had become more clearly pronounced during the war. Thus a 'victorious peace' and a 'peace by mutual agreement' were the two battle-cries under which the poor and the rich, the ruler and the ruled, fought for power in Germany. When the leaders of the Fatherland Party talked of a 'will to victory', the working class interpreted their exhortations to mean the satisfaction of the territorial ambitions of the industrialists and the arrogance of the militarists. Both parties were equally convinced that their own policy would turn out to be for the benefit of the entire nation. But they talked two languages and were incapable of understanding each other's point of view.

From a tactical standpoint it would have been wiser if the supporters of the Supreme Command had not attempted any political action against the Reichstag. Since it was impossible to overthrow the powerful Party organization of the Centre and the Social Democrats, it would have been wiser to have preserved the fiction which came into being on July 19. It would not have been difficult to have maintained publicly that the Supreme Command and the Reichstag pursued identical aims while in reality the Supreme Command took all the decisions. This was the method cleverly used by Count Hertling to avoid for a whole year any open conflict between the Reichstag and the Supreme Command.

The supporters of the Supreme Command felt that their feet were planted on sand. Before their eyes was a vision of the catastrophe which would overwhelm the old Germany if the 'democratic pacifist' movement were to gain the upper hand. The diplomatic phraseology employed by Bethmann-Hollweg in his speeches had been particularly obnoxious to them. Now Bethmann-Hollweg had been overthrown and the decision rested with the Supreme Command. Hence the Fatherland Party was determined to take up the challenge, and to unite the nationalist elements in the nation in support of a victorious peace. The existence of the Fatherland Party and its propaganda was a cause of offence to the majority in the Reichstag, who nevertheless did not feel themselves strong enough openly to attack the Supreme Command. Michaelis and his successor in the Chancellorship, Hertling, sought to come to an understanding with the Reichstag. But the agitation carried on by the Fatherland Party only served to enrage the war-weary masses of the populace to the uttermost, and the fight against this Party served to close the ranks of all the supporters of the majority in the Reichstag. Moreover, the members of the U.S.P.D. were on the whole in agreement with the ideas of the majority parties in the Reichstag, although the U.S.P.D. itself refrained from joining the coalition owing to its refusal to participate in the voting of any further war credits.

Two political camps had thus come into existence in Germany since July 1917: the Supreme Command and the Parties composing the majority in the Reichstag. Although the former was the more powerful, the majority in the Reichstag did not permit itself to be dissolved, and remained at its post until in September 1918 the Supreme Command was destroyed and power passed to the Reichstag. The nature of the relationship between the Supreme Command and the Reichstag was most clearly revealed in the negotiations in connexion with the Papal peace move in August and September 1917.[11]

A Papal Note addressed to the Governments of the belligerent nations was handed in at Berlin in August. This intervention on the part of the Pope had been in preparation since June, and it was in order to clear the way for it that Erzberger sought to induce the Reichstag to pass his Peace Resolution. The Papal diplomats set no great hopes on the success of their action. The English Minister to the Vatican, Count Salis, was in sympathy with the peace party in England, and had undoubtedly represented its influence to the Vatican as being greater than it actually was. It is true that in making this peace move the Pope was not risking much, since, even if he failed to bring about a pacification, his authority was certain to be strengthened among the nations, who would be impressed by the fact that the Head of the Catholic Church had made a serious attempt to restore peace on earth.

The English reply to the Papal Note of August 21, while politely worded, gave little ground for hope in laying stress upon the Entente demands for restoration, compensation, and guarantees for the future. This triple formula was subsequently to become the basis of the Peace of Versailles. The great majority of the English middle class interpreted 'guarantees for the future' to mean the destruction of the military power of Germany on sea and on land and of German competition. It was clear that such demands presupposed the complete victory of the Entente and the capitulation of Germany; and they therefore rendered fruitless any mediation such as that attempted by the Pope. Nevertheless, the Papal diplomats continued their negotiations in the hope at least of being able to strengthen the hands of the peace party in England. The English answer to the Papal Note emphasized that not even in regard to Belgium had Germany ever made any official statement of her war aims. Hence the Papal diplomats were desirous of securing a German declaration to the effect that Germany was willing unconditionally to restore Belgium; the possession of such a declaration would have enabled them to work upon circles in England that were favourable to peace.

On September 11 a Crown Council was held to determine the German attitude towards Belgium. General Ludendorff was prepared to give up the coast of Flanders, but demanded the economic union of Belgium with Germany, the independence of Flanders under German administration, the cession of Liége, and a lengthy occupation of Belgium by the German army. The Emperor was of the opinion that if the annexation of Belgium was no longer possible Germany must be compensated elsewhere. Apart from the complete destruction of English influence in Belgium, he had in mind the solution of the Flemish Question and economic guarantees. On the question of Liége William II expressed no opinion. Since his ideas were thus approximately those of the Supreme Command, Hindenburg and Ludendorff gained the impression that William II had not sought in conjunction with Michaelis to contest their opinions. Otherwise a crisis would immediately have arisen.

On September 12 Michaelis wrote to Hindenburg to inquire whether the Supreme Command would be content with a German occupation of Liége for some years after the conclusion of peace. Liége could be evacuated when Belgium had satisfactorily fulfilled Germany's economic demands. Hindenburg replied on September 15 that he shared in Ludendorff's opinion that for the safety of the Rhineland it was necessary that Germany should remain in permanent occupation of Liége. All this only serves to make it clear that the German Government was at that time not prepared to agree to an unconditional restoration of Belgium. In their formal reply to the Pope they contented themselves with a general reference to the Peace Resolution which, as we have seen, could be interpreted to mean anything. Subsequently, when the Pope pressed for a confidential statement as to Germany's intentions in regard to Belgium, Michaelis gave an evasive reply, notwithstanding the fact that the Pope had given him to understand that without a precise declaration as to Belgium's future his mediation was rendered useless.

Such was German policy as directed by the Supreme Command. At the same time the Reichstag directly sought to influence the course of the negotiations with the Pope, and Michaelis announced his readiness to consult with the Party leaders as to the answer to be returned to the Papal Note. The Reichstag elected a Committee of Seven, consisting of two Social Democrats, two Members of the Centre, a Progressive, a National Liberal, and a Conservative, that is to say, five representatives from the majority and two from the minority of the Right. This was not a Reichstag Committee in a constitutional sense; it was simply an unofficial conference of Party leaders. Nevertheless, in a formal sense, it denoted a great triumph for the Reichstag. In defiance of the Constitution Bismarck had excluded the Reichstag from any direct control over foreign policy. Now, however, the Reichstag went so far as to seek to take part in diplomatic negotiations. Such an action could never occur in States with a well-established parliamentary government, since it would render it impossible for a Foreign Minister to carry out effectively a line of policy if he were compelled to discuss every detail with a parliamentary committee. In these parliamentary States, however, a Minister's tenure of office can at any moment be terminated by a vote of no confidence passed by the Parliament, which does not therefore need to supervise the details of his policy. The German Reichstag, on the contrary, had in 1917 neither the power nor the right to dismiss the Imperial Chancellor or the Secretary of State for Foreign Affairs. And because the Reichstag had in general too few rights, it was compelled to demand too much in individual cases. The then Secretary of State for Foreign Affairs, Kühlmann, sympathized with the majority in the Reichstag, and looked upon the political power of the Supreme Command as dangerous. This suffices to explain the want of confidence which Michaelis publicly displayed towards Kühlmann. Kühlmann was present at the Crown Council on September 11, yet he was not informed of the correspondence between Michaelis and Hindenburg in regard to Liége. Such was the way in which in those days the rulers of Germany administered the foreign affairs of their country! Kühlmann was personally in favour of the restoration of Belgium. Nevertheless he looked upon the Papal peace move as a forlorn hope because he knew—at any rate in general—the views held by the Supreme Command with regard to the future of Belgium. Hence he neither could nor would take upon himself the responsibility of making a public statement in regard to Belgium. For from a constitutional standpoint the Secretary of State was at that time no more than the assistant of the Imperial Chancellor, and was incapable of taking upon himself the responsibility for German foreign policy.

The Committee of Seven met on August 28 and September 10. The Social Democrats demanded a precise statement as to Belgium. The Government replied that a reference to the Peace Resolution in the German reply to the Papal Note was of itself sufficient. Thereupon the Party leaders expressed themselves as satisfied with the reply of the Government, and the German reply was drafted accordingly. The attempt made by the majority in the Reichstag to avail itself of this opportunity to interfere decisively in the conduct of foreign policy resulted in a complete failure. Despite the existence of the Committee of Seven, the Reichstag continued to remain in the dark as to what was being done. The Reichstag did not know that, in conjunction with the Supreme Command, Michaelis had drawn up a programme in regard to Belgium which provided for a permanent occupation of Liége. The Reichstag did not know that the Papal diplomats had expressed their dissatisfaction with the German reply, had pressed with all the means in their power for a precise statement as to Belgium's future, and had not received any such statement from Michaelis. Such was the way in which the rulers of Germany treated the Reichstag after three years of war! It was only when everything was lost that they turned to the Reichstag, placed all the power in its hands, and called upon it to save Germany.

During the weeks occupied with the discussions on the Peace Resolution in the Reichstag disturbances unprecedented in the history of Germany broke out in the High Seas Fleet.[12] Thanks to the conjunction of a number of special circumstances the German cruisers became a centre of revolt against the governing class and naval discipline. Throughout the entire war, with very brief intervals, the German battleships lay in harbour in Kiel, Wilhelmshafen, &c. The overwhelming superiority of the enemy made an attack on the English fleet impossible, while the English for their part did not attack the German coast. All the German High Seas Fleet could attempt were a few short sallies of which one led to the battle of Jutland. Exceptional conditions of service came into being on board the cruisers which can only be described as a peace-time routine in the midst of war. The troops standing in Flanders in water-logged trenches with death staring them in the eyes every moment would perhaps have looked upon life on board a cruiser as idyllic. The lack of food began to affect the navy during 1916 and 1917, and the sailors were justified in their complaints about the rations. Nevertheless conditions in the great battles on the Western Front were incomparably worse, while the crews of the submarines had far greater dangers to face and sufferings to endure than those of the battleships. The test of discipline, however, arose among the crews of the High Seas Fleet and not among those of the submarines, or amongst the troops at the Front.

The problem cannot be solved by simply accusing the officers of the High Seas Fleet of brutality or want of consideration for their subordinates. It is unquestionable that instances occurred of brutality in the handling of the sailors. But no one has ever come forward to explain why the naval officers were so far below the standard of the army officers during the war. The naval officers, through their trips abroad before the war, had acquired a knowledge of the world and of men that brought them more into sympathy with civilian ideas than were the regular army officers. The shameful instances of the mishandling of men, which were so frequently the cause of military court martials before the war, were scarcely ever known to occur in the navy. During the war it was often a matter of pure chance whether a naval officer was appointed to a cruiser or to a submarine. Although one may disapprove of the submarine campaign from a political standpoint, the brilliant achievements of the German submarine commanders cannot be questioned. It is impossible to believe that similarly educated and trained officers on board the cruisers were in general wolves in sheep's clothing in comparison with the heroes of the submarines.

It was, in truth, the close proximity in which for three years officers and men had lived that in the summer of 1917 made possible a fierce outbreak in the navy of the class hatred which was at that time sweeping across Germany. The officers were socially completely cut off from the men, and empowered with illimitable authority. They ate apart from the men, and were better fed than the men; a fact which in itself was a cause of embitterment at a time when famine dominated the thoughts of every man. It is probable that the sailors imagined that the difference between their rations and those of the officers was greater than was actually the case; but the fact remains that the worst form of class warfare—the fight for bread—invaded the navy.

The soldier in the trenches and the sailor on the submarine saw that his officer shared in the same risks. Hence class differences tended to disappear in the trenches and on the submarines. On the battleships and cruisers, however, danger was virtually non-existent, and the crews had practically nothing to do. Their days were passed in drill, coaling, &c., while the officers, as the sailors complained, wandered about in spick and span uniforms and with 'well-manicured' hands. The severe discipline was looked upon by the sailor as the device employed by an arrogant ruling class to hold down a crowd of slaves. The lower ranks in the navy were united in a common opposition to their aristocratic officers. Sailors of middle-class origin were no less embittered than their Social Democratic comrades. Letters and other documents written by Roman Catholic sailors, and members of the Centre Party, are in existence which far exceed in their revolutionary sentiments similar documents emanating from Social Democrats. Nevertheless, only a minority of the sailors were members of political Parties. The great majority held no definite political opinions, were thoroughly patriotic, and were only depressed by the famine. For the most part their desires did not go beyond a speedy peace and the creation of a state of things in which officers would no longer wield a dictatorial authority over the nation. The political ideal of the majority of the sailors would have more nearly approached a vague constitutional monarchy than a Socialist republic.

Into this tense atmosphere came the news of the Russian Revolution and the struggle over war aims. The Russian Revolution was hailed by the sailors in the hope that out of it peace would come. It was for this reason that they closely followed the discussions of the International Socialist Congress which met in the summer of 1917 in Stockholm. The Stockholm Conference owed its origin to the initiative of the Russian Social Democrats, who hoped that a basis for peace might be found through discussions in which Socialists from all the belligerent countries would take part. Since, however, the English and French Socialists were politically too powerless to overcome the embargo placed on the Conference by their Governments, the Conference ended in failure. The endeavours made by Russian, German, Italian, and Austrian Socialists to lay down moderate conditions for peace failed because they met with no response from England and France.

High hopes were set by the German sailors on the outcome of the Conference. Moreover, the Russian navy had shown how officers could be dealt with by the sailors under their command. Hence, whenever the German sailors felt peculiarly aggrieved, they played with the notion of following the example set them by their Russian comrades. The controversy over war aims also helped to induce them to adopt the Russian model. The position of Germany as a world power was a matter of deep concern to the naval officers, who saw in England Germany's most dangerous enemy, and for this reason they were almost unanimously in favour of an unrestricted submarine campaign. A retention of the Flanders coast seemed imperative in their eyes in order that Germany might in the future have a weapon ready for use against England. The majority of the naval officers was thus in favour of a victorious peace, and was in sympathy in the autumn of 1917 with the Fatherland Party. The officers were not party politicians in the customary sense of the word, and they did not trouble themselves much as to whether the Conservatives or the Centre were the better Party. But they looked upon it as a national duty to insist upon a German victory, and they regarded any one who either through slackness or doubts of victory paralysed the fighting spirit of Germany as a traitor.

The sailors, on the other hand, were no less enthusiastically in favour of a peace without annexations and no less determinedly opposed to the war aims of the Pan-Germans. The political and social cleavage within the German nation was thus mirrored on board the battleships of the German navy. Since their ships lay in harbour, the sailors could spend a good deal of their time on land in reading political newspapers and informing themselves as to the aims of the various political parties. Karl Liebknecht roused their sympathy as a pacifist rather than as a revolutionary Socialist, while Scheidemann was particularly popular with them as an outspoken supporter of peace by mutual agreement. It is true that the sailors did not recognize the differences between Scheidemann and Liebknecht any more than those which separated the U.S.P.D. from the S.P.D.

The U.S.P.D. was popular among the sailors as the Party which had been the first and most determined advocate of a peace without annexations, as the opponent of war credits, and as the champion in the Reichstag of all those with a grievance. The sailors supported the U.S.P.D. because it seemed to them to pursue the policy of the majority in the Reichstag more ruthlessly than any other Party. A number of sailors joined the U.S.P.D. in the summer, and began enlisting others. A suggestion was then made that membership of the U.S.P.D. should be made conditional upon the signature of a formal declaration of belief in a peace without annexations and in the aims of the Stockholm Conference. A declaration on the part of four hundred sailors, signed on July 31, 1917, on board the battleship *King Albert*, ran as follows:

PEACE PROCLAMATION

'We, whose names are appended to this declaration, herewith proclaim our membership of the U.S.P.D. and our approval of its policy. At the same time we wish it to be known that we are in favour of a peace without annexations and reparations, and that we are therefore anxious for a conclusion of hostilities. We hope that the Conference of Socialists from all lands now being held in Stockholm will be crowned with success, and that a peace will be brought about on the principle of the right of self-determination of all peoples which will bring to an end the racial and fratricidal slaughter of the international proletariate. We desire to send our best wishes to the Stockholm Conference for the success of its work, and we trust that the work of the U.S.P.D. will also meet with success. The U.S.P.D. has up to now been the most determined champion of our interests in Germany, and hence alone possesses our confidence, as is proved by our entry into its ranks.'

This declaration voiced the political beliefs then common among the broad masses of the German nation, especially among the working class, and at the same time revealed no trace of any revolutionary spirit. A similar declaration on the part of soldiers, like the subsequent professions of sympathy with the Fatherland, a Party to which officers gave expression, would have been permissible from the standpoint of military discipline. Similar declarations to that published on the *King Albert* were also drawn up on other ships. In proclaiming their desire for a peace without annexations the sailors knew that for the most part their officers were of another mind. The Captain of the *King Albert* took advantage of the anniversary of the Battle of Jutland to deliver an address to the crew in which he declared that Germany must go on fighting until her enemies were beaten to their knees and she could dictate peace. He added that he was convinced that the entire crew shared in his belief. In delivering this speech the Captain was only giving voice to sentiments which appeared to him natural in the mouth of an officer in time of war. He certainly had no idea that he had used the very expressions that were most intolerable to the sailors and in which they thought they heard the echo of the overweening arrogance of their political opponents. As a result of his speech, nine sailors sent on July 24 to the *Vorwärts* in Berlin an article entitled 'The voice of the lower deck' in which the Captain's speech was fiercely criticized, and in which, *inter alia*, it was stated: 'The captain can now report to his equals that his crew will have nothing to do with the Scheidemann Peace. If, however, we were once questioned, and allowed to vote without coercion, the truth would come out. Why is it not done? Answer—because it would not serve their interests.' This article shows that the lower deck was not asked for its opinion, and that instead the 'lord spoke for his serf'.

The *Vorwärts* refused to publish the article through fear of the censorship, and returned it to its authors. The manuscript fell into the hands of the officers, and naval justice was so narrowminded that the writer was condemned to six months' arrest. The article was written five days after the Reichstag had passed its Peace Resolution, and serves to reveal how keenly the sailors followed the course of political events. It also reveals that the sailors made little distinction as between the Social Democrats, the U.S.P.D. and the majority in the Reichstag. The existence of the illegal Spartacists was scarcely known to the sailors. The sailors next endeavoured to get in touch with the Reichstag, and letters of complaint were addressed to members of the Centre, Social Democratic Party, and the U.S.P.D. Visits were paid to members of the Reichstag by sailors who were on leave in Berlin. Thus Reichpietsch, a member of the crew of the battleship *Frederick the Great*, who was later shot by order of a court martial, was received in June by the Social Democrat Stücklen and by Dittmann of the U.S.P.D.

At this juncture an instrument was placed in the hands of the sailors by means of which they were enabled to air their grievances. Food committees, with members elected by the ratings, were established for the purpose of controlling naval rations. These committees could either be of little service, or they could make their authority felt in regard to the task which had been entrusted to them. In the eyes of the excited sailors of the High Seas Fleet, however, they were invested with a very different character. The sailors saw in their establishment the concession of a right to a voice in affairs; almost indeed the establishment of legalized Sailors' Councils. It seemed to them that the old ruthless discipline was no longer in force, and that the ratings were no longer compelled to permit themselves to be made the victims of obvious injustice.

The food committees from the individual ships soon got into touch with one another, and the members met each other on their shore leave. A network of associations grew up and spread over the greater part of the High Seas Fleet of which the centre was the energetic committee of the flagship *Frederick the Great*. All shades of political opinion were represented in these nebulous organizations in which were to be found members of the U.S.P.D., S.P.D., some Left Radicals, and many who were wholly indifferent to politics. The men discussed among themselves their rations, their grievances, and peace. Although all sorts of schemes were debated, there was no sign of any definite political policy much less of a revolutionary movement.

The movement among the sailors in 1917 reflected the social and political condition of Germany within the narrow framework of the High Seas Fleet. It is untrue to say that the discontent among the sailors was stimulated by certain political Parties. The Spartacists knew nothing of what was going on in the Fleet, while it was the sailors who came to the U.S.P.D. and the S.P.D. and not the Party agitators to the Fleet. Nevertheless, between June and August 1917, a state of things arose in the German navy which was contrary to the traditions of Prussian discipline.

On June 6 the crew of the *Prince Regent Leopold* went on hunger-strike, and refused to eat the dried vegetables served out to them. Similar instances occurred in July on board the *Frederick the Great* and the *Posen*; while on July 19, the day on which the Reichstag passed its Peace Resolution, a second hunger strike occurred on board the *Prince Regent Leopold*. On this occasion the crew refused to eat mangolds. On July 20 one hundred and forty men of the crew of the *Pillau*, which was lying in dock, left the ship without leave as a protest against what they deemed to be an unjust refusal to grant them leave. On August 2 four hundred men of the crew of the *Prince Regent Leopold* also deserted their ship as a protest against what they considered to be the unjustifiable punishment of some of their comrades. After some hours they were peaceably induced to return to their ship. It is worthy of note that on no single one of these occasions was blood shed or any attack made upon the officers. The sailors assumed for themselves a certain right to strike in consequence of the establishment of the food committees, and, as they believed, concomitant relaxation of discipline. These demonstrations created the greatest alarm among the naval authorities, who instituted a rigorous investigation as a result of the demonstration on board the *Prince Regent Leopold*. This investigation led to the discovery of the organizations among the sailors which had grown out of the food committees. The naval authorities believed that in these organizations they had found the secret source of the revolt.

The members of the Court Martial entrusted with the investigation showed themselves lacking in a knowledge of human psychology, and still more in any knowledge of the political tendencies then prevalent among the working class. The Court Martial interpreted the sequence of events so as to make it appear as if the U.S.P.D. had organized a great conspiracy among the crews of the Fleet in the hope of forcibly overthrowing the Government and bringing about a peace without annexations. The sailors who were questioned by the Court Martial were threatened with the death penalty, and in consequence frequently agreed with the interpretation put upon their actions by the President of the Court Martial in the hope of saving their lives. The defence afforded the sailors was wholly inadequate in view of the secret nature of the proceedings. Hence the proceedings of the Court Martial resulted in a tragic miscarriage of justice.

Ten sailors were condemned to death, of whom two were executed, and the sentences of the remainder subsequently commuted to varying terms of penal servitude and hard labour. On August 26 the sailors Reichpietsch, Weber, and Sachse, all members of the food committee of the *Frederick the Great*, and Beckers and Köbis from the *Prince Regent Leopold*—all so-called leaders of the movement—were court martialled and condemned to death. According to military law death was the punishment to be meted out to any soldier who in time of war attempted to promote a rebellion. The Court Martial justified its judgement on the ground that the sailors' organizations, although they had failed to achieve their object, intended to promote a mutiny. But distinguished experts in maritime law placed a different interpretation upon the law in declaring that by the word 'promote' the drafter of the law had in mind only the accomplished fact. The death penalty therefore did not apply in this particular case.

The Commander-in-Chief of the High Seas Fleet, Admiral Scheer, before whom the sentence of the Court Martial was laid for his confirmation, agreed with the Court Martial's interpretation of the law. He signed the death warrants for Reichpietsch and Köbis at the same time as he commuted the death penalty in the case of the other three sailors to fifteen years' penal servitude. On September 5, 1917, Reichpietsch and Köbis were shot. It is unquestionable that the members of the Court Martial and Admiral Scheer sincerely believed that they had rightly interpreted the law; that they had come upon the track of an exceptionally dangerous revolutionary movement which threatened to incapacitate the fleet; and that they had evidence to prove that the agitation in favour of a peace without annexations was intended to lead to a revolution. Nevertheless, objectively considered, Reichpietsch and Köbis were the victims of a miscarriage of justice. The question at issue was not the interpretation of the word 'promoted'; the actual charge itself was untenable. The conclusion arrived at by the Court Martial that Reichpietsch and Köbis had sought to incite a rebellion was based upon false deduction coloured by political bias. An impartial Court of Appeal would unquestionably have revised the judgement. Further, if the naval authorities had possessed a shred of political understanding, they would not have acted so ruthlessly towards the sailors. The Admiral should have understood the abnormal psychological condition of the crews of the cruisers and battleships. His stern sense of naval discipline rendered him incapable of doing so. An improvement in their rations, and a clear explanation of the military and economic situation in which Germany found herself, would have sufficed to pacify the sailors. The naval authorities in destroying the secret organizations among the sailors aroused in them the greatest resentment. The great majority of the lower ratings only rendered obedience to their officers after the summer of 1917 under the pressure of physical force. Such a situation in the navy of a nation in arms is both a military and political disaster. From the summer of 1917 onwards the armed forces of Germany were hampered by an Achilles heel— the High Seas Fleet. It was Admiral Scheer, and not the U.S.P.D., who created the revolutionary mob of November 1918.

Reichpietsch and Köbis were the martyrs of the political movement that seized upon the German nation in the summer of 1917, and that led to the adoption of the Peace Resolution by the Reichstag. It is of little importance in judging the historical significance of these events in the navy whether the views held by Reichpietsch, Köbis, and their associates on the subject of peace were right or not. It is the gulf that at that time made its appearance between the governing classes and the broad masses of the nation and the lower ranks in the army and navy that is significant for an historian. The Supreme Command still held Germany in its grasp. The nation nevertheless had become inimical to the ruling system and was seeking a way of escape from it.

NOTES TO CHAPTER V

1. On the subject of Germany's inner development during the important three first months of 1917 see Bergsträsser in REPORT, vii, part i, pp. 234 et seq.; also Bredt, ibid., viii, pp. 159 et seq.

2. On the subject of the Constitutional Committee of the Reichstag see Bredt in REPORT, viii, pp. 162 et seq.; Scheidemann, ibid., vii, part i, p. 280. See also ibid., vii, part i, p. 12; vii, part ii, pp. 160 et seq.

3. For the events leading up to the Easter Proclamation see Bergsträsser, ibid., vii, part i, pp. 237 et seq.

4. The genesis of the Peace Resolution has been tested with particular care by the Committee of Inquiry, and pretty well all the questions connected with it have been cleared up. All the material will be found in vols. vii and viii of its Report. For details see especially Bredt, viii, pp. 69 et seq.; Scheidemann, vii, part i, pp. 282 et seq.; Bell, ibid., pp. 307 et seq.; Müller-Fulda (Centre member of the Reichstag in 1917),

ibid., p. 384: 'I met Erzberger in the Reichstag (on July 2) and discussed with him the dangerous feeling which had been aroused in many places because of the food shortage. He told me that Germany could have peace if she were really in earnest about it. He mentioned the proposed attempts at mediation on the part of the Pope, and said that it was now a case of backing it up by a demonstration on the part of the Reichstag for a peace without annexations.' Philipp, vii, part ii, p. 169. Von Richthofen, ibid., p. 217, on the subject of the journey which he undertook with Erzberger in 1917 to 'Oberost'. Von Richthofen's criticism of Erzberger's action: ibid., p. 218. Attitude of the National Liberals, ibid., p. 219. The swing of the Centre towards the left: Spahn, ibid., p. 239.

5. On the subject of the tendency of the Parma Party see Victor Naumann's report to Hertling on February 21, 1918, of his impressions in Vienna, in REPORT, ii, pp. 145 et seq.: 'In my conversations with my friends among the members of the high aristocracy, I found in just the same way a kind of feeling of bitterness against Germany, which I tried vainly to dissipate, and a tremendous longing for peace. It may be assumed that certain Court circles, to which I will give the collective name of the Parma Party, are strenuously at work trying to arrive at an understanding with the Entente.' Further and most important material on the subject of the Habsburg Monarchy during the war can now be found in Naumann's book *Dokumente und Argumente* (1928). Naumann points out perfectly justly that Czernin had nothing to do with the intrigues of the Parma Party, but instead was the strongest opponent of this tendency. It is very doubtful whether Naumann judges the Emperor Karl's personality correctly. But for historical purposes all that is important is the political line taken by the Viennese Court in 1917–18, and this is quite clear.

6. On the subject of the Pope's efforts for peace see Bredt in REPORT, viii, pp. 132 et seq.

7. Erzberger and Scheidemann in the Chief Committee: cf. Bredt in REPORT, viii, pp. 73 et seq.; cf. pp. 108 et seq.

8. Bethmann's fall: Bredt in REPORT, viii, pp. 77 et seq. Prince Max of Baden: *Erinnerungen*, pp. 110 et seq.

9. For the interpretation of the Peace Resolution: David, in REPORT, vii, part i, pp. 170 et seq. Prince Max of Baden: *Erinnerungen*, p.114.— Erzberger knew exactly what he stood to gain from the ambiguous phraseology of the Resolution with regard to foreign policy. Prince Max tells of an interview he had with Erzberger on the subject of the Resolution, during which Erzberger explained: 'You see, Your Highness—this way I get Longwy-Briey by means of negotiations.'

10. The letter from Michaelis to the Crown Prince about the Reichstag session of July 19 may be found in REPORT, vii, part ii, p. 390. Impression made by the remark 'As I understand it' on the Majority in the Reichstag: see Scheidemann, Landsberg, and Bell, ibid., vii, part i, pp. 294 et seq.

11. Germany's negotiations with the Pope in August and September 1917 have been thoroughly investigated by the Committee of Inquiry; cf. especially the minutes of the examination of Michaelis and Kühlmann by the Committee in vol. vii, part ii. The controversial questions are in

some cases very complicated. The views presented by Bredt in his capacity as an expert (viii, pp. 132 et seq.) have not been substantially altered (cf. also the essay by Bredt in the *Preussischen Jahrbüchern*, 1927). Bredt's idea that the Emperor at that time shared the opinion of the majority in the Reichstag on the Belgian question is certainly wrong (viii, p. 152). The minutes of the Crown Council of September 11 reveals the contrary. The statements made in subsequent books of memoirs are of no importance in comparison with this. Kühlmann also stated before the Committee of Inquiry that the Crown Council had not empowered him to make any statement as to an unconditional restoration of Belgium; the German Government was only to make a public statement about Belgium if it had no assurance that this would bring about immediate peace negotiations (Kühlmann in REPORT, vii, part ii, p. 122). There had at that time been no such assurance. 'The second limitation or aggravation was the echo of the annexationists' efforts consisting in a reference to commercial ties, &c. To have made a direct attempt to do away with this, possibly by holding a second Crown Council, would have led to disaster—of that there is no question' (Kühlmann, ibid.). Cf. also Kühlmann, p. 140: 'The formula of the Crown Council was the one which I have frequently proposed. I saw no purpose in informing the Papal Curia definitely that there were certain tendencies in the Crown Council in favour of economic protectorates and temporary occupations of territory.'—Concealment from Kühlmann of the exchange of letters between Michaelis and Hindenburg (about Liége, &c.): REPORT, vii, part ii, pp. 68, 131.

12. Certain external considerations have led the Committee of Inquiry to devote a very large part of its work to the unrest in the navy in 1917. Compression and shortening would have been quite possible here. The whole mass of minutes of the sessions and interrogations, of expert opinions and written statements of persons involved, has been published in vols. ix and x of the Committee's Report. All controversial questions concerning the disturbances in the navy in 1917 have now been definitely cleared up. A short summary of the results by Bredt entitled *Die Marineunruhen 1917* can be found in the *Preussischen Jahrbüchern*, 1927. The two chief reports of the proceedings of the Committee of Inquiry have already been published separately: Dittmann, *Die Marinejustizmorde von 1917 und die Admiralsrebellion von 1918* (1926); and Brüninghaus, *Die politische Zersetzung und die Tragödie der deutschen Flotte* (1926). Dittmann's report especially contains a great deal of material in the way of documents. The statement that the U.S.P.D. wished to rouse a revolt in the navy at that time has been completely disproved by the investigations of the Reichstag Committee. This idea could only be supported by people who were quite unacquainted with the currents and tendencies in the German Labour movement. A few subsequent communist publications (several articles by the former sailor Sachse and the pamphlet by Anti-Nauticus, *Deutschlands revolutionäre Matrosen* (1925)) give the sailors' movement of 1917 a political and revolutionary character which it did not in reality possess. At his examination before the Committee of Inquiry Sachse also modified his former assertions considerably.

The next important source of information regarding the unrest among the sailors is the diary of the clericalist workman Stumpf which he kept from 1914–18 when he was a sailor on the *Helgoland*: Richard Stumpf, *Warum die Flotte zerbrach*, 1927. It is not necessary to weigh each one of Stumpf's words in a delicate balance. Isolated statements which Stumpf makes can be disproved. But the bitterness with which this clericalist, monarchist, and patriotically-minded man regards the officers and the ruling Prussian system as early as 1914 makes a very strong impression.—The Stockholm List: Dittmann, op. cit., p. 23, the letter to the *Vorwärts*, ibid., p. 25, the death sentences, ibid., pp. 62 et seq.—Stumpf, p. 148: 'Often when I hear my comrades railing at circumstances, I go among them and ask: "Well, what would you do if you were Zeus? Where would you begin to improve our unhappy lot?" And I hear some fine things: "Make peace at once," is the most usual answer. "Demobilize and disband the Army and the Navy!"—"Make Scheidemann Chancellor and Liebknecht Minister for War", and no end of things of that sort.'— On page 151 Stumpf describes the Jutland anniversary celebrations on his ship in 1917. The captain said in his address that the one aim of the enemy was to destroy the bond between the Supreme War Lord and the Army and Navy. 'Then when the Hohenzollerns have been driven out a parliamentary régime like that in England and France is to be forced on us. Then the shopkeepers, lawyers, and journalists will rule here as they do there.' Stumpf comments on this in his diary (p. 152): 'If I were an officer, my agreement (with the Captain's speech) and admiration would know no bounds. But my present point of view—the conviction of an unpropertied proletarian—differs utterly. How could I support an increase in the autocratic power (of the Emperor), of the Army, of the Navy! It is easy for any one to talk who does not have to share in the payment. I would rather be a slave to the English than a German soldier! My ideal is to approach the English-American form of government. I am not afraid of the words "parliamentary government".'— Changed attitude of the sailors to discipline, 1917: Stumpf, p. 159. Impression made by the death sentences on the men: Stumpf, p. 167: 'I should have said that any one was a fool who had suggested that in my Fatherland a man could be condemned to prison and to death without having done anything wrong. Gradually an arc-lamp is lighting up my understanding of why some people fight so passionately against the army and the militarist system. Poor Karl Liebknecht! How sorry I am for you to-day!'

VI

LUDENDORFF AT THE ZENITH OF HIS POWER

THE Supreme Command finally abandoned all hope of a victory by the submarine campaign in the summer and autumn of 1917. At the same time a new path to a victorious peace seemed to open before their eyes. The dissolution of the Russian army in consequence of the revolution made rapid progress. It seemed that the moment would not be far distant in which the enemy Front in the east would have ceased to exist. General Ludendorff would then be able to transfer his forces in the east to the Western Front, and there endeavour to win a decisive victory. The Supreme Command sought to hasten the disintegrative process in the east by means of local offensives: a German counter-offensive in east Galicia was the answer to the Russian offensive in the summer. The Russians were defeated and forced to evacuate the districts which they had occupied as a result of the Brusiloff offensive in the previous year. Other German offensives in the autumn led to the capture of Riga and the Russian islands in the Baltic. From that time forth Petrograd was threatened on land and from the sea by the German forces.

In November 1917 the Bolshevik Revolution occurred in Russia. With the two words 'land' and 'peace', Lenin had won over to his cause the majority of the Russian peasants and soldiers and had thereby rendered the position of the middle-class revolutionaries untenable. The Bolsheviks were determined to conclude peace without any regard for the Entente. Moreover, the Russian armies could not be kept at the Front throughout the winter of 1917–18, since the Tsarist officers had ceased to exercise any authority and no others had arisen to take their place. The peasants wanted to return home in order to be present at the partition of the land; and no power on earth could have induced them to remain at the Front. Lenin, who was not only a Marxian doctrinaire but also a great statesman, knew very well that the choice between war and peace no longer lay in his hands. Peace was being made already by the Russian soldiers in their own fashion. Lenin's skill as a statesman displayed itself in making the inevitable appear the result of his own free will.

Hence Ludendorff had very good grounds for supposing that in

1918 he would be able to remove his troops from the east, and that in consequence an entirely new strategical situation would arise. The German troops on the Western Front in 1917 were compelled to maintain themselves on the defensive. Nevertheless, the interminable and heavy fighting in Flanders finally ended in a victory for the German defence. In the autumn of 1917 Ludendorff had to dispatch six German divisions to Italy, where it seemed likely that the Austrians would no longer be able to hold the Isonzo Front against the Italians. For with each day that passed after the dismissal of Conrad von Hötzendorf the inherent weakness of the Habsburg army became more and more evident. The German troops broke through the Italian Front at the battle of Caporetto and the Italian army was hurled back into Venetia with enormous losses. The German armies thus fought simultaneously and victoriously against the armies of England, France, Russia, and Italy—an unprecedented military achievement that nevertheless failed to produce any political results.

For the spring of 1918 Ludendorff planned an offensive on the Western Front with an army of three and a half million men. The German army was numerically the equal of its opponents in the West, while it was not inferior in munitions thanks to the gigantic efforts made by German industry in spite of the blockade. Ludendorff believed himself to be strong enough to defeat the French and English. Behind them, however, loomed darkly the American menace. In the spring of 1918 America had already been a belligerent for a whole year. The Supreme Command had abandoned all hope of hindering by the use of submarines the transport of American troops to Europe. In the spring of 1918 the number of American troops on the Western Front was relatively small; but by the summer and autumn it had increased to hundreds of thousands. The strategical situation in which Germany found herself at the time of her offensive on the Western Front in 1918 was thus as bad as that in which she had found herself at the time of her offensive in 1914. It was not enough that the German army should defeat its enemies. In order to achieve a real victory the Entente armies had to be utterly crushed within the shortest possible space of time. If the campaign were to last until the summer and autumn of 1918 the Americans would be there. But if the English and French armies were to retain their fighting powers until the arrival of the Americans Germany's defeat would be rendered inevitable by reason of the overwhelming numerical superiority of her enemies. A German victory that resulted in the capture of Paris and Calais would not of itself have been enough. For were the Entente armies to retreat in good order behind the Loire, and there await the arrival of the Americans, Germany was lost.

In order that the danger threatening from the American army should be overcome, it was necessary that the victory to which Ludendorff looked forward in the spring of 1918 should be so complete that the French army would be annihilated and the English troops forced to return to their island. Yet even then the most that could have been achieved would have been a peace based on a compromise between Germany and the maritime Powers, England and America—a dictated peace would have been out of the question. How did Ludendorff expect to destroy an enemy army which was the equal in numbers, morale, military experience, and material equipment of the German army? In the spring of 1918 between seven and eight million soldiers would be opposed to one another in northern France, and, in consequence, the freedom of movement of the opposing armies would obviously be greatly lessened by the enormous masses of men to be manœuvred over a comparatively small area. Only a military miracle, and not a victory over the French and English, such as in fact Ludendorff achieved in 1918, could have saved Germany. Hence nothing remained to Ludendorff except to become a worker of miracles.

Ludendorff was successful in inspiring the entire Supreme Command and also a great part of the army and nation with the conviction that he would prove victorious. The believers in a German victory substituted the coming offensive on the Western Front for the submarine campaign as the last hope of Germany. In considering the political and military situation in which Germany found herself in 1917–18 it is necessary to ask the question whether Germany could have found some other way of escape than by embarking on the great offensive. It is true that to have remained on the defensive on the Western Front would have been useless. For the English and French would have simply waited until the Americans arrived, when they would have assumed the offensive with an overwhelming superiority in men and munitions, and would have destroyed the German army. The losses that were likely to be incurred in a defensive operation which turned out badly would at least have been as great as those that would be incurred by taking the offensive. To remain on the defensive meant the end. An immediate unconditional surrender would have been a wiser course.

During the winter of 1917–18 no German Government, no matter of what political colour, would have capitulated to the Entente. Not even a Haase Government would have done so, for the U.S.P.D. refused to give up a foot of German soil, and still less a Liebknecht Government seeing that the Spartacists even refused in 1919 to consent to the signature of the Treaty of Versailles. A German peace proposal to the Western Powers, even though it had included the surrender of Belgium, would have met with no success. For in England as in France the supporters of a peace by compromise were powerless. Lord Lansdowne achieved nothing against Lloyd George nor Caillaux against Clemenceau. The ruling elements in the English as in the French middle class were determined to fight on to the victory which they knew awaited them—thanks to the support of America. Apart from a military miracle on the Western Front, there was one other possibility open to Germany: the transformation of the peace with Russia into a political alliance. A Russo-German alliance would have compelled the Western Powers to compromise—at least so long as the German army remained capable of taking the field. But a Russo-German alliance was rendered impossible during 1917–18 by the unbridgeable difference between the political conditions in the two countries. A militarist-aristocratic Germany ruled by Ludendorff could not ally itself with a Bolshevist Russia under Lenin. It would first have been necessary to bridge this gulf. There were many in Germany, like General Hoffmann,[1] who thought that Germany should promote a counter-revolution in Russia in the belief that, if the middle class in Russia were once restored to power, they would display their gratitude by allying themselves with Germany. Ludendorff had indeed made an experiment of such a kind in the Ukraine, where the establishment of the Hetman Skoropadski in Kieff resulted in a complete fiasco. A White Government in Moscow supported by German bayonets would in similar fashion have had to contend with a revolution throughout the entire country. An adventure of this kind in the east would have diminished rather than increased the strength of Germany.

Moreover, Germany showed a disposition to follow the Russian example. If, for example, in January 1918 a revolution had taken place in Germany like that which took place in October by which a Socialist and Radical middle-class government came into being, an alliance between Germany and Russia would have been rendered possible. The Entente would have been faced with a revolutionary Russo-German alliance the mere existence of which would have sufficed to strengthen the peace movement in France and England. Here again success could only have followed were the German army to maintain its fighting efficiency. If the Entente were to win a decisive victory, a German revolution could not influence the course of events. In the following pages it will be shown how false is the notion that the revolution in Germany caused her defeat in the war. The exact contrary is the truth. It was because Germany had already lost the war in September 1918 that the revolutionary movement in October and November was powerless to affect the military situation.

A revolution in Germany would not have been possible during the winter of 1917–18 because neither the workmen nor the middle class were strong enough to overthrow Ludendorff. Hence only one hope of salvation remained—the offensive planned by Ludendorff in the west. Ludendorff's opponents of the majority in the Reichstag found themselves in a unique situation throughout the summer and autumn of 1917. They had passed their Peace Resolution and even participated under the guise of the Committee of Seven in drafting a reply to the Papal Peace Note, but they had never succeeded in achieving any real political influence. Moreover, their mistrust of the Imperial Chancellor, Michaelis, increased; a fact that was all the worse for him in that even the Supreme Command had come to recognize his utter incapacity. Michaelis, however, thought he could master the crisis, and resolved in October to attack the opposition.[2]

The events in the navy during the summer of 1917 had roused his anxiety, since he was in agreement with the naval authorities in believing that the U.S.P.D. were the promoters of the sailors' conspiracy. He wished, therefore, to bring the evidence which he thought he possessed before the Reichstag in order to prove that the U.S.P.D. had acted illegally, and to secure its suppression. Michaelis hoped that the majority in the Reichstag would support him through patriotic motives. It would in that case be possible to have the U.S.P.D. dissolved and its leader arrested—an action which would result in the removal of a Party which actively supported a compromise peace. The Majority Socialists had been paralysed by the police measures taken to crush the feeling of opposition among the working class, while the supporters of a victorious peace had in consequence felt themselves placed in a stronger position. The attack on the U.S.P.D. was in reality directed against the majority in the Reichstag.

Michaelis underrated the ability of his opponents. When on October 9 he made his attack on the U.S.P.D., he found himself opposed by the S.P.D. The Social Democrats knew very well that the parliamentary members of the U.S.P.D. had conducted their propaganda within the letter of the law, while the middle-class Parties, notwithstanding their dislike for the U.S.P.D., did not place any trust in the evidence brought forward by Michaelis. The Government's attempt to outlaw an entire Party was fiercely resisted by Ebert, who demanded the Chancellor's resignation. The Centre and the Progressives did not support the Chancellor any more than did the National Liberals, who were desirous of seizing any opportunity to overthrow the feckless Michaelis.

Thus on October 9 Michaelis suffered a defeat. The U.S.P.D. gained an unexpected moral victory, and there was once more a Chancellor crisis. The Supreme Command made no attempt to retain Michaelis and he was dismissed at the end of October. His dismissal spelt a victory for the majority in the Reichstag, since he was overthrown, in fact if not in form, by the Reichstag's want of confidence in him. The Social Democrats were now in control of the political situation, and were determined that the mistake which had been made at the time of Bethmann-Hollweg's fall should not be repeated. The Parties comprising the majority in the Reichstag gave the Emperor to understand that they expected that Michaelis's successor would consult the Reichstag in all the chief questions of domestic and foreign policy. This action on the part of the majority in the Reichstag received the support of the National Liberals, who, under the influence of Stresemann, wished to take a step forward along the path that led to the establishment of parliamentary government in Germany. Apart from certain politico-social demands, the majority demanded the immediate initiation of a Prussian suffrage reform by the introduction of a bill for that purpose into the Prussian Landtag; they further demanded a relaxation of the Press censorship and the removal of the prohibition on public meetings; and, finally, they insisted that in foreign policy the basic principles as they were formulated in the German reply to the Papal Note should be adhered to. The majority in thus acting seemed to take a long step along the road towards the extension of the Reichstag's prerogatives. In a parliamentary state it is not necessary that Ministers should be appointed by Parliament, but only that their ministerial existence should depend upon their enjoying the confidence of Parliament. This was the attitude that was now adopted by the Reichstag majority, which was determined not to accept any Chancellor who did not share their views in all important political questions.

In normal circumstances the success thus achieved by the Reichstag would have been one of quite extraordinary importance. Now again, however, the majority in the Reichstag forgot to take into their calculations the real and dictatorial ruler of Germany, General Ludendorff. The Reichstag made demands on the future Chancellor which he was incapable of fulfilling. The most that any Chancellor could do was to promise that he would try and act in accordance with the majority's desires. For the administration of martial law, control of public meetings, and the censorship of the Press lay in the hands of the Supreme Command and not in those of the civil authorities. As was shown at the time of the reply to the Papal Note, it was the Supreme Command who determined Germany's war aims; and important decisions in matters of foreign policy were not even communicated to the Reichstag. The fate of the Prussian suffrage reform ultimately depended upon the goodwill of the reactionary majority in the Prussian Parliament. The resistance of the Prussian Parliament to the reform could only have been broken by the power which Prussia possessed in the Supreme Command. Thus the assent of Ludendorff was a preliminary condition for the fulfilment of the demands made by the majority in the Reichstag: a fact that was well known to the majority itself, which nevertheless thought it possible that Hindenburg and Ludendorff might be induced to make a 'pact with democracy' and to recognize a parliamentary system in Germany. This opinion was strengthened by the recollection of the action of both Generals in negotiating with the members of the Reichstag over the Peace Resolution. At that time the Supreme Command had at least formally given way on realizing that the majority in the Reichstag insisted on the passing of the Resolution. Was not such a collaboration between the Reichstag and the Supreme Command possible in the future? Field Marshal von Hindenburg himself would certainly not have proved an obstacle to any such co-operation between the Supreme Command and a middle-class democratic government. His conduct during October and November 1918 substantiates this opinion. Ludendorff, however, refused to consent to any further enlargement of the Reichstag's powers. Ludendorff had only used the Reichstag in the summer in order to overthrow Bethmann-Hollweg, and on that occasion had bargained over the Peace Resolution, which, in his eyes, was only a 'scrap of paper'. Ludendorff was not prepared to yield one iota of his own power. He had let Michaelis go simply because his inefficiency prevented his being able to place any reliance on him; but the Chancellor's dismissal did not mean that Ludendorff intended to let slip the reins of government. The Court and the Supreme Command had already chosen a new Chancellor in the person of the Bavarian Prime Minister, the aged Count Hertling.[3]

The Supreme Command's choice of Hertling was extremely clever. Hertling, who for many years had been a member of the Centre in the Reichstag, was a typical conservative Catholic. His great personal influence in the Centre Party was calculated to increase the power of the Right Wing within the Party, to lessen the authority of Erzberger, and to restore the conditions of 1914–16 in the inner relationship between the Parties composing the majority in the Reichstag. For this reason the Centre members of the Reichstag were not specially pleased at Hertling's appointment, and Erzberger, who at once perceived the connexion of events, would greatly have preferred the appointment of Prince Bülow.

As Imperial Chancellor, Hertling certainly moderated the opposition of the Centre to the policy of the Supreme Command, although he did not dissolve the majority in the Reichstag which had passed the Peace Resolution. As a politician Hertling was far superior to his two immediate predecessors. He recognized that it was no longer possible to maintain the pre-War domination of the Prussian military aristocracy, although the last thing he desired was the introduction of parliamentary government, and his ideal was a 'democratic monarchy' after the south German model, i.e. a middle-class constitutional monarchy. If he had been able to give form to his ideal the privileges enjoyed by the landed aristocracy in Prussia would have vanished, and the King of Prussia would have been compelled to co-operate with the middle class after the fashion of the rulers in Bavaria, Würtemberg, and Baden. Hence it was quite logical that Hertling should have been a sincere supporter of a Prussian franchise reform. If the German Empire were turned into a bourgeois monarchy, Hertling was of the opinion that the relation between the Government and the Social Democratic working class would be quite different from the existing one. Hence Hertling welcomed the dissension within the Social Democratic Party, and looked upon it as the Government's duty, supported by the middle class, to endeavour to transform the Majority Socialists into a 'National Labour Party' with whom it would be possible to work in permanent collaboration.

Although the relations between the Government, the middle class, and the less radical elements in the working class would undergo a fundamental change, it would still be possible for the Emperor to retain the reins of government in his own hands. The Government could work with the Reichstag without being dependent upon the Reichstag. It is true that on the day on which he assumed office there was not much prospect of Hertling being able to put any of his ideas into practice for power still rested with the Supreme Command. Hertling, indeed, not only recognized this fact, but reconciled himself to its continuance for the duration of the war. It would in truth have been impossible for him with his aristocratic and Catholic traditions to have adopted any other course, since the Supreme Command could only have been overthrown by a revolution, and since Hertling believed that Ludendorff's plans for a German military victory were capable of realization and was anxious to do nothing that would in any way embarrass the Supreme Command in its task. Moreover, Hertling must have said to himself that the end of the war would automatically bring the dictatorial authority of the Supreme Command to an end. Throughout his Chancellorship Hertling studiously avoided entering into any controversy with Ludendorff and Hindenburg, leaving in their hands the conduct of the war and of foreign policy, and invariably acceding to any special requests made by Ludendorff. Hertling was solely concerned to prevent the occurrence of events in Germany which would in his opinion have a disastrous influence upon the future of the country; as, for example, a dictatorial trampling upon the Reichstag and the suppression of the working classes by the employment of military force. It was to a great extent due to Hertling's influence that the majority in the Reichstag, despite its real powerlessness, was able to maintain its existence at least in a formal and external sense throughout the first six months of 1918.

Hertling entered into negotiations with the majority in the Reichstag and lightly accepted their conditions. Certain important positions had to be filled. Hertling was looked upon as the representative of the Centre in the new Government, although this was only true in a very limited sense, and Hertling never regarded himself during his Chancellorship in this light. Hence the Social Democrats and the Progressives claimed that they should be represented in the Government, and proposed in common the name of the Progressive leader, von Payer. Thereupon Payer was appointed Vice-Chancellor, which meant that he had the right to receive the same information as the Chancellor himself in all important political questions. The Left Wing of the National Liberals also claimed to be represented in the Government, since they had supported the movement towards parliamentary government, and since any reform of the Prussian suffrage could only be passed through the Prussian Landtag with their assistance. As was customary Hertling was at one and the same time Imperial Chancellor and Prussian Prime Minister. He therefore appointed the National Liberal, Friedberg, to the Vice-Presidency of the Prussian Cabinet. The Hertling Government assumed office in November 1917.

A considerable move towards the Left seemed to all outward appearances to have taken place by the appointment of a Government with a member of the Centre as Imperial Chancellor, and representatives of the Progressives and Social Democratic Parties as his deputies. Moreover, in Prussia a member of the Centre had become Prime Minister and a Left Wing National Liberal functioned as his deputy. Such a Government would in 1913 have portended revolution; but in 1917 the balance of power had changed a little since Ludendorff was still in the saddle. An attempt has been made above to describe Hertling's conception of his duties. In Prussia Friedberg did his utmost to achieve a reform of the franchise without meeting with any success until the Armistice. In like manner von Payer, as Vice-Chancellor, utterly failed to fulfil the hopes that had been reposed in him by the majority in the Reichstag. In every decisive issue, such as the strikes in January, the peace negotiations at Brest-Litovsk, and the overthrow of Kühlmann, he bowed before the will of Ludendorff. The Hertling-Payer Government was, in truth, no more than a constitutional cloak thrown over Ludendorff's dictatorship. But the movement that led to parliamentary government in Germany was in a formal sense still in progress, and, viewed from this standpoint, Hertling's Chancellorship forms an interim period between the passing of the Peace Resolution and the Revolution in October 1918.

In fulfilment of his promises Hertling at once laid before the

Prussian Landtag a bill for the introduction of the Imperial suffrage system into Prussia which was read for the first time on December 5 in the Lower House.[4] It was clear from the outset that not only the Conservatives but also the Right Wing National Liberals, and a· Conservative group in the Centre, was opposed to the introduction of equal suffrage. Thereupon all prospect of gaining a majority disappeared. The House went into committee, and the proposed measure was discussed in extraordinary detail and in the most leisurely manner. In truth, the majority opposed to the measure felt themselves protected by Ludendorff, and were therefore in no hurry to bring the debate to an end. It was not until the end of April 1918 that the House again discussed the proposed measures. The Government was powerless in face of these obstructionist tactics, and thus the reform initiated by the majority in the Reichstag came to nothing. Meanwhile the foreign policy of the Empire became the subject of controversy.

In December 1917 peace negotiations between Germany and her allies and Soviet Russia were opened in Brest-Litovsk.[5] The test had come which was to show whether the German Government would hold to the basic principles of the Peace Resolution in the sense in which they had been interpreted by the majority in the Reichstag. As a result of the extraordinary political conditions obtaining in Germany at this time the Peace Delegation presented a hydra-headed appearance. The Imperial Chancellor was represented by the Secretary of State, von Kühlmann, and the Supreme Command by General Hoffmann. Count Czernin represented Austria. The Russians demanded on December 25 that the Entente should be invited to participate in the negotiations on the basis of 'no annexations nor reparations'. The German Delegation gave its assent to this proposal, and the Conference in Brest-Litovsk was adjourned for ten days to await the Entente's reply. There was, indeed, little danger that Lloyd George and Clemenceau would enter into negotiations on this basis. Therefore Kühlmann's acceptance of the Russian proposal was a mere formality. Nevertheless, the Supreme Command and the Pan-Germans were displeased that the formula contained in the Peace Resolution passed by the Reichstag had thus been given effect. On the expiry of the ten days the negotiations were resumed in January with Trotsky as the leader of the Russian Delegation. The instructions that went to the German Delegation were drafted under the supervision of the Supreme Command.

Both Delegations were formally in agreement that the peace should be without annexations and that it should recognize in its conditions the principle of national self-determination. Each Delegation, however, placed its own interpretation upon this basic principle. The Bolsheviks in their desire to revolutionize Europe interpreted the formula to mean that the German troops in occupation of the districts across the German frontier were to evacuate these districts in order that the revolution might spread to Courland, Lithuania, and Poland. The German Government sought to interpret the principle of national self-determination in such a way that vassal States would be created in the three countries occupied by their troops. It was intended that these States should enjoy a certain measure of autonomy, i.e. that their inhabitants would have a certain right of self-determination. Hence the German Delegation refused to assent to the evacuation of the districts occupied by the German troops.

Russia was powerless as against the military might of Germany. The Russian army was rapidly dissolving, and was in any case without arms and ammunition. Nevertheless, Trotsky possessed a terrible weapon—propaganda. The Bolsheviks had insisted that as a new departure from the old secret diplomacy the negotiations in Brest-Litovsk should be carried on in public. Since those days Soviet Russia has accustomed itself to make use of the old methods whenever it seriously desires to achieve its object. At Brest-Litovsk, however, the Bolsheviks were concerned less with the diplomatic negotiations than with carrying on a revolutionary propaganda among the populations of Austria and Germany. Trotsky was well aware of the craving for peace animating the workmen in Germany and Austria-Hungary. He also knew that this desire for peace was clothed in child-like phrases which he knew how to turn to account, while in themselves they were a source of amusement to him.

In a series of brilliant speeches Trotsky demonstrated to the world that Russia's desire for a peace without annexations and reparations was being thwarted by the lust for conquest displayed by the German militarists. Clever as he undoubtedly was, Kühlmann was no match for Trotsky in this verbal duel. Besides, the man in the street was on Trotsky's side in arguing in a logical manner that whoever desired a peace without annexations and reparations must at once be prepared to withdraw his troops from the districts which they occupied beyond his own frontiers. If he were not prepared to do so, then it seemed clear that he must be entertaining plans of conquest. As the German Delegation became more and more entangled in the coils of Trotsky's dialectics, General Hoffmann intervened on January 12 by bluntly informing the Russians that Germany was the victor and that Russia had better take this fact into account in making her proposals.

Trotsky now had the German Delegation at his mercy. The German Government had dropped all pretence of making a peace by mutual consent, and had displayed the mailed fist that had hitherto been concealed beneath a velvet glove. At this juncture the working class in Austria and Germany took a hand in the negotiations. The declaration made by General Hoffmann was in itself no world-shaking event, since what he said was obvious and was looked upon as such by the Russians themselves. The cruellest irony of all was that on the same day on which General Hoffmann threw down the gauntlet in Brest-Litovsk he fell under Ludendorff's gravest displeasure. For Hoffmann did not share in Ludendorff's annexationist plans in regard to Poland and had even attempted to win over the Emperor to his views. Hoffmann's intervention at Brest-Litovsk was nevertheless important in that he rent the veil of illusion which had blinded the eyes of the German nation since July 1917 in regard to the Government's war aims. Since the passing of the Peace Resolution and the publication of the German reply to the Pope, the nation had assumed that the Government, despite all the Pan-German agitation, was in favour of a peace by agreement. At Brest-Litovsk the vague phraseology of the Peace Resolution was put to the test with the result that the Government showed itself to be inspired by the wildest Pan-German ideals. The working class at once gained the impression that the Pan-Germans were still masters of the situation, and that it was useless to agitate for a peace without annexations or reparations.

The moment had now come for the majority in the Reichstag to intervene in defence of its Peace Resolution. The Social Democrats had frequently voiced their disapproval of the way in which the German Delegation conducted the negotiations in Brest-Litovsk. Nevertheless, the Reichstag majority refrained for many reasons from taking any decisive action. In the first place, in the eyes of middle-class Parties, Ludendorff's authority had been strengthened by the military collapse of Russia; a collapse that was credited to the Supreme Command. If the Supreme Command has thus brought the war in the east to a conclusion, why should they not do the same in the west? Moreover, all the declarations in favour of a peace by compromise and without annexations that had been made in Germany had aroused no echo worth speaking of among the Powers composing the Entente. Hence it came about that the middle-class Parties forming the Reichstag majority began to doubt whether their action had been well-founded or not. These doubts crippled the majority's capacity for action.

It was of still greater importance that the Social Democrats, the Centre, and the Progressives were divided among themselves as to the policy to be pursued in the east. All three Parties had approved of Bethmann-Hollweg's policy. For years they had contemplated the creation in Poland, Lithuania, and Courland of new States independent of Russia, and hence they were no less unwilling to permit the Bolsheviks a hand in deciding the fate of these three countries than they had been to permit the Tsar. The majority in the Reichstag continued to hope that they would be able to assert the right to self-determination of the Poles, Letts, and Lithuanians against the annexationist plans of the German militarists. Meanwhile any Russian attempt to interfere in the affairs of the new frontier States must be resisted. Thus the Reichstag could criticize the methods employed by Kühlmann and Hoffmann in Brest-Litovsk in certain aspects, although no criticism could be made in general of the policy followed by Germany in the east. The Supreme Command had thus been able to carry out its plans without any serious interference by the Reichstag.

The great majority of the German people, especially the working class, did not share in the tolerant attitude of the majority Parties in the Reichstag. For three and a half years they had been anxious for peace. Thanks to the Bolsheviks a path now seemed to open that promised to lead to the end of the war. At that very instant the German militarists prevented a conclusion of peace with Russia, which would have been the first step on the road to a general pacification. Moreover, food was becoming scarcer and poorer, and the nation was disappointed in its hopes of reform. For the prospect of any suffrage reform in Prussia had become even more forlorn with the introduction of the Bill for that purpose into the Prussian Landtag. Finally, the Reichstag failed the nation by giving the militarists a free hand. Hence it appeared to the masses that they must attempt to find for themselves a path to peace and to the democratization of Germany. This feeling formed the background to the great strikes in January 1918[6] which were a dress rehearsal for the November Revolution. The conditions among the working class in Berlin were particularly favourable to such an action. The Trade Union workmen had naturally been affected by the discord within the Social Democratic Party. Although the Union Committees were in the hands of the Majority Socialists, a great number of the subordinate officials were in sympathy with the U.S.P.D. in repudiating the *Burgfrieden* which rendered it impossible for the working class to fight for its economic and political rights, and in demanding the resolute pursuance of a peace policy united to the most emphatic repudiation of the Pan-Germans' annexationist schemes. Since the munition workers were for the most part members of the Metalworkers' Union, the attitude of this body was of quite exceptional importance. The chairman of the Berlin Committee was a Majority Socialist named Cohen, while the leader of the opposition inside the Party was the sectional chairman of the Turners' Union, Richard Müller. The Spartacists exercised practically no influence over the hands in the great factories. The leaders of the opposition groups united under the chairmanship of Müller; and it was from their ranks that there subsequently sprang the group leaders of the revolution who were for the most part members of the U.S.P.D. In their dealings with the Party Committee they refused to allow themselves to be dictated to, and sought instead to force the Party leaders to adopt their opinions. The historical importance of these group leaders consist in the fact that they were faithful reporters of the opinions and desires of the factory workers. Hence in the activities of the group leaders are to be found reflected all the hopes and fears of the Berlin working man throughout the war.

The first political strike occurred in Berlin as early as June 28, 1916. On May 1 Karl Liebknecht had been arrested on the Potsdamer Platz, and, although the working class was not in agreement with the tactics of the Spartacists, it was nevertheless animated by a strong personal sympathy for Liebknecht as the fearless champion of peace. On June 28, the day of Liebknecht's court martial, fifty thousand workmen threw down their tools for the day in protest. The organization and conduct of this strike was in the hands of the group leaders. Towards the end of 1916 the discontent among the working men was increased by the passing of a law by which the whole nation was mobilized for war work. The workmen saw in this law a weapon by which the Government sought to deprive them of their liberty of movement, and subject them completely to the arbitrary rule of the factory owners and the military authorities. The appalling state of the food rations gave rise in April 1917 to a strike of two hundred thousand workmen in Berlin that lasted for several days. The workmen only resumed work on receiving a promise from the authorities that in the immediate future their bread, meat, and potato rations would be increased. At the same time strikes occurred in Leipzig, Halle, Brunswick, and Magdeburg, which, in the last three cities at least, were due to purely economic causes. In Leipzig, however, which was a stronghold of the U.S.P.D., the strikers put forward seven demands of a more or less political nature. The demands of the Leipzig workmen were so characteristic that they deserve to be reproduced here in verbatim:

'1. The issue of sufficient supplies of cheap provisions and coal to the populace.
2. A declaration on the part of the Government that it is prepared to conclude peace immediately and that it renounces all acknowledged or secret plans for annexations.
3. Abolition of martial law and the censorship.
4. The immediate removal of all restrictions on the right of public meeting and association.
5. Immediate repeal of the "disgraceful" compulsory labour laws.
6. Immediate liberation of all political prisoners and the abandonment of all political trials.
7. Complete civil liberty and the introduction of a universal, equal, secret and direct suffrage in elections to all public bodies in the Empire, in the federal States, and in the municipalities.'

This was a middle-class programme of reform that followed closely that of the majority of the Reichstag. Point 2 is only another way of expressing the Reichstag's Peace Resolution. Point 7 was in line with the proposed application of the Imperial suffrage system to Prussia. Points 3 and 4 were contained in a somewhat weakened form in the demands made by the majority in the Reichstag at the time of the formation of the Hertling Government. Point 1 is obvious; while point 6 was also in accord with the ideas animating the majority in the Reichstag which, on taking over the reins of Government in October 1918, at once gave orders that Liebknecht should be set at liberty. The sole point in this programme with which the majority in the Reichstag would not have been in agreement was No. 5, which demanded the abolition of the auxiliary service law that the Reichstag deemed a necessity. Hence it is clear that the political desires of the German working class, even including the most radical elements, could have been satisfied by a solution along the lines of that proposed by the majority in the Reichstag. There is not a trace of Socialism in the Leipzig demands, and the only difference was that the majority in the Reichstag refused to resort to extra-parliamentary action to achieve their object. The U.S.P.D. workmen, on the other hand, were prepared in certain circumstances to support this programme by strikes and demonstrations. Although the U.S.P.D. leaders did not incite their supporters to any such action, they knew how to make use of the spontaneous actions undertaken by the masses of the workmen. Thus in the U.S.P.D. in Berlin a gulf was opened between the cautious Party leaders and the revolutionary group leaders. Among the U.S.P.D. members of the Reichstag Ledebour was most in sympathy with these revolutionary group leaders.

The strikes in April 1917 were followed in July by the Reichstag's Peace Resolution. The Michaelis Government fell in the autumn, and its place was taken by the semi-parliamentary Hertling Government which in December introduced a Bill for the reform of the suffrage into the Prussian Landtag. These events were a cause of satisfaction to the working class, who saw in them steps along the road towards the realization of their own plans. Hence their disappointment was all the greater at the result of the negotiations at Brest-Litovsk in January, for the Bolshevik Revolution in 1917 had made a far greater impression on the German working class than had the earlier bourgeois revolution. Russia had now a Socialist instead of a bourgeois Government. Moreover, the Kerensky Government had carried on the war, whereas the Bolsheviks were the first not only to speak of peace but actually to achieve it. The intense longing for peace animating the German and Austrian working class was transformed into an ardent sympathy with the Bolsheviks in the course of their negotiations with the German militarists. Indeed, the working class came to look upon it as their duty to support the Russians as against General Hoffmann. Thus the course of events in Brest-Litovsk resulted at first in a dangerous outbreak of strikes in Austria and Hungary. Hundreds of thousands of workmen threw down their tools in Vienna, Budapest, and other industrial centres. It even seemed that in doing so they enjoyed the sympathy of Court circles in Vienna who could now appeal in support of their apparently 'pacifist' policy to the will of the masses. The strike movement was directed above all against General Hoffmann and the German Supreme Command, in that the Austrian workmen demanded that peace with Russia should not be rendered impossible through the demands of German annexationists. The Austrian Government finally induced the strikers to resume work by proclaiming its complete agreement with the working-class peace programme and by promising the fulfilment of all the strikers' demands.

The news of the success of the strikers in Austria swiftly travelled all over Germany, despite the military censorship, and stiffened the backs of the German workmen. The revolutionary group leaders in Berlin demanded in the middle of January 1918 that the leaders of the U.S.P.D. should call out the workers. The leaders were unwilling to do this, since it was contrary to the tactics they had hitherto pursued, but the U.S.P.D. members of the Reichstag published an appeal to the working class as follows:

'There is no time to lose. A new danger threatens our nation and humanity at large. After all the sufferings and dangers of the past years, we can only be saved by a peace without annexations and reparations, and of which the basic principle is the right to self-determination of all peoples. The hour has come in which you must raise your voices on behalf of such a peace. It is now your turn to speak.'

It was for the workers themselves to decide as to whether and in what form they would 'raise their voices' in favour of peace. The Reichstag would then have been able to take control of the movement by means of a corresponding parliamentary action, since in January 1918 the Berlin workmen were still in agreement with the majority Parties in the Reichstag in the demands which they put forward. It was only because the majority lacked initiative that the masses took matters into their own hands and by so doing enhanced the importance of the U.S.P.D. For the Spartacists enjoyed practically no support among the populace.

A meeting of the Turners' Union was held on January 27 in Berlin to which all the principal industries sent representatives. On the proposal of Richard Müller the meeting unanimously resolved to call a general strike for the following day. On January 28, therefore, four hundred thousand workmen in Berlin and the outlying districts laid down their tools; while on the same day four hundred delegates, representative of all the industrial unions in Berlin, met as a Berlin Workmen's Council in the Trades Union building in order to formulate the strikers' demands. These demands were quite obviously based on the Leipzig demands of the previous year. The strikers demanded above all else a speedy conclusion of peace without annexations, and a radical democratization of the whole governmental system in Germany. They further demanded the abolition of martial law and the auxiliary services law in addition to a political amnesty and improved rationing. Only point 2 of their demands contained anything new: 'The collaboration of workers' representatives from all countries in the peace negotiations.' Such a demand was, in truth, neither revolutionary nor unreasonable, seeing that, apart from revolutionary Russia, representatives of Labour sat in the War Cabinets in England, France, and Belgium, and would therefore as a matter of course participate in the coming peace negotiations.

The absence of any Socialist demands from the Berlin strikers' programme of January 1918 is again specially worthy of emphasis. Thus, for example, nobody thought for a moment of raising the vast question of property, notwithstanding the fact that it would only have been a small step forward on the path to socialization to have included in this programme a demand for the nationalization of war industries, or indeed a Labour control over industry. The leaders of the U.S.P.D., as well as the revolutionary group leaders, had indeed Socialist aims that went far beyond the strikers' programme. Nevertheless, they contented themselves with presenting only those demands with which the mass of the working class was in sympathy. The Berlin workman wanted a reasonable peace, bread, and a middle-class democratic Government that would imply the overthrow of the military and Junker domination in Germany. Socialist demands inspired by class interests lay far beyond their horizon, and it was only the small group of the Spartacists who wished a more revolutionary character to be given to the course of events. A republic was in January 1918 outside the realm of practical politics—not to mention a Bolshevization of Germany.

The fact that the Delegates' Conference at the time of the January strike designated itself as a Workmen's Council must not be misinterpreted to mean that the delegates were inspired by a desire to arrogate to themselves a sort of governmental authority. This Workmen's Council was no more than the mouthpiece of the strikers; it took the place of the Trades Unions, and not of the Reichstag. It is the business of the Trades Unions in countries with a long-established and highly organized Trade Union system to direct the economic activities of the workmen, and especially strikes. In Tsarist Russia, however, Socialist Trade Unions were illegal, and consequently their place was taken in the mass-movements of the day by delegates from the individual industries. Thus the Workers' Councils in Russia were the embodiment of the entire proletariate of a city or of an industrial district. The co-operation between these Workers' Councils and the representatives of the mutinous soldiery resulted in the creation of that typical organization of the Russian revolution—the Workers' and Soldiers' Councils. In Germany, on the contrary, the Trade Unions as a result of their attitude towards the *Burgfrieden* had automatically excluded themselves from the leadership of a strike. Thus the German workmen created for themselves on the Russian model an organization composed of delegates from the various industries to take the place of the Trade Unions—a Workers' Council. It was by no means necessary that these Workmen's Councils should be inspired by Bolshevik or Spartacist ideas. Hence in 1918 the Workmen's Councils in Germany were nothing more than the expression of a mass movement, and bore no resemblance whatever to a Soviet.

The strike meeting of January 28 elected a strike committee composed of eleven members of the Workmen's Council, and invited the committee of the U.S.P.D. to send three representatives to take part in the deliberations of the strike committee. A similar invitation, notwithstanding the opposition displayed by a part of the meeting, was also dispatched to the Majority Socialists. Both Socialist Parties accepted the invitations and sent their representatives to the meetings of the strike committee. The U.S.P.D. was represented by Ledebour, Dittmann, and Haase, the S.P.D. by Ebert, Scheidemann, and Braun. A remarkable degree of unanimity existed among the members of the committee as to what could be achieved by the strike and as to its objects. A general strike of a political nature can never last for more than a few days, for it either develops into an open warfare for political power that ends in victory or defeat, or it collapses through the strikers' want of money or food. There was no intention, even on the part of the revolutionary group leaders, to extend the strike into a political life and death struggle, since it was out of the question that in view of the strength of military discipline and the authority of the Supreme Command the troops would take the side of the strikers. It is true that had the Reichstag been in session, and had the majority proclaimed publicly its sympathy with the strikers, another political solution might have been possible. Of this, however, there was no likelihood at the time. Hence, the only possibility open to the strike leaders was to carry on the strike for a few days, to give it as far as possible the character of a mighty demonstration in support of their objects, and then to extract as many concessions as possible through negotiation with the Government. Such was the policy of the revolutionary group leaders, who at that time never contemplated a revolution in Germany, as well as of the U.S.P.D.

Although the S.P.D. disapproved in principle of strikes in time of war, it was in agreement with the views of the U.S.P.D. and the revolutionary group leaders. Moreover, as the strike had occurred, as the strikers were to a large extent members of the S.P.D., and as their aims were in the main also those of the S.P.D., it would have been mere pettiness on the S.P.D.'s part to have refused to share in the responsibility for the strike. The defence of Germany was not materially affected by a strike of a few days' duration, and the Supreme Command, notwithstanding the strike, was able to embark on its offensive in March with enormous reserves of ammunition. The refusal on the part of the S.P.D. could hardly have been looked upon by the strikers as a betrayal of their cause, for none of the strike leaders intended it to last for more than a couple of days, nor that it should have any other character than that of a peaceful demonstration.

The strikers' programme revealed their ideological sympathy with the majority in the Reichstag, which was given practical expression by the participation of Ebert and Scheidemann in the deliberations of the strike committee. The Spartacists took a completely different view of the situation. They demanded that the strike should be given a revolutionary character, and their pamphlets warned the workers against the participation of the S.P.D. leaders in the conduct of the strike. 'Take care that Trade Union leaders, Government Socialists, and other 'see-it-through' men are in no circumstances elected among your representatives. Down with the Workmen's Councils! These jobbers and voluntary agents of a Government that is the deadly enemy of great strikes have nothing in common with the fighting and working man.' If the strike had been conducted by the Spartacists and U.S.P.D. alone, and with a deliberate exclusion of the S.P.D., it would have taken on a completely different character. It would in that case have become a proletarian class action of a Socialist nature instead of a pacifist demonstration with middle-class democratic aims.

The Spartacists failed to secure the adoption of their views. It was the S.P.D. and not the Spartacists who were represented on the strike committee. Thus the great issues of the Revolution in November had already been brought to the surface in January by the general strike.

On January 29 the strikers in Greater Berlin increased to half a million, while at the same time the strike extended to Kiel, Hamburg, Leipzig, Brunswick, Cologne, Breslau, Munich, Nuremberg, Mannheim, Magdeburg, Halle, Bochum, Dortmund, and other towns. The U.S.P.D. estimated the total number of men on strike at a million—certainly a conservative estimate. The strike was in truth a tremendous mass protest against the military dictatorship and against Ludendorff himself. If Germany had at that time been governed by a true statesman, he would have recognized that the possessors of power were seated on a powder magazine. Who, for example, would have been found to guarantee that the soldiers composing the reserve armies did not sympathize with the million strikers? How was it possible to imagine that such a movement could be suppressed in the middle of a war by a simple application of military discipline? And, even if the Government had proved successful in suppressing the movement for the moment, what of the future? The strike in January demonstrated beyond all question that the German governmental system was doomed. The unconstitutional military dictatorship which Ludendorff had now been wielding for a year and a half was opposed at the very least by the entire working class in Germany.

The Supreme Command recognized that its existence was at stake. Ludendorff brushed aside the civil Government and himself took over the task of fighting the strikers. His aim was a ruthless suppression of the strike without conceding an iota of their demands to the strikers. The General Commanding the Berlin District acted in accordance with Ludendorff's wishes in proclaiming on January 31 a state of siege and in establishing special court martials. The publication of *Vorwärts* was forbidden and all meetings of the strikers were dispersed by the police. On seeking to address the strikers at a meeting in the Treptower Park, Dittmann, an S.P.D. member of the Reichstag, was arrested and subsequently condemned by court martial to five years' confinement in a fortress. In obedience to the Supreme Command the Government refused to negotiate with the strikers and called for their unconditional submission. Hundreds of strikers were arrested, and thousands of workmen on the Army reserve ordered to join their regiments. Finally, the General Commanding the Berlin District announced that he had placed seven of the great industrial concerns, including Borsig and the A.E.G. in Henningsdorf, under military control. The workmen employed in these factories were ordered to resume work at seven o'clock in the morning of February 4. Disobedience would meet with severe punishment in accordance with the regulations of martial law. Such workmen as were on the army reserve received their mobilization papers and were ordered to resume work immediately as soldiers.

On February 3 the revolutionary group leaders called off the strike in Berlin as there seemed no hope of its accomplishing its purpose. Meanwhile the strikers in the rest of the country had also gone back to work. For the time being the victory was with Ludendorff. Among the conquered were not only the working class, but also the majority in the Reichstag, for the strongest weapon in the hands of the majority in the Reichstag had hitherto been the possibility of appealing to the support of the Social Democratic working class. The S.P.D. and the U.S.P.D. had organized the strike jointly, and had achieved nothing. Thus the authority of the majority in the Reichstag had received a severe blow, and the supporters of a victorious peace had gained the upper hand. Ludendorff had a free hand both in the east and the west. He resolved to make full use of his political triumph. He demanded that the Imperial Chancellor should formally rescind the Peace Resolutions. As far as foreign politics were concerned that would not have mattered, but within the country it would have been tantamount to setting up a military and Junker domination in the eyes of the majority of the nation. It would have either brought about a cleft within the Parties composing the majority in the Reichstag or an open conflict with the Reichstag and its supersession by the military dictatorship.

Count Hertling at least prevented this latter eventuality. The Peace Resolution remained, although only on paper, and this held the majority in the Reichstag together. It survived the critical first six months of 1918, though not always very heroically, and sometimes only by playing 'possum' as at the treaty of Brest-Litovsk and the fall of Kühlmann.

The January strike was a sound warning to the German working class. It cannot be said that the Labour programme was radicalized by its failure and the lack of consideration shown by the authorities ; but neither did the Labour Party permit itself to be dissuaded from its convictions. The German proletariate held unanimously to the watchwords of peace and democracy. Meanwhile, after the experiences of January, the masses no longer believed in the goodwill of the Reichstag to extricate them from the war and the military dictatorship. They relied instead on their own power, and hoped for a better opportunity than had been afforded them in January 1918.

Thus there were in Germany in 1917 and 1918 enormous masses of the nation whose political aims were identical with those of the majority of the Reichstag, but whose tactics were different and who gradually accustomed themselves to the idea of direct opposition to the military dictatorship. The first act of this direct mass opposition was the naval rebellion in 1917, the second act was the strike in January 1918, and the third act was the Revolution in November. When the masses moved towards the political goals of the majority in the Reichstag, the U.S.P.D. joined them. The Spartacists, on the other hand, did not sympathize with the aims and theories of the national movement of 1917 and 1918. The national movement, which had identical aims to those of the majority in the Reichstag, created its own executives such as the food commissions in the navy in 1917, which had grown to have a political significance, and the Workers' Councils in January 1918 and the Workers' and Soldiers' Councils in November 1918.

The S.P.D., being a powerful factor both in the majority in the Reichstag and in industry, acted as the link between the majority in the Reichstag and the national movement. This double role of the S.P.D. explains to some extent why, in spite of dissensions and the weakness of its political programme, its power grew as the national movement conquered the military dictatorship. The progress of the German Revolution can only be understood if this curious parallelism is realized. It was a middle-class revolution won by Labour fighting against Feudalism.

When the crisis of the general strike had been surmounted, the Supreme Command was able to settle matters in the east according to its own ideas. General Ludendorff planned a Napoleonic policy by which the sphere of German power was to extend as far as Finland and the Caucasus. When the general strike failed in Germany, the Bolsheviks were obliged to yield. Trotsky declared the war to be at an end without making any special peace treaty.

The Supreme Command was not satisfied with this, and the new German advance on Livonia, Esthonia, and the Ukraine followed in February. On March 3 Russia was obliged to agree to the conditions of peace dictated by Germany.

On March 22 the Reichstag approved the Treaty of Brest-Litovsk. The S.P.D. announced by the mouth of Scheidemann that the treaty in question was not a peace by understanding but was the outcome of a German policy of conquest; that the S.P.D. demanded the real democratic right of self-determination for Poland, Lithuania, and Courland; and that the S.P.D. refused to vote in the division over the peace treaty. In the existing circumstances a serious opposition by the majority in the Reichstag to the eastern policy of the Supreme Command was impossible.

Ludendorff kept a garrison in the Baltic States. He sent an expeditionary force to Finland to help the middle-class Finnish Government against the Bolsheviks. In Poland the Austro-Polish solution was to be replaced by German supremacy. In the Ukraine the Supreme Command tried the experiment of ruling by a local hetman who had no power beyond the range of the German bayonets. Ludendorff dealt with Russia as Napoleon I had dealt with Germany after 1807, or as Caesar had dealt with Gaul. Germany undertook these enormous conquests in the east in spite of the fact that she was still waging war in the west with America, England, and France. Ludendorff's eastern policy does not even deserve to be made the subject of serious political criticism.

From a military point of view the occupation of Rumania was the only part of the whole eastern policy which was justified during the war. For it was impossible for Germany to carry on the war without Rumanian petrol for her aircraft, submarines, mechanical transport, &c. The safeguarding of Rumania, with whom peace had also been concluded by the treaty of Brest-Litovsk, would nevertheless not have demanded more than a fraction of the troops which remained in the east in 1918. On March 21, 1918, when the great offensive began in the west, more than a million German soldiers still remained in the east.[7] They consisted, indeed, predominantly of older men—those under 35 years of age having been mainly transferred to the Western Front. The French army, however, also contained a good many older men. If Ludendorff had had even half these troops in the west in March, this half million men might have occupied quiet sectors and thus have released other divisions for the offensive. At the end of March and the beginning of April a decisive German victory in the west hung by a thread.

If Ludendorff had had only twenty of the divisions which he was using for his eastern campaign, he would probably have been victorious. Thus the mistaken eastern policy, the desire to 'liberate' or to conquer countries which had formed part of the Tsarist Empire, was the fatal lodestar of the German Great General Staff from 1915 to 1918.

When in the course of the spring and summer the German losses reached fantastic figures, Ludendorff had after all to transfer his Eastern troops. On October 1, 1918, only half a million German soldiers remained in the east. The same number had gradually been transferred to the west. But they came little by little and too late. They were needed during the first battles of the offensive which were actually decisive. While Ludendorff the Soldier was collecting every man for the decisive battle, Ludendorff the Politician was wasting an army a million strong in the east.

An attempt was made even after the conclusion of peace to justify the existence of the large German army in the east on account of the Bolshevik danger and the necessity for obtaining foodstuffs from the Ukraine. Neither argument is valid. At that time Lenin was very anxious for peace. He would indeed have been glad to see a German proletarian revolution, but in 1918 he would never have made a military attack on Germany. The attempt to obtain foodstuffs from the Ukraine by military force and against the will of the population failed utterly. The comparatively small quantity that the Ukraine delivered in 1918 went almost entirely to Austria, and therefore the Austrian troops should have been used for requisitioning instead of German. To imperil the success of the offensive on the Western Front for the sake of getting a number of horses and oxen from the Ukraine was criminal. The usual method of obtaining goods from a friendly country, especially one with whom peace has been made, is by trade. By this means and by making use of the local commercial customs, Germany and Austria would have got far more foodstuffs from the Ukraine than by the use of troops and machine-guns.

In reality the million German soldiers had to remain in the East in order to enforce the victor's peace. The political and economic conditions which the Supreme Command imposed upon the eastern nations were so insupportable that this political system could only be maintained by the ruthless application of force.

Thus the decisive mistake of the German offensive in the west was once again of a political nature and was made before ever the first shot was fired.

The number of men for whom provisions had to be supplied on the Western Front on March 21, 1918, was over three and a half millions in one hundred and ninety-two divisions.[8] After four years of war and blockade the German army in the west was twice as large as in 1914. All kinds of supplies were provided in profusion by German industry—in itself an enormous military and organizing achievement. The strength of the Entente army in the west was at that time approximately equal to that of the German army. The Entente had about one hundred and seventy divisions; but the fighting strength of an Entente division was usually somewhat greater than that of a German division. The English had about 1,800,000 men in the field, and there was an equal number of French, Belgians, and Portuguese. In March 1918 there were only about 300,000 American troops in France, and only one fully trained division; the others were still in training. If the German army had been able to fight the decisive battle in the spring, the main body of Americans would have come too late.

As has been remarked above, it was not enough that the German troops beat the enemy: the German army, in order to achieve its goal, must win a decisive victory which would annihilate the Entente armies. And this would only have been possible against an enemy which was in every respect as strong and well equipped as themselves by an overwhelming superiority in leadership. Seven million soldiers were crowded in a small space in northern France and Flanders. Hence great strategical movements were impossible. The attacker must depend upon surprise to achieve his object. His endeavour must be to break through a sector of the enemy front by a surprise offensive, thus forcing the enemy armies to retreat along the whole front, and thereby to gain terrain on which to fight a decisive action.

General Ludendorff chose as the sector to be attacked that which promised the most rapid result—the southern sector of the English Front at the point where the French and English lines met. Roughly speaking, the English Front at that time ran north and south, from Flanders to just north of Paris, while the French ran east and west from north of Paris to Verdun and thence to Alsace-Lorraine. Thus—in a manner of speaking—a vertical English beam had been set across a horizontal French beam. If the lower extremity of the English beam could be cut off, the remainder of the beam would be left floating in the air. Ludendorff could then have surrounded the English armies on all sides, driven them towards the Channel, and forced them to leave France with tremendous losses. The French alone would have been powerless in face of Germany's superiority in men and munitions. The achievement of such a victory depended solely on the success of one such operation against the enemy. The occupation of isolated fortified places such as Ypres, Amiens or Verdun was quite unimportant by comparison.

The German attack on the Arras–Cambrai–St. Quentin–La Fère Front began on March 21. In the southern sector the German offensive met with an immediate success. The southernmost sector of the English Front was overrun, and the adjoining French troops were involved in the fate of their English allies. The Entente army had to retreat hastily from this sector. In a very few days the German troops advanced sixty kilometres. The war had thus once more become the war of movement that it had been in 1914. But the Entente reserves, which were rushed up from all sides, brought the German advance to a standstill by the end of the month. The attempt to drive back the northern sector of the English Front from the seacoast to Arras had not succeeded. The troops on the southern continuation of the English Front were now driven back to Amiens where they were able to connect up again with the French.

The German tactical victory in the March offensive is among the greatest in the history of war. The English losses in prisoners alone amounted to ninety thousand men. According to the English Commander-in-Chief, Earl Haig, the Germans only needed a few cavalry divisions on that critical day at the end of March to have made the breach in the enemy line so wide that a general retreat would have been inevitable. On that very day three German cavalry divisions were idling away their time in the Ukraine. Ludendorff had been obliged to use ninety German divisions in this great battle, and they suffered enormous losses.

In order to make the most of the blow dealt to the English army Ludendorff began a fresh offensive in Flanders on April 9. So great had been the German losses in March, however, that only thirty-six German divisions could be put into the field for this offensive. Yet it also proved successful. The English were obliged to evacuate a number of important positions with heavy losses.

Moreover, the English had exhausted their reserves to such an extent that a number of French divisions had to be rushed up to Flanders in order to prevent an utter collapse. Attempts have been made to prove that tactical errors were made by the Supreme Command in the March and April offensives. But, viewed objectively, all Ludendorff's expedients were correct. A decisive victory had not indeed been won. In spite of the dent that had been made in it the Entente Front still held out. Communication between the French and English had not been cut. Indeed, under the impression made by Germany's victory, Lloyd George, ignoring national sensibilities, subordinated the English army to the French High Command. General Foch became the Generalissimo of the Entente armies on the Western Front.

The military situation would nevertheless have been in every way satisfactory for Germany if Ludendorff had only had to deal with the English and the French armies. If the Americans had not been in France, the offensives in March and April would have definitely secured the German superiority on land. Ludendorff now planned to deliver a blow at the French that should exhaust their reserves, after which he proposed to engage the English in a third, and this time decisive, battle. Much time was necessarily lost owing to the immense technical difficulties which had to be surmounted in preparing for this offensive. The attack on the French armies north of the Aisne did not begin until May 27. The French were forced to retreat across the Aisne, and were then pursued as far as the Marne. Once again the German troops were very near to winning a decisive victory, that is to say, to making a definite breach in the enemy line. But it was impossible to achieve a decision with forty-one divisions, which were all that were available for this offensive, and the battle dragged on into June.

In July Ludendorff planned a further attack on the French at Rheims, and intended attacking the English directly afterwards. The Supreme Command realized very clearly that every delay in forcing a decision increased the danger from the Americans. In July 1918 the number of American soldiers in France rose to 1,200,000. Ludendorff had certainly not reckoned on so many Americans, and was therefore still hoping for a victorious end to the German offensive in the summer.

After the collapse of the January strike, after the victorious peace in the east, and after the great successes against the English and the French, Ludendorff's position seemed invincible in domestic politics. The 'victorious peace' Party and the Fatherland Party held all the trumps. The majority in the Reichstag existed only in name. It amused itself with polemics against the Pan-Germans, and from time to time Vice-Chancellor von Payer made a speech against the Conservatives. But the majority was unable to carry any of its ideas into effect as was most clearly shown in the fate of the Prussian electoral reform.

The Government suffrage scheme had been upset in its most important point by the Commission which had been occupied all through the winter with Hertling's proposal.[9] The majority in the committee of the Landtag agreed, indeed, to universal, direct, and secret voting, but refused to agree to equal suffrage. A suggestion was instead made of plural votes, dependent on age, number of grown-up children, and also on property, income, independent enterprise, education, and public service. The workers could, generally speaking, only hope for supplementary votes on the ground of age and number of children. The remaining plural votes could benefit hardly any except the middle class and the farmers. Politically, it was a matter of indifference whether the working class was shut out of the polling booths for the Prussian Landtag by being excluded from the second estate or by being refused plural votes.

Hertling announced that after such an alteration the proposal could no longer be accepted by the Government. But the party in the Lower House which was opposed to the reform knew that Ludendorff was on its side; a fact which at that time was more important than the wishes of the Imperial Chancellor. The proposal for equal suffrage was defeated by two hundred and thirty-five to one hundred and eighty-three votes. The majority consisted of Conservatives, apart from four members of the 'Independent Conservative Party', who had the discernment to support the motion. Among the four were two members of the present Reichstag—von Kardorff and Professor Bredt. Besides those already mentioned, the Right Wing of the National Liberals and the openly conservative group in the Centre voted against equal suffrage. Finally, unequal suffrage was adopted on the recommendation contained in the report of the Commission.

The Landtag at that time was under the influence of the German victory over the English in March and April. The landed proprietors and the industrialists were convinced that the Supreme Command would win a victorious peace by force of arms. In that case the ruling classes in Germany would keep power in their own hands, and it would be unnecessary for them to make any concessions. This calculation was at least as narrow-minded as it was mistaken. The old Prussian system of government had been overthrown by the war. If the war had ended favourably for Germany, the movement would have been all the more definitely towards the Left. The millions of men from the working class who had fought in the war would also have won the constitutional conditions which they considered necessary. The power of the Supreme Command would have ended with the conclusion of peace, and the disrupted Imperial authority could never have been resurrected. Middle-class democracy as well as the Socialist movement in Germany would have been far less hindered in its development if it had not been burdened with the Treaty of Versailles and reparations. In the spring of 1918, however, the majority in the Prussian Landtag could not realize that its day was done.

In June the Landtag once again altered the suffrage proposal. Each voter was to be allowed only one supplementary vote. They were first to be given to all men over 50 years of age, and then to all who were occupied in independent undertakings, who were officials, or employees or workmen in high positions. This was the form in which the law was eventually adopted by the Lower House on July 4. At a first glance this appears to be a considerable concession in the direction of equal suffrage. Actually, a Prussian Lower House elected on this system would have hardly differed from the old three-estates parliament. For under the three-estates system the decisive voice lay not with the great landed proprietors and industrial magnates, who were only a part of the first estate, but with the rural and urban middle class of the second estate. If the first and second estate voted together, the workmen of the third estate were powerless.

According to the law of July 1918 the supplementary votes on account of age would have fallen pretty equally to the working and middle classes. Thus the results would have been unaltered. Besides the farmers, manual labourers, shopkeepers and higher employees, as well as employers under 50 years of age, would also have had a second vote. These extra votes were not given to the proletariate of corresponding age. Owing to the vast numerical strength of the voters belonging to the middle-class categories the Labour candidates would be placed in a hopeless minority in at least ninety per cent. of the electorates as a result of the plural voting system. If the Protestant farmers cast their votes with the Conservatives as in pre-War days, and if the division into electorates continued to favour agrarian interests, the representatives of the old Prussia had nothing to fear from the new suffrage system. A suggestion to give all who had fought in the war the supplementary vote was rejected by two hundred and fifty-one votes to one hundred and forty-seven, for the acceptance of this proposal would have practically meant equal suffrage, and the majority in the Landtag was not sentimental. It is significant that such treatment of unpropertied front-line soldiers was possible in the fourth year of the war and at the time of the great offensive in the west. When the Lower House refused the supplementary vote to the soldiers, Ludendorff had just pushed back the French as far as the Marne and fresh victories were expected. According to the Prussian Constitution the suffrage law after having passed the Lower House had to go to the Upper House.

When the Upper House began to consider the suffrage reform in September after their summer recess, the military collapse of Germany was public knowledge. Ludendorff now suddenly declared himself in favour of equal suffrage. A suggestion from the Supreme Command, which was conveyed to the Upper House by various Ministers, resulted in that body adopting equal suffrage. On October 15 the Conservatives, National Liberals, and the Centre unanimously declared for equal suffrage. They had, however, no opportunity of putting their twelfth-hour enthusiasm for reform into action. Before the Prussian Lower House was able to revise its July decision it had been swept away by the Revolution of November 9.

The somewhat farcical conclusion to the suffrage dispute in Prussia shows clearly two things. First that the real power lay with General Ludendorff. An indication from the Supreme Command to the Conservatives and National Liberals that equal suffrage in Prussia was necessary on military and nationalist grounds would have had the same result in 1917 as it did in October 1918. Second, it showed that the majority in the Lower House was not specially concerned with the actual principle of suffrage but was simply following an opportunist policy according to the military situation. As long as Ludendorff's offensive on the Western Front was successful they were in favour of plural voting. When the offensive collapsed the same men were suddenly unanimous for equal suffrage. The organic connexion between the movement for a victorious peace, Ludendorff's authority and the defence of the privileges of the old Prussian ruling classes, is obvious.

Bismarck had always emphasized the danger of judging political measures by their working under the most favourable conditions. What kind of statesmanship was it that created a suffrage system which could only be maintained by great military victories? Yet this is how the Prussian Lower House acted in July 1918. It will be argued, on the other hand, that Bismarck himself often sharply criticized the three-estates suffrage system, although he never actually altered it. During the eighties Bismarck indeed went so far as to play off the Prussian three-estates Parliament against the inimical Reichstag on several occasions. In order, however, to avoid making concessions in the domestic policy of Prussia, Bismarck after 1871 never again engaged in a war. The fight which the greater part of the Prussian nobility and Prussian industrialists waged against equal suffrage during the fourth year of the World War is almost inconceivable to posterity. It becomes more comprehensible if one can put oneself in the place of those classes who knew that they stood on the edge of an abyss, but who thought that they might escape disaster by a rigid fixity of purpose.

While Ludendorff was at the height of his power he had removed the only German statesman who might have been dangerous to him—the Secretary of State, von Kühlmann.[10] The history of the events leading up to von Kühlmann's fall is not uninteresting. The representative of the Supreme Command at the Foreign Office was at that time Colonel von Haeften who enjoyed Ludendorff's complete confidence. At the beginning of June Haeften submitted to General Ludendorff a memorandum for a German 'political offensive' which was expected to supplement and assist the military offensive. Haeften's intention was to strengthen the peace party under Lansdowne in England by a well-calculated move on the part of Germany; for even the most ardent supporter of the Supreme Command and the peace by conquest must have realized that, even if the military offensive was completely successful, the war against England's sea-power could only end in a compromise. Ludendorff himself never questioned this fact, but he hoped to be able to arrange the compromise so that Germany was left in control of Belgium.

Haeften wished a number of influential and independent men to express their opinion on the subject of peace. They were to emphasize that Germany's peace aims were most moderate and that she was interested in upholding universal ideals such as the protection of Labour and the freedom of the seas. Haeften further proposed to make the Treaty of Brest-Litovsk palatable to the English by suggesting that Germany was obliged to defend the interests of Europe against Bolshevism. That was at least an attempt to create a German political ideal. For it was obvious that any one who wished to fit the Supreme Command's far-reaching eastern plans into any kind of system must at least try to obtain England's assent to Germany's eastern policy. The formula which was given for such a German-English compromise was a speculative united front against Bolshevism. Against this it can be urged that since the entrance of America into the war England was reckoning on the complete defeat of Germany and was not likely to agree to any compromise. Besides, it would have been a most degrading role for Germany to play the part of jailor to the Baltic peoples on behalf of the English.

Haeften laid particular stress on the idea that the procedure which he advocated was to seem to be entirely independent of the German Government and the spontaneous utterance of influential but non-official Germans. Haeften wished to give the impression that a patriotic 'realpolitik' peace party, the German counterpart of Lansdowne's group, was bringing pressure to bear on the German Government. Haeften's plan contained nothing contrary to Ludendorff's ideas. Hence General Ludendorff accepted the suggestion willingly, and wrote to the Imperial Chancellor recommending him to begin a political offensive along the lines of Haeften's scheme. When Kühlmann heard of this, he interpreted the situation quite wrongly. It appeared to him that Ludendorff had altered his opinion fundamentally, that he no longer believed in a decisive victory on the Western Front, and that the Supreme Command was now preparing to seek a peace of understanding by political means. So Kühlmann decided to take the bull by the horns, and to make public the change of front simply and openly in a speech in the Reichstag.

Kühlmann's much debated speech in the Reichstag on June 24 was exactly contrary to the terms of Haeften's memorandum, in which great stress was laid upon the necessity for keeping the Government out of the peace movement. As a matter of fact, Kühlmann's speech contained nothing that was not obvious. He emphasized that in order to achieve peace an understanding must be sought between Germany and the Entente. An absolute end to the war by purely military means and without any diplomatic negotiations could hardly be expected. If Kühlmann's speech is dissociated from the true situation, it consists purely of truisms. The Secretary of State, however, was speaking after the great victory of the Marne, and at a time when every one expected another and still greater German advance. Thus Kühlmann's speech was bound to give the impression publicly that neither the German Government nor the Supreme Command any longer believed in victory in the west, and were therefore obliged to seek to end the war by diplomatic means.

It was thus that Kühlmann judged the situation, and, as the developments of the next few months proved, he was right. But neither the Imperial Chancellor nor the Supreme Command had ever commissioned him to speak in this sense. Kühlmann's speech was, on the contrary, an indirect call to the majority in the Reichstag to return to the Peace Resolution and to take the initiative once more. The Secretary of State's speech came as a political bombshell. Count Westarp protested in the name of the Conservatives in the Reichstag against Kühlmann's attitude. The majority in the Reichstag was still sufficiently cowed not to dare to stand up openly for Kühlmann. The Secretary of State had, indeed, judged the military situation correctly, but had assumed the existence of dissensions among the supporters of a victorious peace which did not actually exist. Ludendorff saw a challenge in Kühlmann's speech. The Supreme Command declared that it could no longer work with Kühlmann. On July 1 a conference was held at Spa by the Imperial Chancellor, Hindenburg, and Ludendorff to decide Kühlmann's fate. Fortunately the brief minutes of this meeting are extant—an astounding document.

Hertling was obliged to apologize for the Secretary of State to the Generals like a 'teacher excusing a pupil's bad essay to the school inspector' (Bredt). Amongst other things Hertling said: 'Circumstances contributed towards the unfortunate impression made by the Secretary of State's speech—such as fatigue and lack of time for preparation owing to a previous committee meeting; no time for luncheon, and hence exhausted tone of voice and the impression that Kühlmann was losing the thread in the latter part of his speech, since there would have been nothing to complain of in the first part.' Among other remarks Hindenburg said: 'The Secretary of State must find time to prepare speeches as important as this one. He is backed by the *Frankfurter Zeitung* and the

Berliner Tageblatt. An impression is given that there is a conflict between Kühlmann and the majority of the Reichstag on the one hand and the Imperial Chancellor on the other.' Moreover, the apparent similarity between Kühlmann's utterances and George Bernhard's articles in the *Vossische Zeitung* was held to incriminate still further the Secretary of State.

According to the Imperial Constitution the Secretary of State for Foreign Affairs was responsible to the Imperial Chancellor, and through him to the Emperor, but no Prussian General had the right to interfere with the way in which he performed his duties. Actually the Supreme Command's attitude towards the Secretary of State was that of an ill-humoured absolute sovereign towards his Minister. The Supreme Command regarded Kühlmann's speech as an attempt to undermine their authority in domestic politics, in which the Secretary of State together with the Left Wing Liberal Press was endeavouring to mobilize the majority in the Reichstag against the Supreme Command and the Imperial Chancellor. It is again obvious how the formulation of German war aims acted as an indicator of the balance of power in domestic politics. On July 8 William II was obliged to dismiss Secretary of State von Kühlmann, although his political views coincided exactly with those of the Emperor.

Von Kühlmann's place was taken by the former ambassador von Hintze, who was reputed a determined supporter of a victorious peace. The Reichstag allowed all these events to pass without any protest. Even the Vice-Chancellor von Payer, the confident of the Progressives and the Social Democrats in the Cabinet, had no better counsel to offer than to submit to the inevitable. He and Hertling were responsible for there being no outcry in the Reichstag over Kühlmann's dismissal.

Kühlmann's fall coincided precisely with the final rejection of the equal suffrage bill in the Prussian House of Commons. The programme which the majority in the Reichstag had drawn up on the formation of the Hertling Government had been torn to shreds by General Ludendorff. The Supreme Command now dominated the Emperor, the sovereigns of the federal States, the Reichstag, the army and the nation. But Ludendorff had no objection to German dynasties achieving new crowns.[11] William II was to become Duke of Courland, and thus re-establish the traditions of the Teutonic Knights. As compensation the Emperor wished to obtain the Crown of Lithuania for the King of Saxony. Other men—among whom unfortunately was also Erzberger—would have preferred to see a Würtemberg prince on the throne of Lithuania. The King of Bavaria was to receive a part of Alsace, and the Grand Duke of Baden the rest of Alsace. A dominion was also planned for a German prince in Finland. All this irresistibly recalls Napoleon I's king making. But while the Kingdom of Westphalia at least survived for a few years, the Kingdom of Lithuania never got beyond the paper on which it was planned. It was the farce following on the tragedy of Brest-Litovsk.

NOTES TO CHAPTER VI

1. On his plan for a counter-revolution in Russia General Hoffmann writes in his book, *Der Krieg der versäumten Gelegenheiten* (1923), p. 224.

2. On the subject of the fall of Michaelis see Bredt in REPORT, viii, pp. 97 et seq.; von Richthofen in REPORT, vii, part ii, pp. 221 et seq.

3. Hertling's political ideas are best expressed in a memorandum by the Under-Secretary of State in the Imperial Chancellery, von Radowitz, dated January 17, 1918. The memorandum was compiled by the order of Hertling, and was signed by him with the addition of the remark, 'I quite agree' (see REPORT, ii, p. 337).—Hertling and the Centre: Bell in op. cit., vii, part i, p. 316.

4. Hertling's campaign for the reform of the suffrage: Bredt in REPORT, viii, pp. 184 et seq.

5. On the subject of the negotiations in Brest-Litovsk see Hoffmann, *Der Krieg der versäumten Gelegenheiten*, pp. 197 et seq.; Bredt in REPORT, viii, pp. 218 et seq.; Trotsky, *Von der Oktober-Revolution bis zum Brester Friedensvertrag* (1918), p. 102: 'General Hoffmann brought an air of reality into the negotiations. Without paying any great attention to Kühlmann's diplomatic instructions, the General several times put his feet up on to the table round which involved legal discussions were raging. For our part, we did not doubt for one moment that the one actual reality in the whole of these negotiations were General Hoffmann's top boots.'

6. Unfortunately, the Committee of Inquiry did not investigate the strike of January 1918 in detail. The most thorough account of these events is to be found in Richard Müller's book, *Vom Kaiserreich zur Republik*, i, 1924. Especially valuable are the records and documents published by Müller. Cf. also the report of the *Büros für Sozialpolitik* written immediately after the end of the strike, in REPORT, v, p. 103, with a clear, well-informed analysis of events.

7. Strength of the German Eastern army in 1918: von Kuhl in REPORT, iii, pp. 6, 8, 10 et seq. On the subject of Rumania, ibid., p. 10; the Ukraine, pp. 16 et seq. General Hoffmann, *Der Krieg der versäumten Gelegenheiten*, p. 221: 'The organization (of Germano-Ukrainian trade) was brilliant on paper, only it produced relatively small results. . . . I believe we should have got a great deal further if, instead of having

a great central organization, we had simply commissioned a large number of Jewish dealers to obtain corn for us by ordinary trade methods.'

8. An excellent military presentation of the 1918 offensive: von Kuhl in REPORT, iii.—Also the important memorandum by General Wetzell, the Chief of the Operations Department of the Supreme Command in 1918, in REPORT, i, pp. 305 et seq.—Haig's opinion of the prospects of German victory: Kuhl in ibid., iii, p. 138.—The German cavalry divisions in the Ukraine: Kuhl in ibid., iii, pp. 22 et seq.

9. For the suffrage negotiations of 1918 see the review by Bredt in REPORT, viii, pp. 187 et seq.—All details are in the *verbatim* (shorthand) reports of the meetings of the Prussian Lower House from April to July 1918.—The very complicated compromise which was accepted on July 4 is only reproduced as a political précis in the text.

10. For Haeften's 'Peace Offensive' and Kühlmann's dismissal see the thorough description by Schwertfeger, with all the documents, in REPORT, ii, pp. 193 et seq.; also Bredt, in REPORT, viii, pp. 273 et seq.

11. Cf. in REPORT, ii, p. 347, the note on a remark made by Hertling to William II on July 13, 1918: 'Concerning Lithuania, His Majesty has himself discussed with the King of Saxony the prospects of a union with Lithuania, and he is holding to this idea. His Majesty will supply the military officials with the necessary instructions, according to the expressed wish.'—Erzberger and the Duke of Urach's candidature for the throne, see Bredt in REPORT, viii, p. 344.—Much new material on these dynastic projects by Naumann in *Dokumente und Argumente*.

VII

THE COLLAPSE

AT the beginning of the German offensive on the Western Front there were 300,000 Americans in France. By July the number had risen to 1,200,000.[1] In March the German army had been equal in strength to that of the Entente. In July the Entente, thanks to the Americans, had a considerable majority. The reserves of the German army grew weaker from month to month, for in the four years of war millions of men of active service age had been eliminated either by death, severe wounds, or illness. There were no longer enough young sound men in Germany in the spring of 1918 to keep up an army of three and a half millions on the Western and one million on the Eastern Front. Even the gradual transfer of German troops from the east to the west could not fill the gaps.

Among the Entente the position of the French was bad, for they had also suffered tremendous losses; the man-power of the British Empire, on the other hand, was not nearly as exhausted as that of the French and Germans. In March 1918 600,000 men were available as reserves for the English army. In addition 900,000 more men were added to the British reserve battalions between March and November. In March and April the British army had suffered severely under the German offensive, but the three months May, June, and July, during which the offensive was directed against the French, gave the British time to recover. All gaps in the battalions were filled up and lost guns replaced. Thus the positive advantage which the Germans had gained was quietly destroyed. The German successes in the spring had not been a question of a territorial advance, which would have been important, but had consisted in the weakening and harassing of the enemy troops. In these circumstances the English and French combined were at least equal in strength to the German army of the west in July, and the million and a quarter Americans formed an absolute majority for the Entente. It was unnatural that the vastly superior army of the Entente should have left the Germans to take the initiative in attack. The time was approaching when Marshal Foch would be able to use his superior army for a counter-attack.

The future counter-offensive on the part of the Entente had not only the advantage of greatly superior numbers, increased from month to month by fresh American divisions, but Foch also had a mechanical means of attack to which the Germans could oppose nothing of equal value—the tank. Neither poison-gas nor aircraft had any decisive influence in the World War; for the former was counteracted by gas-masks and the airmen of one side by those of the other. Such means of attack as were not countered by corresponding means of defence were far more important. During the first part of the war, the German heavy artillery, the 42 cm. guns, &c., destroyed all enemy fortifications within a few days. Only thus was the first great German offensive through Belgium and Northern France made possible. The superiority of the German 42 cm. ordnance destroyed all the Entente plans of defence which depended on fortifications. Hence trenches became the distinctive means of defence in the World War. Obviously no trench, however well constructed, could save the weaker army, if the opponent was able to bring into action the necessary superiority of forces and élan. This was demonstrated in the German offensive against the Russians in 1915, against Italy in 1917, and against the English in March 1918, as well as, for instance, Brusilow's offensive against the Austrians in 1916.

Nevertheless, a successful attack on a fortified enemy position, in which the aim was not merely to capture a few trenches but to conquer the enemy army, needed complicated and arduous preparation. The concentration of the necessary artillery above all needed much time. If success had crowned their efforts and the enemy had occupied another position some miles farther back which could not be enveloped, the whole tedious process had to be repeated. Now, however, the English technicians discovered a new weapon which hastened and simplified these proceedings enormously. This was the so-called Tank,[2] or armoured car, which overcame all natural obstacles. If tanks had been used in large numbers, say in hundreds, as a complete surprise, they must have broken every Front.

The first English tanks appeared in September 1916 at the Battle of the Somme. They were first used in large numbers on November 20, 1917, at Cambrai. Arriving without any preliminary artillery bombardment, several hundreds of tanks overran the German Front on a sector some miles wide. The English themselves had not counted on such a success, and had no reserves with which to follow up the tanks. Thus the Germans were able to force back the English in a counter-attack and to regain their old front line. Meanwhile the French had also built tanks. As early as

October 1916 the German Supreme Command requested the Ministry of War to design a German tank and to have it produced in quantity. For reasons which cannot be explained satisfactorily neither German industry nor the technical branch of the army were able to carry out this demand. This is the more curious in that the German army did not suffer from technical difficulties as a rule. By 1918 only a few German tanks had been produced, and were not altogether satisfactory. The tank played no part in the great German offensive in the west. If Ludendorff had had a few thousand efficient tanks in the spring of 1918, the long intervals and arduous preparations between one attack and the next would have been avoided. Possibly a decision might then have been forced on the Entente before the arrival of the Americans. From July onwards Foch relied largely on tanks in his counter-attacks and with very telling effect.

In continuation of his offensive Ludendorff planned to attack the French on both sides of Rheims on July 15 in order to use up the French reserves so as to be able to deliver a fresh and crushing blow at the English. The German preparations had not been kept as secret as they should have been. In the weeks before the new offensive the men on leave in southern Germany spoke openly of the attack that was to be delivered on the French at Rheims towards the middle of July.[3] Hence the enemy Supreme Command also got to hear of the German plan of attack. The main requisite for success—the element of surprise—was lacking, and the French simply avoided the German attack. As there was no use in pursuing the attack on Rheims, Ludendorff discontinued the offensive against the French, which was in reality only a blind, and hurried on the preparations for the next great push against the English.

On July 18 the Allies began their counter-attack. French and American troops with six hundred tanks rushed the Western flank of those German troops which had been pushed forward to the Marne. After several days' fighting the German High Command was indeed able to bring the enemy attack to a standstill, but the German troops had to retreat from the Marne to a more northern line, and so many of the German reserves were exhausted that Ludendorff was obliged to give up the big attack he had planned against the English. The German loss of territory at the Marne was unimportant; but what was of extreme importance was that Foch had prevented the continuance of the German offensive. It was the definite turn of the tide. The war was lost there.

The main body of the German soldiers felt this at once. The German army had entered on the great Western offensive with all its might and with the will to win. The soldiers told themselves that the German offensive, if it succeeded, would at least secure peace on land, and they had therefore performed prodigies of valour at the crossing of the Marne on July 15 in spite of four years of war. If, however, the Americans were to arrive before the victory had been won, all would have been in vain. During the latter half of July the men in the front line realized that the German armies were obliged to retreat, and that the Entente was attacking. In addition the Americans were now occupying positions all along the enemy lines. Nine strong American divisions took part in the battle of July 18 and the following days. Thus a deep depression filled the German army. The last despairing effort with which they had thrown themselves into the offensive had evaporated. The terrible collapse of the morale of the German troops had nothing to do with propaganda: it resulted automatically from the change in the military situation.

The higher officers were also convinced that the war was lost after July 18, as is witnessed, for example, by a memorandum addressed to the Supreme Command on July 20 by Staff Major Niemann who was serving on the Western Front.[4] Niemann suggested in guarded terms that Germany should try to save herself by offering to cede the Fleet to England. England might then be prepared to give way in the matter of the Berlin–Bagdad railway. Colonel Bauer, who was highly influential in the Great Headquarters, made comments on Niemann's memorandum on July 28 which in the main indicate agreement, although Bauer wished Germany to expand in the future towards the east into the Ukraine, the Caucasus, &c., instead of through Turkey. Bauer, too, was prepared to give up the German navy to England, and expressed himself in somewhat unjustifiably contemptuous terms about the High Seas Fleet. These General Staff Officers like Colonel von Haeften were also preoccupied with England. It showed astounding political shortsightedness on their part to have persuaded themselves that England would consent to such a compromise with a conquered Germany after four years of war.

At the beginning of August Ludendorff felt rather more hopeful about the general position. He thought the Entente's counter-attack was ended, and he began planning fresh German offensives on a smaller scale. But on August 8 Foch continued his offensive.

This time the English attacked near Amiens; four hundred tanks broke through the German positions; and the German Second Army was forced to retreat with heavy losses. Henceforward Foch continued his offensive without a break up to the time of the Armistice. During three months of heavy fighting the German army gradually retreated. When hostilities ceased in November, the German troops were occupying the so-called Antwerp–Meuse line. The continuation of this line ran across Lorraine to the Vosges mountains.

The position grew worse and worse for Germany as regards numbers. On October 1 the German Western army consisted of no more than two and a half million men; at the same time there were two million Americans on the Western Front alone; and, if the French and English troops are added, it is seen that the Entente had a clear hundred per cent. majority during the last months of the war. The Entente possessed in addition a vast superiority in munitions, as well as the hundreds of tanks which allowed Foch to continue his offensive almost without a pause. The German troops, who never got any rest, were indescribably overstrained and exhausted. To this was added the conviction that the war was hopelessly lost for Germany. Nevertheless, a part of the German army held on doggedly to the very end. Others, whose power of resistance had given out and who saw no point in continuing to fight, simply deserted from their units and collected in the base camps. These so-called 'shirkers' behind the Front were a characteristic sight during the last part of the war.

The material conditions prevailing in the German army afford a complete explanation of this situation. To the very end active revolutionary propaganda had played no real part in the Western army. But in the fifth year of the war, and after all the starvation and suffering, a part of the army was no longer prepared to sacrifice itself for something which appeared to be completely vain. Nevertheless, the majority of the front line troops did not become conscious revolutionaries until much later. Disloyalty to the officers occurred only in isolated cases, and after the Revolution the front line soldiers were bitterly opposed to what was then called Spartacism. If successful revolutionary propaganda had been carried on in the army on the Western Front, the men would have behaved very differently after November 9.[5]

It is astonishing in view of all these circumstances that Foch, with his overwhelming superiority of men and munitions, could

not force a decisive victory up to the end of the war. During the
three months from August 8 to November 11 the Entente slowly
gained ground. Nevertheless, at the time of the Armistice, the
German army still stood on enemy territory in fighting trim. The
final military catastrophe did not really occur on the Western Front,
but was the result of the defection of Bulgaria and Austria, which
opened the way for the Entente armies to enter Germany and
attack the German forces in the rear.

The German Supreme Command had known since August 8
that the war was lost. There was, of course, some doubt as to how
long the last act would take. The considerable diminution in
Ludendorff's authority following on the military disaster somewhat raised the Emperor's status. After August 8 William II held
a conference with Ludendorff in Avesnes. He allowed himself to
criticize the Supreme Command in certain details and emphasized
that 'too much had been expected' of the troops. William II
announced that Germany had come to the limits of its endurance
and that the war must be ended. He commanded Hindenburg and
Ludendorff to a Crown Council at Spa in order to take the necessary resolutions. Had the Emperor been really determined, he
might have picked up the reins again at this time for the Reichstag
was still without a definite leader. But neither William II's mental
powers nor his strength of character were sufficient to enable him
to take up the leadership of the German people at such a crisis.

The Crown Council was held in Spa on August 14.[6] On August
13 Ludendorff had held a conference with the Secretary of State
for Foreign Affairs, von Hintze. Ludendorff said to him: 'In the
middle of July I told you that I was certain I could break the enemy's
spirit by my present offensive. I am no longer certain.' At the
same time Ludendorff still held the very problematic hope that he
might still succeed in dragging on the war for a few more months by
a strategic defensive policy, and meanwhile find the opportunity
for making a fairly satisfactory compromise with England. The
deliberations in the Crown Council of August 14 were conducted
on this basis. The Emperor, the Crown Prince, Hindenburg,
Ludendorff, Hertling, and Hintze were present at the Council. It
was decided to approach the Entente at the first favourable
opportunity through the King of Spain or the Queen of the
Netherlands—it did not appear expedient to make such a move in
favour of peace at a moment when the Entente army was making
a victorious advance in the west. It was decided to wait instead

for a pause in the hostilities during which the German army might consolidate its position somewhat. From all previous experience in the World War it was to be expected that such a pause would soon occur. Nobody in influential circles as yet considered the possibility of a German capitulation.

The reproach which has been levelled against the Supreme Command that it concealed the full gravity of the military situation from the Imperial Government is unjustified. Moreover, the situation was not at that time so serious that the Crown Council would have been justified in deciding on capitulation, a plea for an armistice, and peace at any price. Nevertheless, it is curious that no inferences were drawn from the alteration in the military situation and applied to domestic politics. After the collapse of the great German offensive Ludendorff's political dictatorship no longer had any foundation. The Emperor or the Imperial Chancellor might have announced on August 14 that the Imperial Government would itself seek the means to end the war without consideration for the Supreme Command. The elimination of the Supreme Command from the discussion of war aims would have automatically ended Ludendorff's dictatorship. At this time General Ludendorff could not have raised any serious opposition to his removal from political life. But no successor to Ludendorff had as yet presented himself.

The Reichstag was at such a low ebb, and so cowed by its failures since January 1918, that it utterly failed to appreciate the political significance of the collapse on the Western Front. It is characteristic of the situation that it was not considered necessary to summon Vice-Chancellor von Payer, the confidant of the parties forming the majority, to the Council on August 14. To re-establish the Imperial power on pre-War lines was impossible. Von Hertling, the Imperial Chancellor, was indeed in favour of a 'democratic monarchy', but was opposed to a parliamentary system. At this moment he did not desire an upheaval in home politics, and so everything remained as it had been. The shadow of General Ludendorff continued to reign in Germany until the end of September. The change in the political situation was not clear to the nation at large, because nothing was altered politically, because all the old officials remained in their posts, saying the same old things, though in a slightly less peremptory manner.

At this time nothing short of a great upheaval in the domestic politics of Germany could have indicated the path to salvation.

The majority in the Reichstag should have overthrown Ludendorff in August and have formed a parliamentary government. The middle-class democratic revolution which followed in October could equally well have taken place in August. The new German Government should then have stopped the Supreme Command's ventures in the east, should have denounced the peace of Brest-Litovsk of its own free will, and have recalled all German troops from the occupied eastern countries. An understanding and a political alliance with Soviet Russia would thus have been made possible. During August and September Germany might have initiated the conversion of Austria-Hungary into a working confederation of States; it might have achieved an understanding with Poland; and have created an autonomous Alsace-Lorraine. If Germany and Russia had made a pact, the situation would also have been altered in the Balkans, in Rumania, and Bulgaria. A strong political coalition between Germany, Russia, and Austria would much more easily have achieved favourable peace terms from the Entente than did an isolated and defenceless Germany later at Versailles.

The premise for all this was that no immediate military catastrophe should intervene. The events in Bulgaria and Austria at the end of September and during October closed even this avenue of escape. In order to have initiated an attempt on such a large scale in August and September to save Germany the Reichstag would have had to possess a degree of statesmanship in which it was quite lacking. When Herr von Payer [7] received the report of the Crown Council at Spa, he considered neither a revolution nor a transference of power; instead he decided, in the manner of July 1917, to induce the Supreme Command to announce their assent to a 'peace by understanding'. According to the traditional views of the majority in the Reichstag, the German desire for a 'peace by understanding' was dependent primarily on a declaration in favour of the unconditional restoration of Belgium.

On August 25 Payer went to the Great Head-quarters in order to demand the assent of the Supreme Command to this formula. Payer believed in all sincerity that a German declaration to this effect would be the preliminary to peace negotiations. The conferences between Ludendorff and Payer in Avesnes from August 25 to 27 are a grotesque historical farce. Ludendorff, the vanquished General, still played the part of dictator and tried to save the last rags of a victorious peace, while the representative of the Reichstag tried to persuade the Supreme Command to be so kind as to let Belgium go. At that time the opinion of those in power in Germany in the matter of Belgium was of no importance whatever. The question was no longer what was to become of Belgium, but what was to become of Alsace-Lorraine and Posen. The vital question was no longer what were the Supreme Command's war aims, but for how much longer the German Emperor would continue to wear his crown.

Since the political parties still left the decision with General Ludendorff, he made his reservations: the decision over Belgium which was taken on August 27 was the last victory of the Supreme Command over the Reichstag and the Imperial Government. In the introduction, indeed, is the statement: 'At the conclusion of peace we will return to Belgium her complete independence without burdens and without reservation.' But at the end is the remark: 'We do not doubt that in the understanding which we expect to reach with Belgium details such as the Flemish Question will be settled to the satisfaction of both sides and will contribute to the furtherance of peace.' According to this Germany assumed the right to take up certain national guarantees for Flanders in the peace treaty and to guarantee their fulfilment. This clause about the Flemings, which was included at Ludendorff's instigation, would have ensured Germany's having a say in the domestic policy of Belgium. Payer was also satisfied with it. He went home with the 'Belgian formula', and made it public in a speech at Stuttgart during September. This declaration on the part of the German Government passed unnoticed in foreign countries in view of the military situation. The discussion over Belgium between Ludendorff and von Payer is like two men playing a game of chess on a sinking ship, taking no notice of the waves which are closing over them, but continuing to call 'check' to each other. This was the last duel between the adherents of the peace by agreement and the victorious peace.

On September 27 von Hintze informed the Committee of the Reichstag of Bulgaria's defection; and that it was to be expected that in a few weeks the Entente's Balkan army would again be in occupation of Rumania. The loss of Rumania's petroleum would make it impossible for Germany to carry on the war.[8] The Supreme Command began at the beginning of October to consider whether the loss of Rumania made it necessary to begin peace negotiations at once. The decision was arrived at that the Air Force could continue operations for another two months after which it would be completely at a standstill. Motor transport also could be carried on as usual for two more months; after this time it could have about half rations. There was lubricating oil enough for six months; but of oil for purposes of illumination there was no more than would last for two months. The decisive factor was the complete elimination of aircraft without which a modern war cannot be waged.

Any one with any insight must have realized in addition that very shortly after Bulgaria's desertion a decisive step on the part of Austria-Hungary would follow. The Viennese Court had only been kept true to the alliance during the past year by the military successes of Germany. Since the tide of victory had turned in August the loyalty of the Habsburgs was no longer to be relied on. Austria's attempt to make a separate peace in the middle of September had already shown what was to be expected. As soon as Austria was out of the war the Italians could pour into Germany through Tyrol. The Entente's Balkan troops could use the Austro-Hungarian railways to come through to the frontiers of Bavaria and Saxony. Thus, while the German army in the west was fighting against overwhelming odds, great masses of enemy troops would break into Germany in their rear—and who would there be to defend her against them? No new army that was worth anything was to be made out of the remains of the German Eastern army.

At the best only a few months could pass before the Entente would march into Bavaria and Saxony. But the German Government and the Supreme Command dared not let matters get to that pitch—the war must be ended at all costs. Ludendorff arrived at this decision, which in the existing circumstances was unavoidable, on September 27, when he realized how events were developing in Bulgaria.[9] He was also troubled by the constant fear that the Entente would still manage to break through and annihilate the German army. It was, as a matter of fact, a miracle that the Entente was never able to achieve such a victory before the Armistice. On September 27 Ludendorff was unable to furnish a guarantee that there would not be a German collapse in the west. Thus the situation in the south east and in the west had brought the German High Command to the point at which they declared that an immediate armistice and peace must be demanded.

Ludendorff's judgement of the military situation was once more absolutely correct. He recognized, moreover, that such a peace move on the part of Germany necessitated an immediate change in the German governmental system; for the Entente would not negotiate with the old rulers of Germany. Thus the German confession of collapse must rob those men who had hitherto been Germany's leaders in military and political matters of all their authority. In order to avoid chaos within the country a new Government was essential. Ludendorff now finally decided to give up his dictatorship, and to hand power over to his rival, the only other real authority in the country, the Reichstag. During the week following September 27 Ludendorff concentrated all his energies on putting power into the hands of the Reichstag. The Reichstag Committee had met during the very days of the Bulgarian catastrophe at the end of September. The Social Democrats as well as the other Parties composing the majority realized that Germany's situation had become hopeless. The Reichstag had to prepare to take over much greater responsibility. Plans for a more far-reaching parliamentarization of Germany and for the easing of the blockade began to crop up. Since Hertling, the Imperial Chancellor, was not prepared to make any such concessions, a fresh ministerial crisis occurred. Nevertheless, the Reichstag gave no real sign of announcing its programme publicly to the German people or of demanding the immediate retirement of the old authorities. The parliamentarization of Germany was not fought for by the Reichstag; it was arranged by Ludendorff.

This kind of revolution is without a parallel in the whole history of the world. It has frequently happened that arbitrary military rulers and dictators have surrendered power of their own free will; but it has never happened that a dictator took such infinite pains to secure power to his antagonists as Ludendorff took at the end of September and in October 1918. His conduct and that of the Reichstag is only comprehensible when it is remembered how extremely backward politically the whole of Germany was at that time. As has been stated above, Ludendorff never sought power in Germany before August 1916; he had no intention of becoming an autocrat like Caesar or Napoleon I; he became German Dictator because there was no one else who had the courage to command and because he was able to insist on being obeyed. He was utterly devoted to the cause of his country, as he understood it, and showed a disinterestedness which is rare among great Dictators.

It would have served his own interests better not to have published the request for an armistice but to have held out to the end as an 'indomitable hero'. For when the catastrophe came it would have been easy to find a scapegoat, and so to have perpetuated an heroic legend. In a similar situation in 1814 Napoleon I fought to the last drop of his soldiers' blood. But Ludendorff, with all his self-assertion, was free from selfish personal motives. It was only the deplorable internal condition of Germany which had forced him to play the dictator for two years. Thus in September 1918 he did not consider his personal future, his position, his historical reputation, but quite loyally thought of his troops, as an honourable colonel at the Front would think of his regiment. The fate of the German army might in a few weeks' time be a matter of days or even hours. Ludendorff was, therefore, anxious to make known his desire for an armistice as soon as possible. At best the negotiations must last some weeks before hostilities could cease—and what would meanwhile happen at the Front nobody knew.

Ludendorff was not indeed prepared to accept the enemy's conditions in their entirety. He thought that the decision to make one last desperate effort could still be taken; but that the first thing to do was to make an effort as quickly as possible to get the German army extricated from the war under tolerable conditions. The preliminary to the achievement of an armistice and peace was the rapid formation of a new Government. Hence Ludendorff concentrated his energies on this point. On September 28 he sent a message to Hertling, the Imperial Chancellor, to say that an 'alteration in the Government or its re-constitution on a broader basis' had become necessary. Hertling was absolutely dumbfounded at finding the Supreme Command so suddenly in favour of a parliamentary régime; he himself was determined not to join in this *volte face* but rather to resign his office.

On September 29 the decisive conferences took place at Spa between Hindenburg, Ludendorff, Hertling, Hintze, and the Emperor. The Supreme Command announced that the military situation demanded the immediate institution of negotiations for an armistice. The Emperor and his Ministers did not dare to question the inevitability of such a step. It was decided to address an appeal to President Wilson to bring about an armistice and peace, and in doing so to announce Germany's acceptance of Wilson's famous Fourteen Points.

The upheaval in domestic politics, the 'revolution from above' as Hintze called it, demanded primarily a new Imperial Chancellor, for Hertling, not wishing to countenance parliamentarism, handed in his resignation. Hintze did likewise because he was considered to be a supporter of the Pan-German and Victorious Peace Parties. On the evening of September 29 itself, Count Roedern, the Secretary of State of the Imperial Treasury, left by special train for Berlin to form a new Government with the help of the Vice-Chancellor, von Payer, and the political Parties. Ludendorff sent Major von dem Bussche, one of the officers on the staff of the Supreme Command, with Roedern to Berlin. His task was to explain the gravity of the military situation and to press for the immediate formation of a new Government. Ludendorff himself did not go to Berlin because he did not wish to let the military leadership out of his own hands at this critical time. But he spent the next few days unceasingly urging over the telephone and by telegraph the necessity for haste in Berlin. For until the new Government existed an armistice could not be asked for.

On October 2 Major von dem Bussche delivered his memorable address to the Party leaders on the military situation. At this meeting there were present Count Westarp (Conservative), Gamp (Empire Party), Stresemann (National Liberal), Gröber (Centre), Fischbeck (Progressives), Ebert (S.P.D.), Haase (U.S.P.D.), and Seyda (Polish). The Major only elaborated what any one with any insight must have realized since the recent events on the Western Front and in Bulgaria. The gist of his statement was: 'The German army is still strong enough to hold the enemy in check for months, to gain territorial advantages, and to inflict fresh losses on the Entente. Nevertheless each successive day brings the enemy nearer to his goal, and will leave him less inclined to make peace on terms which are at all supportable for us. No time must therefore be lost.' The *Vorwärts* had on September 28 published an article which aroused much comment, stating the position in much the same terms, though it had no information as to Ludendorff's opinion. Nevertheless Major von dem Bussche's speech came as a terrible shock to his listeners, for General Ludendorff, who for four years had been the embodiment of the German 'Will to Victory', told the Reichstag officially by the mouth of Major von dem Bussche that he had lost the war, and that the Reichstag must take over the executive power immediately.

Thus the Reichstag had attained to full political power without any exertion on its own part or without any struggle. Once more it is characteristic of the weakness and instability of the parties composing the majority that they had nobody to suggest to put at the head of the Government. The era of middle-class democracy in

Germany began with the Imperial Chancellorship of a Liberal South German prince. The Chancellor of the new 'People's Government' was Prince Max of Baden. The Baden dynasty was the first to compromise with the middle class. Ludendorff gave the order for parliamentary government to be instituted in Germany and a Prince of Baden carried it out.

As a matter of fact Prince Max expressed the strongest doubts as to the wisdom of Germany's asking for an armistice.[10] He was of opinion that such a step on the part of Germany would be an open avowal of defeat and would destroy all hopes of tolerable peace terms. Moreover, as he pointed out to the Supreme Command, the whole 'atmosphere favourable to peace created by the formation of the new Government would be lost in the sensation which the request for an armistice would create'. Prince Max's view was correct as far as it went, but it was already too late to take the longer way to peace. The 'formation of the new Government', i.e. the victory at least of middle-class democracy, should have taken place in Germany at a time when the military situation was still favourable. Prince Max was determined not to forward a request for an armistice to the Entente unless it was expressly demanded by the Supreme Command in writing. Thereupon Hindenburg wrote the historic letter of October 3 to the Imperial Chancellor:

'The Supreme Command continues to hold to its demand expressed on September 29 of this year that a request for an armistice should be sent to our enemies immediately. As a result of the collapse on the Macedonian Front, the consequent weakening of the reserves on our Western Front, and the impossibility of making good the very severe losses which we have suffered in the last few days, there is, as far as it is humanly possible to judge, no further chance of forcing a peace on the enemy. Our adversaries are continually bringing up fresh reserves. The German army still stands firm and is successfully resisting all attacks. Nevertheless, the situation becomes daily more critical; and the Supreme Command may be forced to take very grave decisions. The circumstances call for a cessation of hostilities in order to spare the German nation and its allies needless sacrifices. Each day that is lost costs the lives of thousands of brave soldiers.'

This declaration was given by Hindenburg with Ludendorff's full approval. The Supreme Command in thus acting was inspired by highly creditable motives. Moreover, it had unquestionably formed a correct estimate of the military situation. It nevertheless assumed the entire historical responsibility for the manner in which the war was ended. The attempts that have subsequently been made to place the responsibility for the disastrous end to the war on the German Republic are quite unjustifiable. Prince Max pointed out to the Supreme Command that this peace move would very likely lead to the loss of Alsace-Lorraine and of the purely Polish districts in east Prussia. The Supreme Command replied that they were quite prepared for the loss of the small French-speaking portion of Alsace-Lorraine, but that there could be no question of tampering with German territory in the east. In a speech on October 3 Hindenburg stated that in case the enemy's peace terms should prove too hard 'we shall fight to the last man!' Hindenburg and Ludendorff were prepared to go on fighting if the Entente made conditions that were too crushing—nevertheless, as Count Roedern pointed out to the Field Marshal, to 'fight to the last man' was not to be expected of a nation of sixty-five millions.[11]

The Supreme Command's attitude was comprehensible from a purely logical standpoint: a rapid attempt was to be made to come to reasonable terms and, if the attempt failed, the war must simply be carried on. The Supreme Command judged the psychology of the German nation wrongly. If, after more than four years of tremendous sacrifices, it was officially announced that the war was lost, then the masses both in the army and in the country itself could not be expected to go on fighting simply for glory. In the existing circumstances the Supreme Command's move for an armistice and peace meant the end of the war.

It has been said in France that if the Germans had had a Gambetta[12] they could have gone on fighting in November 1918, and that peace might have been concluded on a different footing. In answer to this it might be asked why the French did not go on fighting in 1815 after Waterloo instead of allowing the Allies to enter Paris. From a purely military standpoint the situation in France after Waterloo was considerably better than it was in Germany in November 1918. To continue fighting was impossible in either case for reasons of racial psychology.

It must in fairness be pointed out that in the very thorough discussions that took place in every influential quarter from September 29 to October 2, all possible loopholes and peculiarities of the situation were considered. But no one cherished the fantastic idea that Germany might still win the war by a victorious naval action against the Entente. It would be an insult to the military judgement of the Supreme Command if it were to be even remotely suspected of such an idea. It was not until the so-called 'stab in the back' discussions after the war that this possibility was mooted.

As soon as Prince Max had Hindenburg's written declaration in his hands, he sent off the German Peace Note to President Wilson on the night of October 3–4. The delay which ensued upon Wilson's various Notes and the German answers in October did not allow of the Armistice being concluded until November. Meanwhile the collapse and disintegration of the Habsburg Empire took place. During the last days of the war German troops entered Tyrol, Salzburg, and northern Bohemia in readiness to offer resistance to the enemy who might be expected to invade the country at these points. Although it never again came to fighting in these particular districts, the German army and navy nevertheless guarded all the frontiers up to the last day of the war.

Prince Max of Baden's Government relied on the support of the three parties comprising the majority in the Reichstag:[13] Social Democracy was represented by Bauer, Secretary of State for the Ministry of Labour, and by Scheidemann, Secretary of State without portfolio; the Centre was represented in the Government by Trimborn, Secretary of State for the Interior, and by Gröber and Erzberger, both without portfolios; the Progressive Party was represented by the Vice-Chancellor von Payer and by Haussmann, Secretary of State without portfolio. Friedberg, the Vice-President of the Prussian Cabinet, constituted the link with the National Liberals. By the formation of Max of Baden's Government, Germany had changed over to middle-class parliamentary democracy without any immediate alteration in the Constitution. The fact that the Government could only remain in power so long as it kept the confidence of the Reichstag sufficed for the present.

After the Supreme Command had resigned its political powers, no autocratic or feudal method of government was conceivable in Germany. The new order of things was regularized by making the necessary alterations in the Constitution in October. The Bismarckian Constitution was repealed in the necessary details, and a political system was created whose main ideas survive in the Weimar Constitution of 1919. The parliamentarization of Germany was made constitutionally more difficult by the existence of the Federal Council. Bismarck had never really formed an actual Imperial Cabinet. Instead the Federal Council (*Bundesrat*), a collection of delegates from all the separate States, was to act as the Imperial Cabinet. The Imperial Chancellor was legally nothing more than the executive chairman of the Federal Council. His actual power consisted in the fact that he was at the same time the Prime Minister of Prussia, and was thus able to lead and instruct the Prussian delegates in the Federal Council. The old Constitution had no place for a responsible Cabinet Minister in the modern sense of the word; the Secretaries of State of the various ministries were nothing more than expert assistants to the Imperial Chancellor. It was, indeed, customary for Prussia to charge these Secretaries of State with her representation in the Federal Council. But they had no personal political responsibility. They were expected to vote in the Federal Council as the Prussian Government instructed them. For Bismarck's Federal Council was not a collection of men; it was a collection of States. It was not the persons X, Y, Z, &c., who were voting: it was the States Prussia, Bavaria, Hamburg, and so forth.

According to the old Constitution it was not permissible for any one to sit both in the Reichstag and in the Federal Council. This prohibition in Article 9 of the Constitution of 1871 has frequently, though quite erroneously, been looked upon as the real hindrance to parliamentary government in Germany. Article 9 was an unessential part of the Constitution, and its omission would have involved no material alteration, as witness the fact that before 1914 the Imperial Chancellor and various Secretaries of State did at the same time occupy seats in the Reichstag. There could obviously be no parliamentary government as long as the Imperial Chancellor was appointed not by the votes of the Reichstag but at the pleasure of the Emperor; and as long as the Secretaries of State were nothing but the obedient subordinates of the Chancellor. The reform of the Constitution would have to be undertaken from quite a different point of view.

The Federal Council would have to resign the functions of government and turn itself into an Upper House for the German Empire, which role it plays in the Weimar Constitution under the title of 'Reichsrat'. The Secretaries of State must be released from their leading strings by the Chancellor and turned into responsible political officials. A vote was taken on the constitutional question in the Reichstag on October 26. A motion on the part of Ebert (S.P.D.), Fischbeck (Progressives), Herold (Centre), and Junck (National Liberals) added the following words to the old

Article 15 of the Constitution: 'The Imperial Chancellor must possess the confidence of the Reichstag in order to remain in office. The Chancellor is responsible for all acts of political importance which the Emperor undertakes according to the powers granted him by the Imperial Constitution. The Imperial Chancellor and his representatives are responsible for their conduct of affairs to the Federal Council and the Reichstag.'

The actions of the Majority Parties were obviously supported by the National Liberals. In connexion with the alteration of Article 15 the declaration of war and the conclusion of peace was made dependent upon the assent of the Reichstag. Finally, the Emperor's absolute authority over the fighting forces was abolished: the appointment and dismissal of naval officers was made dependent upon the assent and counter-signature of the Imperial Chancellor. The appointment and dismissal of army officers was made in the same way dependent upon that of the Minister for War in each separate State—i.e. the Minister for War of Prussia, Bavaria, &c. These local War Ministers were made directly subordinate to the Reichstag by the introduction of a new clause into the Constitution: 'The Ministers for War are responsible to the Federal Council and to the Reichstag for the administration of the contingents for which they are severally responsible.'

On October 26 the Reichstag completed the revision of the Constitution in spite of the opposition of the Conservatives. That marked the complete victory of the middle-class revolution. The assent of the Emperor and of the Federal Council followed immediately. On October 28 the new clauses came legally into force. Bismarck's Germany thereby became a thing of the past. The German Empire had become a constitutional monarchy of the same type as England. The Emperor had been transformed into an hereditary President with considerable outward dignity. But the real power now lay with the Imperial Parliament—the Reichstag. The Federal Council had become the Upper House of the German Empire; it represented the individual States, and stood beside the Reichstag as a Second Chamber. The corresponding parliamentarization of the individual States would follow automatically. Meanwhile the last obstacles in the way of the introduction of the Imperial suffrage system into Prussia had been abolished. The formation of a Prussian parliamentary government similar to the Imperial Government was to be expected. Parliament and not the Emperor now held political power over the army. Thus the World

War overthrew the Prussian military aristocracy and smoothed the way for a middle-class democracy.

The classes which had hitherto been in power in Prussia—landowners, regular officers, and the higher officials—followed the course of the Revolution with the liveliest sense of their own material and political losses. But they could do nothing to prevent it since the Militia was not at their disposal, and the immense majority of the population was opposed to them. The great industries, on the other hand, began as early as October 1918 to adapt themselves to the new conditions by adopting the idea of a 'Co-operation in work' with the Trades Unions; for a middle-class democracy offered at least as good opportunities to industrialists as had the former militarist empire.

The adherents of the old order fired a Parthian shot at the Reichstag majority by the question whether Germany was preparing to accept Wilson's terms unconditionally or whether it was ready to try a last desperate fight. In the Notes which the President of the United States sent to the German Government in October he demanded as a preliminary to an armistice the immediate cessation of submarine warfare. In addition, he made it clear that the Entente would only consider an armistice on conditions which would make it impossible for the German army to continue fighting. The Supreme Command was not in favour of accepting Wilson's conditions. It was ready to move back the German army to the western frontiers of the Empire. But in Ludendorff's opinion Germany ought to remain in a position to continue the war in case the peace negotiations failed.

It was obvious that if an armistice were concluded according to Wilson's plan the conditions of peace would be entirely determined by the Entente. But was it still possible for Germany to avoid this in October and November 1918? Although Ludendorff was in favour of continuing to fight, he laboured under no military illusions. In a memorandum he wrote on October 31, 1918, under the immediate influence of recent events, Ludendorff said: [14]

'Our situation could certainly not have improved. Events in the southeast were bound to take their course—of that there could be no doubt. But a tremendous effort on the part of the German nation would have had a sobering effect on the peoples and armies of France and England, and probably also of America. We could have held out for a few more months. The garrison of a fortress which capitulates before it is utterly exhausted lies under the stigma of dishonour. A nation which accepts humiliation and allows conditions to be forced upon it which destroy its existence without having fought to the uttermost is on the down-grade. If the same things happen to it after it has made every possible effort, it will survive.'

A final effort on the part of the German nation might indeed have lasted for several months. It could not have materially altered the situation. Only a formal military notion of honour favoured a continuance of hostilities. Ludendorff's theory that the German nation could only 'survive' if it made a final effort, even though that led to no result, was even then untenable, and has been completely disproved by the history of the last ten years. The German nation demonstrated from 1914 to 1918 a power of resistance that far surpassed all expectation, and it could no more be 'destroyed' by unfavourable peace terms than was France in 1814, 1815, or 1871. That the Supreme Command and the Corps of Officers rebelled against capitulating to the enemy is quite comprehensible, as is also the fact that the Conservatives again took their stand by Ludendorff's side in October 1918, for in these circles militarist ways of thought were the rule, and the collapse of the form of government to which they had been accustomed for centuries encouraged their wish to die fighting.

Nevertheless, the political leaders of Germany could not permit matters to go so far as to allow a completely exhausted people to sacrifice further hundreds of thousands of lives; and to let not only the Rhineland but also Bavaria and Saxony become battlefields to no purpose. Germany had no further choice. When all efforts to achieve a satisfactory end to the war had failed under the old system and Ludendorff's dictatorship, Prince Max's Government was obliged to agree to the enemy's terms. The suggestions of the Supreme Command to reject Wilson's conditions and to continue fighting were refused. Hindenburg and Ludendorff had laid their point of view before the Emperor on October 25 in Berlin. William II referred them, quite constitutionally, to the Imperial Chancellor, and, since he was ill at the time, to von Payer, the Vice Chancellor.

In the memorandum of October 31, Ludendorff writes of the conference with Payer:

'In the evening we had another meeting with von Payer. It was very depressing. I had no further doubt that the Government did not wish to continue fighting, and that it was prepared to yield everything and to accept any terms however harsh. To some people who were waiting to see me after the interview I could only say that I considered that all was lost and that I expected to see the country given over to Bolshevism.' The last sentence is interesting. Ludendorff considered that a determined national resistance would introduce a certain stability at least in domestic affairs that would prevent a Bolshevik, i.e. a Radical Socialist, revolution in Germany. Ludendorff was by no means alone in this idea. Up to the very last days of the war military questions and those concerning the balance of political power ran parallel.

Since Ludendorff was now in open opposition to the new parliamentary Government, he was obliged to withdraw from his post. On October 26 he requested the Emperor to allow him to resign and his resignation was accepted. After the internal political upheaval in Germany at the beginning of October Ludendorff's dismissal was the easiest thing in the world. The fact that Ludendorff himself had contributed considerably to the formation of Germany's first parliamentary government was not taken into account. It was not to be expected that the Reichstag majority would demonstrate any particular gratitude to Ludendorff. Since the assumption of power by Max of Baden's Government, Ludendorff was no longer the Dictator of Germany but only a General who was subordinate to Parliament. The calm and frictionless dismissal of Ludendorff was the first great test of strength of the new system. Field Marshal von Hindenburg remained at his post, and thereby demonstrated his readiness to co-operate with middle-class democracy. General Groener became First Quartermaster-General in Ludendorff's place.

At that moment Ludendorff's dismissal was a proof that the Government was making the best of a bad job, and considered that resistance to the Entente was henceforth useless. The Armistice would have been signed even if the Revolution of November 9 had not overthrown Max of Baden's Government.

Prince Max himself still clung to the hope that at a given moment a call to the nation to resist would be possible. But on this point the Imperial Chancellor was in opposition to the very men who were the most influential members of his Government. Prince Max hoped to draw out the negotiations with Wilson until the Entente submitted each of the humiliating terms of the Armistice singly. A national outburst of fury would then occur in Germany, and the war would be carried on for a time with the result that the Entente might be induced at least to modify the harshest of the conditions. Since the great majority of the German people was no longer considering individual terms, and was only animated by a desire for peace at any price, Prince Max's psychological deductions are open to criticism. Any one in Germany who was still considering individual political details could gather everything that was necessary about Wilson's and the Entente's intentions from the American President's Third Note of October 23. If negotiations with Wilson were still to be broken off, it should have been done after this Note and on the lines suggested by Ludendorff. If the German Government quietly accepted the Note of October 23, it was tacitly informing the German nation and the world at large that it laid Germany's fate unreservedly in Wilson's hands. The reservations which Prince Max made mentally or which he uttered among his intimates did not alter the political facts in any way.

Moreover, the most influential part of the Cabinet was opposed to Prince Max when he hoped for future national resistance. The Social Democratic Ministers had never allowed any doubt to persist that they considered a continuance of the war as out of the question. At a meeting of the Cabinet on October 24 Erzberger announced that the Centre Party in the Reichstag 'had unanimously declared against national defence'. The political power of the Government lay not in the person of the Imperial Chancellor but in the co-operation of the two parties representative of the great mass of the people—the Centre and the S.P.D. Of the parliamentary Secretaries of State only one—Haussmann—was definitely on Prince Max's side. The real distribution of power in the Government was shown in the preparation of the German answer to Wilson's Third Note. A draft of the reply by Prince Max, in spite of its compliance with Wilson's ideas, contained the sentence: 'The German Government expects suggestions for an Armistice, and not for surrendering arms.' Even this wording caused considerable misgivings in the Cabinet, although it was finally accepted. Then the Government received information of the letter of the Emperor Karl to William II of October 27, in which Karl wrote: 'Therefore I write to inform you that I have irrevocably decided to request within twenty-four hours a separate peace and an immediate cessation of hostilities.' While still under the impression of Austria's defection, the majority of the Ministers no longer considered it possible to refuse to 'surrender arms'. Prince Max reluctantly yielded to the pressure of circumstance. Thus the

German reply went out on October 27 without the clause about 'surrendering arms'. That was two days before the beginning of the unrest in the fleet. Thus even then Max of Baden's Government held it to be no longer possible to avoid a 'surrender of arms' in view of the hopeless military and economic situation of Germany.

The Reichstag majority did nearly everything in October that the mass of the people wanted. It had declared itself unreservedly for an armistice and peace, and by the end of October the cessation of hostilities was to be expected any day. Within the country, the old military power had been set aside, as Ludendorff's fall witnessed. The officers were no longer the masters but the servants of a Reichstag elected by the people. The old semi-absolutist State of the Hohenzollerns no longer existed. Universal suffrage was assured in Prussia. Many political prisoners had been amnestied; Karl Liebknecht had been discharged from prison. Only the minorities among the nation were now in opposition to the new wielders of power: the old Conservative sections of the Right, and, on the Left, the supporters of the U.S.P.D. and the Spartacist Association who were dissatisfied with a middle-class government and wanted a Socialist State.

A new revolution could logically only have been caused after October 28 in one of the following ways: the supporters of the old system might have tried to promote a counter-revolution; or the radical Socialists might have attempted revolution after the manner of the Russian Bolsheviks. Either of these attempts was doomed to failure from the outset, since it would be resisted by the great mass of the middle class and the workers among the nation and in the army. The masses at that time were anxious for peace and a middle-class democracy—and nothing more. Their political voice was the Reichstag majority. They had the power and had achieved their desires. How should a new German revolution be possible that should destroy Max of Baden's Government, i.e. in reality Erzberger's and Scheidemann's? Nevertheless in November 1918 the most curious of all revolutions took place. The masses behind the Reichstag majority rebelled against Max of Baden's Government, that is to say, against themselves. How was this revolution made possible?

Since the winter of 1917–18 the Reichstag majority had lost contact with its supporters. The masses, indeed, still shared the political aims and ideals of the Majority Socialists and of the Left Wing of the Centre; but they no longer had any confidence that their representatives would do anything against the ruling military caste. The Supreme Command went from victory to victory; the January strike failed; the peace of Brest-Litovsk was signed; the army advanced steadily in the east; the great offensive in the west was successful; Kühlmann fell. The masses felt that they were powerless in the mailed fist of the militarist power. Ministers such as Payer and members of the Reichstag such as Scheidemann could effect nothing. At the beginning of July came the military reverses. The German army was continually in retreat. Germany's allies failed her. Germany begged for an armistice. The war was manifestly lost. Respect for the Supreme Command and military officials diminished. The terrible embitterment of workmen, farmers, and the middle class was united with the wish to bring the now completely purposeless war to an immediate end.

At the beginning of October the formation of Max of Baden's Government was announced in the newspapers. At the end of October the journals were discussing the constitutional changes. The real significance of this peaceful revolution never reached the masses. They were taking revenge for the fact that the Reichstag majority had not won all these changes by fighting for them but had received them as a gift from above. If a great battle over constitutional reform had raged publicly for months, the workers and middle classes would have taken sides about it and looked upon the victory as their own. In 1918 the sudden complete victory of German middle-class democracy followed on nine months of deathly silence politically. In order to have faith in the new system the masses would have had to see it in working order. The man in the street could not understand the change.

A Prince from Baden had taken Count Hertling's place. This did not bear any obvious stamp of democracy, for nine-tenths of the German people knew nothing of Prince Max and supposed him to be a prince like any other prince. The Vice-Chancellor—von Payer—was the same as under Hertling. The Prussian Ministers also remained in office. The Minister for War was as hitherto a General, the Secretary of State for Foreign Affairs a diplomat. Everything was as it had been in the old days. A few of the parliamentary Secretaries of State were new; but what reason was there to suppose that Erzberger and Scheidemann would achieve more than Payer against the military and absolutist rulers? Prussian generals were still ruling over the Prussian provinces and other Federal States. Up to November 9 the

General in Command published his regulations in Berlin, pro-
hibited political labour meetings, arrested offenders; while the
censorship prevented the Berlin Press from publishing anything
about the events in Kiel.

All this did not look particularly democratic nor was there
anything new about it. Apparently it was the same old system
under which Germany had been ruled since August 1914. The
masses of the people could discern no difference between Bethmann-Hollweg's government and Max of Baden's. Nor did it
seem that anything had been changed in the army and the navy.
The authority of the officers and military disciplinary powers were
the same as before. But what was most important of all in the eyes
of the populace was that by the end of October armistice and
peace had been under discussion for a month: yet the war went
on. Who could guarantee that the officers would not drag out the
war through the winter and into the new year? While Wilson's
Notes were being debated, the idea of national defence was
publicly mooted and of an appeal to all German men to rise in
a last desperate resistance. Such proposals embittered the masses
as had the earlier talk of a peace of conquest and annexations.
They felt that there had been enough suffering and starvation and
that an end must be made of these things.

On October 24 Hindenburg had published an army order containing *inter alia* these words: 'Wilson's answer demands military
capitulation. It is, therefore, impossible for us, as soldiers, to
accept. It is a proof that the desire for destruction which led our
enemies to loose the war on us in 1914 remains unaltered. Wilson's
answer can therefore only be taken as a challenge to continue our
resistance with every means at our command.' Thus, if things
depended on Hindenburg, thought the workers and soldiers, the
war would be carried on for a long time, and the masses had no
assurance that Scheidemann would be able to prevent this. Any one
examining the events of the autumn of 1918 critically must be
surprised that Ludendorff's dismissal made no more impression,
and that the masses were not convinced by it how much things
had altered in Germany. But Ludendorff had never been much in
the limelight. It was enough for him to be actually exercising
power. That Ludendorff had been the Dictator of Germany since
the summer of 1916 was known to the higher officers and other
authorities, to the politicians, and to the Press, which had been
prevented by the censorship from publishing it. The people as

a whole realized the military dictatorship of the Supreme Command, but they felt it as a general system and not as the power of a single man. Field Marshal von Hindenburg seemed to the nation to be much more the outward representative of the Prussian-German military rule than Quartermaster-General Ludendorff, who indeed signed the communiqués, but otherwise did not appear very much in the public eye.

Ludendorff's successor, General Groener, was known to the workers on account of his having dealt very severely with the strikers in the munition works. He was considered to be a man of inflexible determination. War to the death was expected of the Supreme Command under Hindenburg and Groener, and equally of the Navy under Scheer and Hipper. Thus at the end of October the masses realized that the War was hopelessly lost, but the decision as to whether peace was at length to be concluded still apparently lay with the higher officers. Even the supporters of the Reichstag majority did not believe that there had actually been a decisive revolution in Germany and that the Reichstag now possessed the power. This lack of confidence and of contact between the Reichstag majority and the nation became one of the chief causes of the November Revolution.

During those weeks in October the majority had perfectly clean consciences concerning their supporters. Thus in an appeal from the Committee of the Social Democratic Party warning its members against 'indiscretions' are the words:

'Since our comrades have become members of the Government, an offer has been sent to the enemy which is bound to lead very shortly to an armistice and to peace; equal suffrage has been achieved in Prussia; the Reichstag has become the real executive power in the State and autocracy has been abolished; military power has been made subordinate to civil power and thus militarism has been deprived of its strongest support; freedom of the Press and of public meeting have been increased; Liebknecht and many others have been released from prison.'

All this was founded on fact. But this and similar enumerations were not sufficient to demonstrate to the masses the fact of the German Revolution. Not only the sparse political education of the nation as a whole was to blame for this lack of understanding. The Reichstag majority was guilty of serious mistakes.

At the outset it had been a mistake not to make Erzberger, Scheidemann, or one of the other well-known members of the Majority, Chancellor, instead of putting a Prince at the head of the

'People's Government'. Utterly incomprehensible are the lengthy recesses which the Reichstag took during October and November 1918. On October 5 the Reichstag heard Prince Max's speech in which he introduced the new Government. Then it adjourned and did not meet again until October 22. Subsequently the Reichstag adjourned again and did not reassemble until November 9. During the first weeks of the new order in Germany, with all the tremendous home and foreign problems of the day, the Reichstag should have been at work unceasingly. The Government would have had quite a different authority in dealing with the events in Kiel if it could have relied on the support of the Reichstag.

An equally great mistake was the fact that the People's Government did not immediately abolish the state of martial law and relieve the Generals Commanding the Home Districts of their commands. The masses found it intolerable, for instance, that General von Linsingen wielded the legitimate authority in Berlin until November 9. Finally, it might have been demonstrated to the troops by suitable measures, even without loss of military discipline, that the old system no longer existed. If, for instance, the same rations had been introduced for officers and men, discipline would not have suffered nor would any reasonable officer have felt himself injured. As things were, it would have worked like a charm on the soldiers and sailors. None of this was done. The Reichstag actually possessed the power in the country, but it was still so little accustomed to its new authority and felt so insecure in itself that it was incapable of demonstrating its superiority to the men and the regulations of the old régime.

Thus a period of danger arose which would have been overcome by the signing of the armistice. If Max of Baden's Government could have given the people a cessation of hostilities on land and sea, they would thereby have stabilized their authority. As long as the war continued there was danger of some incident occurring which would incite the masses to seek to take things in their own hands in their longing for peace.

If it came to more serious disturbances, nothing much could happen to the Reichstag or the Majority Parties; for the fundamental unity between the Reichstag and the great masses of the nation was bound to emerge in spite of confusion. The propertied middle class had nothing to fear. The overwhelming majority of the German workers could not imagine life clearly in a Socialist State in spite of the fifty-years' existence of German Social Democracy, and they had no immediate socialistic demands. Neither could Germany's traditional system of officials and administration be abolished by a spontaneous movement of the populace. The German nation was not trained in self-government in the Anglo-Saxon fashion and could not develop the capacity overnight. The weakest part of the German State edifice, as it existed since October 1918, was the monarchy—the Imperial throne and those of the federal princes.

The hatred that whole classes of the people felt for the officers was also directed against the dynasties as heads of the military organization. Much more dangerous even than hatred was the indifference and lack of interest evinced by the people for the Emperor himself during the past four years. William II had quitted the political stage in 1914—he continued to exist only as a figurehead. Since October 1918 this fact had also been recognized constitutionally. The old tradition of the autocratic Hohenzollerns was dead. Nobody as yet knew or cared about the new parliamentary monarchy. The remaining federal princes at best had only a very narrow circle of adherents. The 'Question of the Emperor' grew pressing through Wilson's Notes. Public opinion in the Entente countries saw in William II, as a matter of fact quite unjustly, the conscious instigator of the World War. According to some of the statements in Wilson's Notes, it seemed probable that the Entente would refuse to make peace with Germany as long as William II remained the head of the State.

Thus in October the wish was uttered in many quarters that William II should abdicate so as to make peace negotiations easier for Germany. Since the Crown Prince seemed equally unsuitable as ruler, his eldest son would have had to be William II's successor. William II, however, would not hear of abdicating. He had long ago renounced all effective Imperial power: but in view of his character it is comprehensible that he clung the more firmly to the appearance of power. Nevertheless, the idea is quite false that there would have been no November revolution if the Emperor had abdicated earlier. The Revolution among the sailors would have broken out just the same if the navy had sailed out under the Regency of Eitel Friedrich instead of under William II. The 'Emperor Question' played no part in the first decisive days of the naval upheaval.

It is just as little true to say that it was the fault of the Entente that the German monarchical crisis arose. Although Wilson made the question an urgent one, he did not create it. The Entente was indeed resolutely opposed to William II, but not to the South German princes. Influential politicians in Paris would have been pleased if, for example, the kingdom of Bavaria seceded from the German Empire. The ease with which the dynasties fell during November in Munich, Stuttgart, Darmstadt, and Karlsruhe cannot be explained by Wilson's demands. The truth is that the overwhelming majority of the German people had broken away from the idea of monarchy as a result of their experiences in the war. It needed only the smallest push to cause the German dynasties to topple.

As early as 1917 Government circles were in no doubt as to the weakness of the Empire. On May 25, 1917, a meeting [15] took place in the Ministry of War in Berlin for the purpose of considering 'the enemy's anti-monarchist efforts and what steps were to be taken to counteract these'. Colonel von Wrisberg was the Chairman; and amongst others, Lewald, a high Government official, and Colonel von Haeften were present. The meeting ascribed the prevalence of anti-monarchist feeling to 'enemy propaganda', which was very convenient but not quite correct. The resolutions passed by the meeting are very characteristic but remarkably naïve. The main theme was: 'His Majesty the Emperor as well as his whole family must once more be brought into close touch with the people.' It was believed that the Church, the schools, and the hospitals could be effective channels for monarchist propaganda. 'Monarchist lectures should be delivered frequently by teachers or other suitable persons such as wounded officers. Lectures to children are better given outside school hours in the evenings, with a certain amount of ceremony (by artificial light and with the parents present, &c.').'The clergy and the educational authorities must be given definite instructions on this point, since the magnitude of the danger is not fully recognized in the country.'—'The Press must publish articles and more especially pictures and films about the hard work and the strict attention to duty displayed by the Emperor and the members of his family; about the simplicity of their lives; their deeds in the face of the enemy; their sacrifices &c.' An end must also be made to the 'rumours about the Crown Prince'. The lower ranks of court officials and servants must be 'prevented from indulging in any gossip'. Government measures for the amelioration of social conditions and for the improvement of rationing were to be attributed by the Press to the Emperor's initiative. The Emperor was to visit large factories; more decorations were to be distributed; women's associations were to be enlisted for work on behalf of the monarchy; and so forth. One wonders whether such meetings were found to be necessary to bolster up Frederick the Great's throne in the year 1759 after the battle of Kunersdorf! Attempts to save a monarchy by such means as the meeting on May 25, 1917, prove that that monarchy is already dead.

The victory of middle-class democracy in Germany in October spurred on the groups that inclined to the Left to greater activity. A secret conference of the Spartacists in Berlin on October 7 issued an appeal to the workers and soldiers [16] not to be satisfied with the introduction of parliamentary government, but to carry through the Socialist Revolution in Germany. The following were announced as some of the aims of the revolutionaries: the repudiation of all war loans; the expropriation of all bank capital, of mines, foundries, and great estates; and the abolition of the individual States and dynasties. The Workers' and Soldiers' Councils were to assume power as executives of the Revolution. The Party Committee of the U.S.P.D.; led by Haase and Dittmann, was as sceptical as ever before about the prospects of a Socialist revolution in Germany. In the autumn of 1918, on the other hand, the Berlin revolutionary group approached nearer to the views of the situation held by the Spartacists. [17] A number of the Berlin workers in the great industries had come to hold the opinion, as a result of the events of 1918, that a revolution on the Russian model was also possible in Germany. The workmen's leaders therefore busied themselves with the prospects of a militant revolution. Among the revolutionary leaders, besides Richard Müller, Emil Barth had also come into the limelight during the year 1918. The revolutionists were advised in political matters by Ledebour, a member of the Reichstag, and by Däumig, the well-known Socialist writer. Representatives of the Spartacus Association, especially Karl Liebknecht since his release from prison, appeared at the meetings of the revolutionaries in October. The Party Committee of the U.S.P.D. was also called into consultation. Karl Liebknecht was in favour of immediate action; the Committee of the U.S.P.D. in favour of delay. The leaders themselves were all in favour of action, but only after due preparation.

Emil Barth obtained money from the Russian Embassy with which he bought a few weapons [18]—a work of supererogation, for were the army to remain loyal to the Government the revolution would fail, while if the troops mutinied there would be no need for Barth's revolvers. The Soviet Government saw no reason at that time for affording support to Max of Baden's Government. The new German Government had indeed declared itself on principle in favour of a revision of the Peace of Brest-Litovsk; but it had not actually done anything to change the former eastern policy of Germany. The Soviet Government had every excuse for fearing that Max of Baden and his colleagues would try to form a united front with the Entente against Bolshevism. A new German revolution which would bring to the helm a Russophil Labour Government was obviously in the interests of Soviet Russia.

More important than the obtaining of arms were the attempts made by the revolutionaries to get in touch with the soldiers who were in Berlin in October and at the beginning of November. But no clear picture of the temper of the troops in Berlin was to be obtained up to November 8. The outstanding revolutionary leaders, such as Richard Müller, knew that they had undertaken a tremendous task. The success of a Socialist revolution in Germany, as the leaders and the Spartacists visualized it, was not possible by a compromise with the Majority Socialists, but only by their complete defeat. The revolution must not only overthrow the kings and the officers but also those Social Democrats who were in favour of middle-class democracy, and, in fact, the Reichstag majority and the whole middle class. It was not even certain whether such a revolution would be successful in Berlin. The revolutionaries knew practically nothing of the state of feeling in the country at large and at the Front. Thus their hesitation is only too comprehensible.

At a meeting as late as November 2 the leaders did not think that the time was ripe for immediate action. They knew nothing of the events of the past few days in the navy. November 11 was the day appointed for the revolution in Berlin. Meanwhile the whole of Germany was swept by quite a different revolutionary movement in which neither the revolutionary leaders nor the Spartacists were concerned. It was a 'wild' spontaneous rising without leaders of the supporters of the Reichstag majority against the military rulers of the country. This movement, chiefly by the Majority Socialist masses over the heads of their Party leaders, coincided with the organized attempt at a Socialist revolution in Berlin on November 9.

Imprisonment on a large scale and court-martial decrees had dissolved the secret associations among the sailors of the High Seas Fleet in 1917. Any connexions which had existed with the U.S.P.D., and possibly with the Left Wing Radicals, had since then been ruptured. But the hatred of the men for their officers and for the system which they embodied grew continually fiercer. When at the beginning of October it became known in the Fleet that Germany was asking for an armistice, and that a People's Government had been formed with Erzberger and Scheidemann as Ministers, satisfaction was general among the sailors. The officers, who saw all their hopes extinguished, were filled with forebodings. The Captain of the *Thüringen* told his men that Germany had lost the war, and that the Emperor was now nothing more than a lay figure.[19] One of the sailors who were afterwards arrested on the *Thüringen* for mutinying in order to prevent the Fleet from putting out to sea told the following story: A sailor had been to see the First Officer and had said to him that he did not think that the proposed naval attack could be in accordance with the wishes of the present Government. Thereupon the First Officer was alleged to have said: 'Yes that is *your* Government!' It does not matter whether this story is true or not; it shows what the sailors judged to be their position and that of the officers with regard to the new Government.

When in the course of October the news appeared in the Press that Germany might perhaps make a last united attempt at resistance, the sailors were profoundly alarmed. The utterances of various officers were hawked about: 'Rather ten years more war than such a peace!' or 'Rather an honourable death than a shameful peace!' It is quite possible that officers in the Navy may have said such things. If they did, it reflects no discredit upon them. Class conflict lay behind the different conceptions of the war and its termination. The antithesis which in 1917 had been 'Peace by compromise or a victorious peace' was now 'Immediate cessation of hostilities or a last desperate attack'. If the officers and the old Prussian Conservatives in general were in favour of continuing the fight, it was not only that they were filled with a deep concern for the honour of the nation but also by the wish to escape from the present political misery through a fight to the death no matter what might be the ultimate outcome. On the other hand, the sailors saw in the continuation of the war nothing more than a subtle Pan-German manœuvre: the ruling class wished to show its power by every means; to destroy the prospects of peace; if possible, to overthrow the People's Government by means of a military *coup d'état*; and, if that proved impossible, to involve the sailors in their own ruin. It was in this political atmosphere that the High Seas Fleet received the order on October 30 to sail for the purpose of making a great raid, ostensibly on England.

The German Admiralty, especially since the submarine campaign had failed, hoped to relieve the hard-pressed troops on the Western Front by making a raid. While the submarine campaign lasted, the Fleet had been able to interrupt communication between France and England, although the counter-measures of the Entente, who were in command of the seas, had grown more and more effective. In October the German Government had stopped the submarine campaign because Wilson had announced that its cessation was an essential preliminary to an armistice. The German Admiralty now planned a cruiser raid in the Channel in order suddenly to cut off communication between England and the Continent. Battleships were to follow to cover the cruisers. The base of the English Grand Fleet lay far away to the north at Scapa Flow in the Orkneys off the northern coast of Scotland. The distance from Scapa Flow to the Channel is twice as long as from Wilhelmshafen to the Channel. Thus there was every prospect that the German cruisers would return without any very serious loss before the English Grand Fleet would have arrived and attacked them.

To mask the German cruisers the entire submarine force could be used since it was no longer needed for its former purpose. Moreover, the English had scattered mine-fields over the whole of the North Sea during the past years in order to make it more difficult for the German submarines to come out. These same mines would now seriously impede the movements of the English Grand Fleet. Viewed from a purely strategical point of view, the proposed naval raid was neither speculative nor suicidal; but a carefully planned action calculated to inflict considerable damage on the enemy with very slight risk. There was never any question of the raid by the German Fleet making a change in the naval situation or in the war as a whole. The fantastic stories that are told about the proposed raid in the so-called 'stab-in-the-back' literature have no interest for scientific historians. At best the German cruisers might destroy a number of enemy transports; at worst the affair would turn into a sea-fight with the same odds as those that had obtained in the battle of Jutland. A turn in the tide of the war could only have

been caused if the German Fleet had broken the sea-power of
England and America at one blow; and that was absolutely impossible. Those who planned the German naval raid never
cherished any such fantastic notions.

The German admirals have been severely blamed for not commu-
nicating their plans to the Government. It would have been
politically advantageous if the Admiralty had informed Prince Max
of its intentions. But the change in the constitution effected on
October 28 placed no obligation on it to do so. Under a parliamentary régime a government can deprive high officers of their
command at any time, and it can dictate to them in broad outlines
the strategy they are to follow. But naval and military authorities
are not bound to ask permission of the civil government before
each individual action. If, for example, the German Supreme
Command had planned a local offensive in Lorraine at the beginning of November in order to relieve the rest of the Front, it would
not have required previously to have obtained the sanction of the
Imperial Chancellor. The situation was exactly the same for the
navy. It would have been mutiny if the admirals had continued
the submarine campaign against the order of the Government.
But so long as the war was in progress the High Seas Fleet could
fight as its commander deemed best. The plans for armistice and
peace could not be upset by a raid on the part of the German Fleet.
And the Entente was daily continuing its offensive on land quite
undeterred by the thought of the coming peace negotiations. The
Entente statesmen naturally wished to frame their armistice terms
so as to render impossible any German naval action or in fact any
further fighting on the part of Germany.

Hence the German admirals were neither mutineers nor were
they taking undue risks; they could completely justify their plans
on strategical grounds. Nevertheless, they made an enormous
political and psychological mistake when they expected the sailors
to undertake this action. It was once again obvious that the higher
officers knew absolutely nothing of the psychology of the sailors.
The sailors would certainly have fought if the English had attacked
the German coast; but once the war was lost they had no wish to
lose their lives in an engagement that was undertaken by the
Germans of their own free will. The conviction spread among the
men that the Government knew nothing of the proposed naval
action; that the officers wanted to bombard the English coast,
and thus destroy all chance of peace negotiations; and that the

whole thing was a *coup d'état* planned by the Pan-German officers.

On October 29 and 30 the men of the *Thüringen* and the *Helgoland* refused to obey orders. The Admiralty was therefore obliged to countermand the proposed raid. It made a further grave error in arresting four hundred men from the *Thüringen* and two hundred from the *Helgoland* and imprisoning them on shore. These men were convinced that they were being punished for their loyalty to the new Government. This was their defence before the court martial which tried them on November 1–3. Actually the mutiny in the Fleet was not in the smallest degree directed against the Government nor against the Reichstag majority. Two small episodes deserve mention. One of the arrested sailors told how on the *Thüringen* a portrait of Admiral Scheer was destroyed and its place taken by a photograph of Scheidemann cut out of a newspaper. The sailors had also cheered for Scheidemann. One of the officers of the *Thüringen* writes in his memoirs that on the evening of October 30 he asked a crowd of excited sailors on board what it was they really wanted; thereupon one of the sailors shouted: 'We want Erzberger,' which was greeted with loud applause by the rest. The crews of the remaining ships were at one with the six hundred men who had been arrested, and they were convinced that the Government was too weak to prevail against the officers. Fearing that there would be further death sentences, the sailors decided to take matters into their own hands. On November 4 mutinous sailors took possession of the town of Kiel. They elected Sailors' Councils, and the workmen in the shipyards who went on strike elected Workers' Councils. The Workers' and Sailors' Councils had all the power in their hands. By November 7 the crews of the whole Fleet with the exception of some thirty submarines and a few torpedo boats had joined the mutineers. The mutineers' demands were entirely non-political. Among the thirteen demands which the Sailors' Council of the First Squadron formulated, the one which came nearest to having a political character was the demand that the imprisoned sailors from the *Thüringen* and the *Helgoland* should be set free, in addition to those sailors who in 1917 had been sentenced to imprisonment. They also demanded that those who had taken part in the present mutiny should go unpunished—'no unfavourable entry should be made in their service books'. The mutineers, in other words, did not want to have the fact of the revolution noted in their service books! The first demand in their programme was equal rationing for men and officers. New food committees were to be formed, also complaints committees for the men, who were to be present at courts martial and who were to be allowed to intervene. The saluting of retired officers was to be abolished. Conditions of service and of leave to be rearranged. Point 9 is incredible: 'The address "Sir" is only to be used at the beginning of an interview —in the course of conversation officers will be addressed as "you".'

The situation needs to be clearly envisaged. 100,000 sailors had mutinied. All the guns were in their hands. The lives of their officers were at their mercy. The German Empire was breaking up under their action. And these same revolutionaries were concerned with the question as to whether they should say 'you' instead of 'Sir' to their officers! The political naïveté and inexperience of the Germans finds adequate expression here. At the beginning of November 1918 the sailors thought neither of a Republic nor of overthrowing the Government, nor even of the introduction of Socialism. What they wanted was to defend peace against the destructive influence of the Pan-Germans, and such modification of Prussian discipline as would give them back their human self-respect. If the U.S.P.D. or the Spartacus Association had had any influence upon the course of the revolt, the sailors' demands would have been very different. The Government sent to Kiel the Majority Socialist Noske, who took control of affairs there without the slightest difficulty. This again shows that the sailors' revolution was not directed against the S.P.D. or the Government. An attempt by Haase to gain the upper hand in Kiel failed.

The collapse of discipline was not confined to the navy. In November 1918 the obedience of the German soldiers to their officers after all that had happened was only a mechanical habit. Since discipline had no longer a foundation in free will and in the soldiers' minds, the army organization collapsed like a house of cards as soon as the navy had set the example. During the course of the naval revolution the army reservists had unhesitatingly joined the revolutionaries. The military revolt spread from Hamburg over the rest of Germany with lightning rapidity. By November 7 the revolution had already reached Munich. The embitterment of the Bavarian peasant soldiers with the ruling system destroyed the Bavarian Government overnight. A notable political change was the outcome of the proclamation of the

Bavarian Republic. The movement now went beyond the October Constitution in so far as this bore a monarchical character.

The Munich revolution is very noteworthy from the point of view of racial psychology. Kurt Eisner, the leader of the Bavarian U.S P.D., gave it the first impulse. At the time he occupied a curious position intermediate between the Right and Left Wings of the Party. The Left Wing of the U.S.P.D., the revolutionaries and their friends, considered a Socialist revolution to be possible in Germany. The Right Wing with the Party leaders did not cherish any hopes of effecting a great change. Eisner also considered a forcible introduction of Socialism into the Germany of 1918 as unthinkable. The task of the German workers and Socialists—as he saw it—was to carry through the radical middle-class revolution. This revolution was to overthrow the power of the militarists and the dynasties, and to assure an immediate peace and a strong democracy in Bavaria under the leadership of the workers and peasants. At the same time Eisner wished to develop the Workers' and Soldiers' Councils into an organized, democratic form of popular government. As the elections in Bavaria showed after the revolution, the U.S.P.D. had behind it only a very small following even among the working class. The Munich revolution on November 7 was made possible by the fact that the soldiers, who were mostly of the peasant class, accepted the watchwords of Eisner and his group. The problem of the Bavarian revolution may be thus formulated: first, why did the Munich peasant soldiers under the leadership of Eisner remove their officers, overthrow the Wittelsbach dynasty, and proclaim the Bavarian Republic? Second, why did all the rest of Bavaria follow the Munich example without further resistance on November 8?

During the first days of November Bavarian political circles were leisurely occupied with preparations for the introduction of parliamentary government without any expectation of an immediate upheaval. Neither the Ministers nor the Bavarian members of the Reichstag majority (Centre, Majority Socialists, Liberals) knew what was really going on among the masses of the people. Eisner's advantage was that he judged the temper of the Bavarian people better. Since the collapse of Austria, i.e. since the end of October, Bavaria had become a frontier State threatened by the enemy. This caused great panic among the workmen, peasants, and middle class, and they wanted to have done with the forlorn war at all costs. From November 4–7 Munich lived in constant fear of an attack by enemy aircraft. The furious protests of the Bavarian peasants against coercive economic measures and against the Central Government in Berlin have been referred to above. The temper of the Bavarians was such that it might in other circumstances have given rise to a dynastic-separatist movement. That it never came to that is to be explained by the fact that the masses discovered the complete impotence of the Wittelsbachs as against 'Berlin'. The necessity for the centralization of the Supreme Army command in Germany in war time had in reality invalidated Bavaria's particular State privileges; 'Berlin' decided all military and economic questions, foreign policy, and war aims. The King of Bavaria had no say at all in any questions affecting the life of the German people, including of course the Bavarians, from 1914 to 1918. The House of Wittelsbach and the Bavarian Ministers appeared to the masses to be only the tools of the hated 'Berlin' system. At the beginning of November the Bavarian peasants, workmen, and soldiers definitely wanted an immediate peace. Nevertheless, it seemed obvious to them that 'Berlin', the Emperor, and the Supreme Command were in no such hurry. Moreover, the Bavarians had lost all confidence in the power of the Wittelsbachs to help them. This was the situation when the Munich Majority Social Democrats arranged a demonstration on the Theresienwiese on November 7. The demonstration, which was joined by the U.S.P.D., demanded peace, democracy, and the abdication of the Emperor. The Majority Social Democrat leaders no more wanted a violent revolution in Munich than anywhere else in Germany.

It is not true of Bavaria any more than of the rest of Germany that the November revolution would have been avoided if the Emperor had abdicated sooner. The Bavarians were indeed most anxious that William II should abdicate, for they considered him to be standing in the way of peace, but the psychological premises for a revolution in Bavaria lay in the continuance of hostilities. The revolution would be successful so long as fighting was still going on at the front, irrespective of whether William II was the theoretical head of the army or any other Hohenzollern Prince as Regent and Governor. Eisner's supporters went to the barracks after the demonstration in Munich; and the troops at once joined them. The soldiers considered that Eisner's tactics would at least bring an immediate end to the war for Bavaria. The power of the House of Wittelsbach as well as that of the Ministers and officers collapsed overnight. By the following morning Bavaria was a Republic. In the Government formed by Eisner the Majority Socialists immediately played a leading part. For in Bavaria, as elsewhere in Germany, as soon as the masses thought that the end of the war was a certainty a retrograde movement set in. The events in Munich on November 7–8 were an exact model for the republican developments in the rest of Germany and especially in Berlin.

The military revolution, which had at first run like an electric current across Germany from Hamburg to Munich, now spread east and west—towards Berlin in the east and across the Rhine to the army on the Western Front. Before the revolution reached the Front, the Armistice had been concluded; and thus the movement lost its meaning. For the chief aim of the military revolution was to assure peace by abolishing the power of the officers. The Workers' Councils everywhere followed close on the Soldiers' Councils as they had at first done in Kiel. The Soldiers' and Workers' Councils took over the executive power. To some extent they took the place of the District Commands which had administered martial law. On the other hand, the municipal and civil authorities were in the main left undisturbed. There was no really serious manifestation anywhere in the country of a wish to carry through socialist measures. Any such intentions would have been frustrated by the attitude of the soldiers, the majority of whom were not Socialists in conformity with the political composition of the German nation. Although the Soldiers' Councils generally co-operated with the Majority Socialists, this radical tendency did not mean a denial of middle-class ideas.

The local political leadership of the revolution was taken over almost everywhere by the S.P.D. and the U.S.P.D. Such a collaboration was possible because the U.S.P.D. and most of its officials throughout the country did not then wish to go beyond the middle-class democratic republic. In Berlin alone there existed a definite Left Wing to the U.S.P.D., led by the revolutionaries, which aspired to a Socialist Republic. The S.P.D. maintained relations, even during the days of the revolution, with the Liberals and the Centre throughout the whole country; and in Bavaria with the Peasants' Federation. In isolated places where the Spartacists had been in power during the first days of the revolution they were soon lost sight of again. The Conservatives were everywhere politically eliminated.

The upheaval in the country at the beginning of November
placed the leaders of the S.P.D. and the Social Democratic
Ministers in an awkward position. The S.P.D. was in reality
making a revolution against itself—Social Democratic masses, and
masses led by Social Democrats, were tearing up a constitution
that had been formed by a government at whose head was the S.P.D.
In order to get out of their difficulty the S.P.D. delivered an ultimatum to the Imperial Chancellor and the middle-class parties
represented in the Government in which they demanded that the
Emperor should abdicate and the Crown Prince renounce the
throne.[20] If this did not take place the S.P.D. would resign from
the Government. The S.P.D. hoped that by sacrificing the two
Hohenzollerns who were most compromised it would be possible
to save the October Constitution with its parliamentary monarchy.
There is no essential difference between a middle-class republic
and a constitutional monarchy. The attempt made by the S.P.D.
leaders to defend the October Constitution had not much prospect
of success in view of the complete bankruptcy of monarchist senti-
ment in Germany. But it was no 'betrayal' of the middle-class
revolution which could not really go substantially beyond the
October Constitution.

Prince Max allowed himself to be convinced by the S.P.D.'s
arguments. Up to November 9, however, he was not able to achieve
the abdication of William II, who remained in the Great General
Head-quarters. The revolutionaries were not planning their coup
until November 11; but two days before there was a lightning
general strike in the great factories in Berlin. Although the troops
of the Berlin garrison at once elected Soldiers' Councils, they
joined the Majority Socialists and not the revolutionaries and
Spartacists. This decided the fate of the revolution in Berlin.

When the Revolution broke out in Berlin on November 9,
Prince Max of Baden on his own initiative announced the Emperor's
abdication. He hoped to save the monarchy by this desperate
step. A deputation of the S.P.D. appeared towards noon to interview Prince Max, and informed him that the Social Democratic
Secretaries of State no longer considered themselves members of
the Government. The Party thereby regained its freedom of
action and Max of Baden's Government fell. The S.P.D. demanded
that the Chancellorship should be handed over to a member of
their own Party. Prince Max resigned in favour of Ebert.

This step can only be justified by the legal fiction that the Prince was acting as Regent or Vice-President. Since the alleged abdication of William II there was no reigning Emperor. The Imperial Constitution recognized no substitute for the Emperor, but contented itself with the statement that the 'Präsidium' in the German Empire belonged to the King of Prussia. If the King of Prussia himself was not fit to govern, a Regent took his place in accordance with the Prussian Constitution. So long as no Regent had been constitutionally appointed, the Cabinet carried out the functions of Regent. If these ideas are brought to bear on the situation in the German Empire on November 9, the following becomes clear: if neither a reigning Emperor nor a Regent is available, the Imperial Chancellor must temporarily take the place of the Regent and wield the supreme power. Thus the right to make some one else Imperial Chancellor could be attributed to Prince Max. As a general rule the Imperial Chancellor cannot hand on his office.

As soon as Ebert became Chancellor, he invited Prince Max to become Regent (*Reichsverweser*). Such a juxtaposition between the *Reichsverweser* and the Chancellor would have been possible. But Prince Max refused. Thus on November 9, by virtue of the existing Constitution and the legal fiction above mentioned, Ebert was at the same time Chancellor and Regent. On November 9 and 10 he only held the title of Imperial Chancellor, for on November 9 and 10 Ebert's Government was still a monarchical Cabinet, not indeed in Bismarck's sense, but according to the Constitution of October 1918.

Further developments in Berlin, however, showed that the people were no longer in favour of a monarchy. The S.P.D. leaders also decided under pressure of circumstances for the middle-class Republic. The new Government could receive its authority neither from William II nor from Prince Max, but only from the revolutionary populace. Once more a legal fiction was required. The Berlin Workers' and Soldiers' Councils were considered as the representatives of all the revolutionary elements in the nation. A general meeting of the Berlin Workers' and Soldiers' Councils held on November 10 in the Busch Circus elected the new Republican Government. Since the Soldiers' Councils pledged the strength of the armed forces of the nation to the S.P.D., the original plan of the revolutionaries and of the Spartacists to form a Socialist Government without the S.P.D. was hopeless. Those who had hoped for a Socialist Republic recognized their failure. As a consequence, Liebknecht, as leader of the Spartacists, and Richard

Müller, as chief of the revolutionaries, refused to become members of the new Government. As a personal concession to the most radical workers, Emil Barth, one of the revolutionary leaders, was taken into the Government. Nevertheless Barth only had a seat in the Government as a member of the U.S.P.D. and not as the representative of the Spartacists and the revolutionaries.

After November 10 Germany was in possession of a supreme governmental organ—the Council of the Representatives of the People formed by a coalition between the S.P.D. represented by Ebert, Scheidemann, and Landsberg, and the Committee of the U.S.P.D., represented by Haase, Dittmann, and Barth. The Reichstag Majority therefore contrived to remain in power, for, apart from the S.P.D., the Centre and the Liberals held several important Secretaryships of State. Thus Erzberger, as Secretary of State, conducted the armistice negotiations, and the Progressive Preuss was made Minister of the Interior. The middle-class Ministers were called 'experts' in November. That was another fiction. Would Lenin have sent the Cadet leader Miliukow to Brest-Litovsk as head of the Bolshevik Peace Delegation? In reality the Government of November 10 was composed of the old Reichstag Majority slightly veiled in Socialism and increased by the Right Wing of the U.S.P.D. Such a government corresponded with the course of the revolution and the then distribution of political power in Germany.

The old Constitution kept curiously atune with the new revolutionary political conditions even after November 10.[21] The representatives of the people expressly recognized the continued existence of the Federal Council, and they declared from the outset that they would cause a National Assembly to be elected. Prince Max had already announced the convocation of a German National Assembly on November 9. This was the Reichstag in a slightly different form. Thus both the law-giving organs of the old Empire —the Federal Council and the Reichstag—were preserved even after November 10. Nor was there any question of a Dictatorship of the Proletariat, for the most important of the Councils, the Soldiers' Councils, were on the whole neither proletarian nor socialist nor desirous of exercising a dictatorship. The National Congress of the Workers' and Soldiers' Councils [22] expressed itself with an overwhelming majority against the adoption of the Councils as a permanent form of government and in favour of the election of a National Assembly. It is significant that neither Karl

Liebknecht nor Rosa Luxemburg were members of the Congress of the Councils.

The Supreme Command under Hindenburg and Groener immediately declared themselves for the new Constitution. William II was obliged to leave the Great General Head-quarters and went to Holland. The last Hohenzollern to reign in Prussia shared the fate of James II and Charles X. The Prussian military nobility and the monarchy had been overthrown. The supporters of a Socialist revolution had not been able to put their ideas into practice. The middle-class Republic was victorious in Germany.

NOTES TO CHAPTER VII

1. Strength of the Americans in France: Kuhl in REPORT, iii, p. 55. —Conditions of reserves in England: Kuhl, ibid., iii, p. 9.

2. The history of the Tank: Kuhl, ibid. iii, pp. 78 et seq.

3. See the diary of Richard Stumpf (p. 199, conversations of the writer with soldiers on a journey taken to Bavaria on leave): 'Being asked for the goal of the next advance, all with staggering certainty gave it as the country east and south of Rheims, and the date as July 16.'

4. Memorandum by Major Niemann, as well as the notes by Colonel Bauer: REPORT, ii, pp. 215 et seq., Niemann writes: 'England must be informed that we are planning our future, i.e. our military-political situation, on land and not on the sea. . . . England will certainly bite at the cheap bait of our maritime withdrawal.'—Bauer remarks: 'Quite agree with your view of the question of the fleet. Our naval policy before the War was absolutely wrong, and was the chief cause of England's enmity. . . . In the War itself the High Seas Fleet has only cost men and money. I can see no military use for it.'

5. Volkmann in REPORT, vi, p. 288: 'The army on active service was at first very little affected by the revolutionary events at home. Only very occasionally was the attempt made to question the authority of the officers and their power to command.'—P. 289: 'The troops crossed the home frontiers with steady military bearing, under the old black, white, and red colours and singing patriotic songs.'

6. On the subject of the Crown Council in Spa, see Schwertfeger in REPORT, ii, pp. 223 et seq., where all the documents are to be found. The notes of the Secretary of State, von Hintze, are a valuable source, but not convincing in their attacks on Ludendorff.

7. On the subject of Payer's action, see Schwertfeger, ibid., ii, pp. 237 et seq., and the note by Payer himself, ibid., ii, p. 384.

8. Rumanian petroleum and the conduct of the War: Kuhl in REPORT, iii, p. 12.

9. On the subject of September 29 and the following days, see the excellent description, besides documents, by Schwertfeger, in REPORT, ii, pp. 260 et seq.—Cf. Prince Max of Baden, *Erinnerungen*, &c., pp. 335 et seq.

10. Hindenburg's letter of October 3: Schwertfeger in ibid., ii, p. 302.

11. Hindenburg and Graf Roedern: Schwertfeger, ibid., ii, p. 303.

12. Marshal Foch's interview with a representative of the Vienna *Neue Freie Presse*, reprinted and reviewed in the Berlin newspapers at the beginning of August 1928 (*Berliner Tageblatt*, August 3, 1928).

13. On the subject of Prince Max of Baden's Government, see Bredt in REPORT, viii, pp. 204 et seq., and the thorough valuable description in the Prince's own *Erinnerungen*.

14. Ludendorff's note of October 31, 1918, REPORT, ii, pp. 361 et seq.— On the subject of Ludendorff's retirement, see Prince Max's *Erinnerungen*, pp. 500 et seq.—The Centre against 'national defence', ibid., p. 499.— The preparation of the German Answer to Wilson's Notes on October 27: ibid., pp. 505 et seq.

15. Session of May 25, 1917: REPORT, v, p. 130.

16. Spartacist activities in October 1918: Paul Fröhlich, *Zehn Jahre Krieg und Bürgerkrieg*, i, 1924, pp. 212, 239.

17. The revolutionary *Obleute* (leaders) in October and November 1918: Richard Müller, *Vom Kaiserreich zur Republik*, i, pp. 127 et seq. (A detailed description. On the writings of Emil Barth on the same subject, see the Preface to Müller's book, p. 8: 'Barth's book is nothing but a piece of vain and foolish braggadocio.')

18. Richard Müller, i, p. 128: 'The revolutionary *Obleute* (leaders) have never received or been offered any money either from foreign countries nor by people in Germany. Emil Barth was given money for buying arms by a body which was closely allied to the German working class. Barth considered that this was an affair for which he need render no accounts.'

19. For the attack which had been planned by the Fleet and the naval revolution, vols. ix and x of REPORT contain all the necessary material.— For the plan of the attack, see Beckmann, *Der Dolchstossprozess in München* (1925), p. 41. Admiral von Trotha's speech: 'Supported by the German capital ships, the cruiser attack could be directed against the Flanders coast, which was already in enemy hands, and against the mouth of the Thames without any risk and in the certainty of inflicting incalculable damage on the enemy. . . . Much could be achieved with very little risk.'— The naval attack and the Government: Prince Max's *Erinnerungen*, pp. 572 et seq.—The protocol of the examination of the sailors from November 1–3 (a primary source) in Dittmann's *Die Marine-Justizmorde usw.*, pp. 94 et seq.— Cf. the statement of Lieutenant-Commander Fikentscher, quoted in REPORT, vi, p. 193. The naval documents relating to the Kiel mutiny will be found in the *Denkschrift zur Frage des Dolchstosses* which is published in vol. ix of REPORT.—Ibid., the thirteen demands of the Sailors' Council of the First Squadron. Very important also is the memorandum published there of the negotiations carried on by von Mann, the Secretary of State for the Navy, with the emissaries of the Third Squadron on November 7. Even as late as this the sailors' spokesmen insisted on their loyalty to the Government and made quite unpolitical demands.—For general information on the naval mutiny, cf. Herz in REPORT, vi, pp. 190 et seq., and Stumpf, *Warum die Flotte*

zerbrach, pp. 206 et seq.—Richard Müller, *Vom Kaiserreich zur Republik*, i, p. 135.—On the revolution in Munich, see the very vivid description by Victor Naumann, who lived through the days of the revolution in Munich, *Dokumente und Argumente*.—The documents concerning the Eisner Government can be found in Richard Müller's *Vom Kaiserreich zur Republik*, ii, pp. 240 et seq.

20. Prince Max and the S.P.D., see Prince Max's *Erinnerungen*, pp. 589 et seq.—November 9, ibid., pp. 630 et seq.—On November 9 an appeal was issued, signed: 'The Imperial Chancellor, Ebert', which began with the words: 'Fellow citizens! Prince Max of Baden, who has hitherto been Imperial Chancellor, has handed over to me the office of Imperial Chancellor' (cf. Bredt in REPORT, viii, p. 350). Prince Max on this subject: *Erinnerungen*, p. 643: 'Between five and six o'clock (on November 9) I went to say good-bye to Ebert. Ebert said to me: "I implore you to remain." I asked: "What for?" Ebert: "I should like you to remain as Regent." This request had been made to me repeatedly during the last few hours by my late colleagues. I answered Herr Ebert: "I know that you are about to make an agreement with the Independents, and I cannot work with them".'—On the subject of the 'substitute' for the King of Prussia, cf. Arts. 56–8 of the old Prussian Constitution. (Art. 57 reads: 'Until the Regent shall take up his post the Cabinet conducts the Government.')

21. On the subject of the constitutional changes see the excellent explanation by Bredt in REPORT, viii, pp. 348 et seq.—The continuance of the Federal Council by order of the Council of the Representatives of the People on November 14, ibid., p. 352.—On the subject of the events in the Busch Circus on November 10, cf. Richard Müller, *Vom Kaiserreich zur Republik*, ii, pp. 32 et seq.

22. On the subject of the Congress of National Councils within the Reich which met on December 16, 1918, cf. Richard Müller, op. cit. ii, pp. 203 et seq.; and Bredt in REPORT, viii, pp. 356 et seq.

INDEX